AUTONOMY
AND FAITH

RELIGIOUS PREFERENCE
IN EMPLOYMENT DECISIONS
IN RELIGIOUSLY AFFILIATED
HIGHER EDUCATION

Robert T. Sandin

Published for

The Center for Constitutional Studies

OMEGA PUBLICATIONS
Atlanta, Georgia

Published by Omega Publications
34 Peachtree Street N.W., Suite 2570
Atlanta, Georgia 30303

Copyright, Center for Constitutional Studies

First published 1990

Printed in the United States of America

ISBN **9626684-0-0**

TABLE OF CONTENTS

PREFACE

This book is the product of a project on Preferential Hiring in Independent and Religiously Affiliated Higher Education, which was conducted by the Center for Constitutional Studies at Mercer University in 1987-89. The project builds upon, extends, and updates research on the legal basis of the exercise of religious preference in employment decisions at religiously affiliated institutions of higher education, previously conducted by the Center at the University of Notre Dame.

The project was funded by a generous grant from The Lilly Endowment, Inc. We wish to express our profound appreciation to the Endowment, and particularly to Dr. Ralph E. Lundgren, Program Director, for their support of the Center since its early days and for the grant which made this project possible. Additional grants were received from the Education Commission of the Southern Baptist Convention and the Board of Higher Education and Ministry of the United Methodist Church. We express our deep thanks to Dr. Arthur L. Walker, Jr., Director of the Commission, and Dr. Julius S. Scott, Jr., former Associate Secretary of the Board and now President of Paine College (GA), for making these grants possible.

A number of individuals have contributed to the project through their participation in workshops and conferences sponsored by the Center under the Preferential Hiring project. These include: Leon S. Conlon, Sally M. Furay, Edward McGlynn Gaffney, Frederick M. Gedicks, Stanley M. Hastey, John Hill, William A. Kaplin, Charles S. Mackenzie, Richard A. Millard, Walfred H. Peterson, Oliver S. Thomas, Kent M. Weeks, and Mark G. Yudof. Each of these people contributed important insights and analyses in the development of our project, but they bear no responsibility for errors and other limitations which may appear in the final report. We express to each of them our deep appreciation for their participation in our project and for their support of the Center for Constitutional Studies.

INTRODUCTION

Religiously affiliated institutions of higher education play an important and distinctive role in the American society. The preservation of these institutions and the enhancement of their effectiveness and viability are important concerns not only for preserving a much-to-be-desired pluralism in post-secondary education, but also for improving the coherence of the system of values which underlies our common life.

In pursuing their distinctive purposes in the formation of values, religiously affiliated educational institutions need to be able to recruit and retain faculty and staff who possess professional, scholarly, and personal qualities suited to the demands of values-related education. Such institutions require a faculty and staff who not only exhibit basic moral and aesthetic sensibilities, but also understand the religious values of the various communities of faith, appreciate the constructive role which religion has played and can continue to play in the American experience, respect the religious traditions of the particular institutions in which they serve, and can contribute to the fulfillment of the distinctive missions of their institutions. Accordingly, religiously affiliated colleges and universities need to have the freedom to exercise religious preference and discrimination in recruiting, selecting, retaining, and developing academic and academic-support personnel.

The right of religiously affiliated institutions of higher education to exercise religious preference in employment decisions is explicitly recognized in recent legislation in civil rights and labor relations, and it has been confirmed by a number of judicial decisions. Yet in many religiously affiliated institutions of post-secondary education, personnel administration suffers from a lack of clarity concerning the legal and administrative basis for the exercise of religiously preferential hiring. Frequently the root of malaise in institutional employment practices is a feeling that the exercise of religious preference is somehow inconsistent with concern for civil rights, with the principle of non-

1

discrimination in employment, or with the traditions of academic freedom.

Furthermore, federal and state law and judicial decisions leave unresolved some significant questions concerning the underlying principles which can be expected to govern legal determination of the conditions under which institutional employment practice might be judged properly or improperly discriminatory. Confirming the legal, administrative, and academic legitimacy of religiously discriminatory employment practices in religiously affiliated institutions of postsecondary education has become a matter of some urgency in efforts to assure the autonomy and viability of this important sector of American education.

1. Autonomy and Accountability

Our study of the legal and administrative basis for the exercise of religious preference in employment decisions in religiously affiliated higher education involves a balanced understanding of the autonomy and the accountability of such institutions in the American social and educational system. By "autonomy" we here mean the capacity of an institution of higher learning to define its purposes, organize its programs, and establish its policies on the basis of the institution's own understanding of truth, social value, and organizational integrity. The autonomy of an institution of higher learning, so understood, is never absolute, of course, but is conditioned by its accountability. By "accountability" we mean the liability of an institution of higher education to an assessment of its educational quality and social utility through monitoring agencies, both governmental and non-governmental, functioning in the public interest.

The autonomy of higher education is essential both to the life of learning and to the adaptability of education to changing social needs. Academic freedom and the right of self-determination in matters of educational policy lie at the foundation of all education, public as well as private. As Ortega y Gasset once put it, education must always be

INTRODUCTION

understood as a social function; but the university serves society in its freedom, or not at all. Particularly in the domain of values, education depends on freedom in the expression of ideas and the pursuit of truth wherever it leads. And this means the independence of the academic system from arbitrary constraints imposed from without.

In the American system the educational autonomy of religiously affiliated institutions is reinforced by the tradition of religious liberty, which is closely associated in the language of the First Amendment with freedom of belief, expression, assembly, association, and speech. The American Constitution, the system of American law, and the larger complex of American institutions and social conventions protect both individuals and religious organizations in the pursuit of their own religious beliefs, practices, and ministries, whatever they may be.

On the other hand, the social importance of education leaves a religiously affiliated college or university - - even a school of theological education - - accountable in certain respects to the society within which it serves; and this accountability is appropriately enforced and monitored through governmental and non-governmental agencies of evaluation, coordination, and regulation. Among the sources of such accountability are the public interest in the quality of education, the need for the protection of individual rights, and the law of contracts. External constraints are appropriately placed, under certain conditions, on a religiously affiliated educational institution not only by legislative, regulatory, and judicial authority, but also by ecclesiastical hierarchies and constituencies, by accrediting agencies, and by professional and academic associations. All of these systems, both governmental and non-governmental, make use of various kinds of sanctions to enforce standards of social accountability on institutions of higher learning, both public and private, both secular and religious, and to protect the public interest in education.

Religiously affiliated institutions of higher education are subject, too, to the accountability which derives from the values which are inherent in the higher learning. Reverence for truth, intellectual honesty in its pursuit, respect for the canons of evidence, and commitment to the principles of academic freedom are virtues on which every enterprise of higher education depends. Indeed, the distinctive emphasis which religiously affiliated institutions place on the worth of human personality makes it especially important for them to avoid any form of instruction which diminishes the freedom of the learner to consider the issues of valuation and belief on the merits.

The dialectics of autonomy and accountability are in constant search of the proper balance between the rights of individuals and the rights of institutions, between the public interest and the exercise of private initiative, between the values of academic freedom and the priorities of public policy. William A. Kaplin observes that in the last three decades there has been something of a trend in American law toward greater accountability and less autonomy for both public and independent institutions of higher education.[1] The trend has been part of a growing emphasis on the protection of individual rights against institutional power. The trend also reflects the progressive reduction of the differences between the public and independent sectors of higher education during the Twentieth Century and the growing recognition of the social, economic, and political importance of education. It seems likely that the trend toward greater accountability in religiously affiliated higher education will continue into the foreseeable future.

This trend is by no means all bad. There have undoubtedly been points where it has been necessary to check the autonomy of religiously affiliated higher education through agencies of evaluation and control, functioning in the public interest. Questions remain, however, concerning the forms of monitoring which appropriately balance the public interest with the concern for religious liberty and educational autonomy. New pathways need to be indicated for dealing more effectively with the problem of institutional accountability within the traditions of academic and religious freedom, in a manner which assures the continued viability of religiously affiliated higher education, ministering with the integrity of faith to human development and the social good.

Our study of the proper balance between these two underlying themes of "autonomy" and "accountability" in the theory of religiously affiliated higher education is addressed to such questions as the following:

1. What are the forms of external monitoring, evaluation, and coordination which should be recognized as appropriate for independent and religiously affiliated institutions of post-secondary education in consequence of their social and educational accountability, and what forms should be recognized as inappropriate?

2. What is the jurisdiction of the various state, regional, and national agencies, both governmental and non-governmental, in the coordination of planning and program development in religiously affiliated higher education and in the evaluation of programs and policies in the public interest?

3. How might different institutional understandings of educational mission in religiously affiliated higher education affect the nature and scope of governmental concern with the internal policies and operations of such institutions and the nature and scope of governmental support for programs and students in such institutions?

4. What are the rights of religiously affiliated institutions of higher education as employers, and what are the rights of their employees, with particular reference to the use of values-oriented and religious tests in the employment of personnel? How does the public interest in civil rights and non-discrimination in employment impact governmental concern with the personnel policies and practices of independent and religiously affiliated institutins of higher learning? And what are the social values by reference to which employment policies and practices at such

5

institutions should be judged?

These are by no means simple issues, and it should not be surprising if gifted and conscientious leaders in both law and education should meet with only limited success in resolving them. The law of religious liberty is not as clear and consistent as theoreticians might like it to be, and the concept of the religiously affiliated college or university is not fully determinate in educational theory either. Still it is important for the best legal and educational minds to collaborate in a continuing effort to reduce vagueness, ambiguity, inconsistency, and unpredictability in the law of religiously affiliated higher education as it affects employment decisions and employment relationships.

2. Previous Research of the Center for Constitutional Studies

Since its founding in 1979 at the University of Notre Dame, the Center for Constitutional Studies has conducted extensive research into the legal basis of the exercise of religious preference in employment decisions at religiously affiliated institutions of higher education. An early Center publication, <u>Church and Campus: Legal Issues in Religiously Affiliated Higher Education</u> (1979), presented an empirical profile of religiously affiliated higher education, developed by the Center for the Sloan Commission on Government and Higher Education. The largest section of this work was devoted to employment policies and practices at such institutions. The authors, Philip R. Moots and Edward McGlynn Gaffney, Jr., presented an extended rationale for the exercise of religious preference in employment policies under existing law.

The exposition sought to interpret Congressional intent in the Civil Rights Act of 1964 and in the amendments to that Act incorporated in the Equal Employment Opportunity Act of 1972. The authors also summarized several recent judicial determinations of the law of non-discrimination, analyzed administrative regulations emerging from federal agencies and reached the following conclusion:

INTRODUCTION

If administrators of religiously affiliated colleges wish to assert a right of religious preference where there is no demonstrable nexus between the employment position in question and the religious mission of the college, they must be prepared to risk litigation which would test the constitutional validity of the broad statutory exemption of these institutions from the law prohibiting religious discrimination. In our opinion such litigation would probably result in a narrowing of the statutory exemption or its invalidation. We also believe that it is not constitutionally permissible to grant religiously affiliated colleges an absolute immunity from the general prohibition against employment discrimination on the basis of religion, because the duty of the courts is to protect both the religious interests of these institutional employers and the religious freedom of their employees or prospective employees.[2]

The authors took the view that neither federal legislation nor judicial precedent would prevent a religiously affiliated college or university from asserting its right to exercise religious preference in employment decisions without thereby rendering the institution or its students ineligible for federal or state funding. The Center researchers found that no case had squarely presented this issue to the Supreme Court to date, but they saw intimations of the way the Court might be expected to answer the question in Tilton v Richardson (1971), Hunt v. McNair (1973), and Roemer v. Board of Public Works of Maryland (1976). The writers expressed their considered opinion that "a college administrator may safely exercise religious preference to create a predominance of faculty members belonging to a particular religious group . . . and would probably not jeopardize the eligibility of the institution for public assistance." They found it less clear, however, how employment policy in a pervasively religious or highly sectarian institution might potentially impact funding eligibility.[3]

In reporting the findings of their survey of religiously

affiliated institutions of higher education for the Sloan Commission, the Center researchers noted that an overwhelming majority (91.7 percent) of these institutions affirmed (not surprisingly) that they thought it important that they should retain the right to exercise religious preference in faculty hiring and promotion, without thereby forfeiting their eligibility to receive public benefits. A lower percentage (72.6 percent) expressed the same view with respect to the employment of non-academic staff.

The actual practice of such institutions in the exercise of religious preference in employment decisions was also reported. Of the responding institutions 37.8 percent indicated that their general practice was to exercise religious preference in the hiring of all faculty positions; an additional 46.1 percent indicated that such preference was exercised in some, but not all faculty positions (for example, faculty in theology or religious studies). The vast majority of these institutions (83.9 percent) indicated that religious preference was exercised either in some or in all faculty appointments, while a minority of only 16.1 percent indicated that religious preference was never exercised in faculty hiring. Only 23.1 percent of those who exercised religious preference in faculty employment indicated that the religious orientation or church membership of the applicant was decisive by itself in the selection process; the remaining 76.9 percent indicated that the religious factor was one among many considered.

Of the institutions participating, 35.4 percent indicated that religious preference was exercised in the hiring of all administrative officers; an additional 52.2 percent indicated that such preference was exercised in filling some administrative positions (for example, the position of president). However, only 29.1 percent indicated that they ever exercised religious preference in filling non-academic staff positions.

TABLE 1[4]

PERCENT OF INSTITUTIONS
EXERCISING RELIGIOUS PREFERENCE
IN EMPLOYMENT DECISIONS

By Denominational Affiliation

	All Positions	Some Positions	No Positions
Administrators			
Baptist	78.3	17.4	4.3
Catholic	8.3	81.9	9.7
Lutheran	50.0	50.0	0.0
Methodist	14.3	66.7	19.0
Presbyter	50.0	15.0	35.0
Others	73.0	10.8	16.2
All Denom	39.3	48.3	12.4
Full-time Faculty			
Baptist	82.6	8.7	8.7
Catholic	12.5	77.8	9.7
Lutheran	62.5	31.3	6.3
Methodist	13.6	40.9	45.5
Presbyter	50.0	11.1	38.9
Others	73.0	16.2	10.8
All Denom	37.8	46.1	16.1
Non-Professional Staff			
Baptist	47.8	13.0	39.1
Catholic	5.5	1.4	93.2
Lutheran	6.7	13.3	80.0
Methodist	4.8	9.5	85.7
Presbyter	10.0	35.0	55.0
Others	43.2	27.0	29.7

TABLE 1 (continued)

	All Positions	Some Positions	No Positions
Faculty Tenure Decisions			
Baptist	42.1	0.0	57.9
Catholic	2.9	7.4	89.7
Lutheran	50.0	6.3	43.8
Methodist	9.1	9.1	81.8
Presbyter	47.1	0.0	52.9
Others	60.0	8.6	31.4

Three years later in <u>Government and Campus: Federal Regulation of Religiously Affiliated Higher Education</u> (1982), the Center published additional information concerning the exercise of religious preference in employment decisions at religiously affiliated colleges and universities, as obtained in the 1978 study for the Sloan Commission. The proportion of institutions exercising religious preference was reported to vary significantly by denominational affiliation, the proportion being much higher for Baptist institutions, for example, than for Methodist institutions. The Center's findings are summarized in Table 1.

The study showed that the religious factor was considered in the selection of all faculty in 82.6 percent of Baptist institutions and in 62.5 percent of Lutheran institutions. By contrast at 45.5 percent of Methodist institutions and 38.9 percent of Presbyterian institutions the religious factor was never taken into consideration in faculty appointments. Catholic institutions tended to be concerned about the religious factor on a more selective basis, discriminating more frequently as to the kinds of positions in which religious preference was viewed as appropriate (e.g., in theology and philosophy appointments).

The Center's study also determined that religiously affiliated colleges and universities were much less likely to exercise religious preference in granting tenure to faculty than in initially hiring them. Table 1 indicates the percentage of institutions exercising religious preference in tenure decisions by denominational affiliation. The table shows that a very high proportion of religiously affiliated colleges and universities never exercised religious preference in making such decisions. A substantial proportion of Baptist, Lutheran, and Presbyterian institutions exercised religious preference in tenure decisions for all faculty, but a very high proportion of Catholic and Methodist institutions never did.

In Government and Campus the Center researchers presented the same "rationale for religious preference" in employment decisions as had been published three years previously in Church and Campus. In the later publication, however, the Center researchers found that two divergent interpretations had arisen more recently in several lower court decisions, so as to raise questions of judicial consistency and predictability in employment discrimination cases.

In EEOC v. Mississippi College, 451 F.Supp. 564 (S.D. Miss. 1978), vacated and remanded 626 F.2d, 477 (5th Cir. 1980), and in EEOC v. Southwestern Theological Seminary 485 F.Supp. 255 (N.D. Tex, 1980); 651 F.2d, 277 (5th Cir. 1981), the Center reported, two federal district courts held that a religiously affiliated institution of higher education (in one instance a college and in the other a seminary) were not subject to the jurisdiction of the Equal Employment Opportunity Commission in seeking to make a factual determination respecting an actual or potential claim of employment discrimination. In the same time period, however, two other federal judges ruled that religious corporations (in one instance a religious press and in the other a parochial high school) were in fact subject to the Title VII prohibition against sex discrimination.

In the Mississippi College case the issue presented to the court concerned the jurisdiction of the Equal Employment Opportunity Commission to exercise its investigative powers in the context of alleged sex discrimination by a religiously affiliated college. The circuit court agreed with Mississippi College's contention that the EEOC had no power or authority to gain access to the college's files in order to seek evidence needed to establish the facts bearing on the allegation of sex discrimination against the college. The EEOC, said the court, "does not have jurisdiction even to maintain its investigation." The basis of this judicial determination was held to be the college's status as a religiously affiliated college.[5] Note that the complaint against the college was for alleged discrimination on the basis of sex.

In the Southwestern Seminary case the circuit court ruled that the EEOC lacked the power to compel a theological seminary to submit a routine information report required by the agency in accordance with the record-keeping and reporting provision of Title VII of the Civil Rights Act. The court based its ruling on a finding that Title VII does not apply to the employment relationship between a seminary and its faculty. The seminary successfully argued "that application of Title VII to any aspect of the employment relationship existing between the seminary and its administrators, faculty, and support personnel would not only infringe upon the free exercise rights of the seminary, but would lead inevitably to excessive entanglement of the government in the process of dissecting employment functions into religious and secular components and in divining the good faith and legitimacy of religious grounds asserted as a defense to a prima facie case of discrimination".[6] Note that no specific allegation of any form of discrimination was brought against the seminary. The case concerned only the question of the jurisdiction of the EEOC and its authority to investigate the institution's compliance with federal law.

In EEOC v. Pacific Press Publishing Association, 21 EPD 812 (N.D. Cal. 1979), on the other hand, a district judge declared that both the language and the legislative history of Title VII clearly indicate that Congress intended to prohibit acts of discrimination (other than religious discrimination as explicitly exempted) committed by religious employers. Furthermore, the court rejected the defense

INTRODUCTION

claims of a religiously affiliated publisher that application of Title VII would offend the Free Exercise clause by colliding with a truly religious cause of conduct, and that it would also offend the Establishment Clause by creating an excessive entanglement of government with religion. "The separation of church and state," the court declared, (is) not thwarted by this Court's decision in a secular employment matter."[7]

Similarly, in Dolter v. Wahlert High School, 483 F.Supp. 266 (N.D. Iowa 1980), a district court found that a religiously affiliated school was not exempt from liability under Title VII for sex discrimination, but was exempt only from liability for religious discrimination. In Dolter an unmarried female teacher was terminated by a parochial school when it was learned that she had become pregnant. The teacher sued, alleging that sex discrimination was the basis of her termination. When the school challenged the jursidiction of the EEOC on both constitutional and statutory grounds, the court found that it was proper to judicially inquire, not concerning the appropriateness of a religiously affiliated instituition's code of moral conduct as a bona fide occupational qualification for continuing employment at the school (in this case the code prohibiting pre-marital sex), but concerning whether the provision is "applied non-discriminatorily on the basis of sex; that is, unequally to defendant's male and female lay employees."

Government and Campus also mentions a case which tested the question how far a religiously affiliated college may go in the exercise of the entitlement under the Civil Rights Act to "employ employees of a particular religion" without offending the Free Exercise rights of individuals under the First Amendment. In Larsen v. Kirkham Civ. No.C. 74-287, D. Utah, an English instructor at Ricks College, a business college affiliated with the Church of Jesus Christ of Latter-Day Saints, brought suit against the college, alleging that the college had engaged in a discriminatory practice when it had dismissed her on the basis, in part, of reports that "her faith, her financial contributions, and her activity in the Latter-Day Saints

Church did not conform to the standards of the college with respect to female employees who are members of the L.D.S. Church." The court dismissed the complaint of the teacher, ruling that Congress had acted within its constitutional authority in allowing (through Title VII) a religiously affiliated school to consider religious belief and practice in establishing bona fide occupational qualifications for teachers. The Center researchers viewed this ruling as significantly broadening the rationale of McClure v. Salvation Army (460 F. 2d 553 (5th Cir.) cert. denied, 409 U.S. 896 (1972)), which had concerned the employment relationship between an ordained minister and her church, to cover the case of an employment relationship between an English instructor and a religiously affiliated college.[8]

The Center's research in the area of religious preference in employment decisions in religiously affiliated higher education has also been reported in the Legal Deskbook for Administrators of Independent Colleges and Universities, originally published in 1981 under the editorship of Kent M. Weeks and updated in 1987 under the editorship of Mark G. Yudof.[9] Two sections of this comprehensive reference manual include materials and analysis which are relevant for our topic. In Chapter IV on "Employment," an extended exposition is presented on the topic of "Nondiscrimination." Chapter IX, devoted in its entirety to "Church-related Colleges and Universities," includes an examination of the topic of "Public Assistance and Exemption from Civil Rights for Church-related Institutions." The comprehensive bibliographic, statutory, and judicial references in the latest edition of the Deskbook are current as of 1987.

In State and Campus: State Regulation of Religiously Affiliated Higher Education,[10] Center researchers Fernand N. Dutile and Edward McGlynn Gaffney, Jr., produced a monumental state-by-state summary of state laws and regulations affecting religiously affiliated higher education in eight categories: 1) corporate status; 2) state financial aid; 3) personnel policies and practices; 4) student admission and discipline; 5) use of publicly funded facilities; 6) taxation and exemption from taxation; 7) charitable solicitation and other forms of fund-raising; and 8) miscellaneous (e.g., laws affecting minors, state coordinating boards, licensing laws, charitable immunity, campus disorders, etc.).

In an introductory chapter the manual presents an extended national overview of state regulation in the area of "Religious Preference in Employment Policies." Detailed information on provisions of state law affecting the exercise of religious preference in employment decisions is presented in the state-by-state summaries. The work presents a legal rationale for the exercise of religious preference in employment decisions in religiously affiliated institutions of higher education, which is essentially the same as was originally presented by the Center in Church and Campus; but State and Campus is a mine of information concerning the diversity of constitutional, statutory, and judicial provisions in the several states. The information is current as of 1984.

3. Aims of the Present Study

Our study builds upon and extends the previous research completed by the Center for Constitutional Studies. The present work brings constitutional interpretation, judicial precedent, and statutory provisions up to date as of 1989. Although a detailed investigation of state law is beyond the scope of this publication, occasional reference is made to representative state law affecting religious preference in employment decisions for illustrative purposes, in the hope that such examples will stimulate institutions to closely examine the specifics of state regulation as it affects them. Our inquiry readdresses the Center's long-standing question of how the exercise of religious preference in employment decisions at religiously affiliated institutions of higher education might be managed without jeopardy to the institution's eligibility for federal and state funding. And our study also addresses the bearing of the traditions of academic freedom and of sound administrative practice on the exercise of religious preference in academic employment.

INTRODUCTION

Among the specific questions which we shall seek to address are the following:

1. What are the major models of religiously preferential hiring among different types of religiously affiliated institutions of higher education and how are these models distributed among such institutions?

2. What is the present statutory basis, both federal and state, for defining the rights of institutions and of individuals, respectively, in the exercise of religious preference in employment decisions at religiously affiliated institutions of higher education?

3. What are the key constitutional concepts and interpretations which establish the context within which such institutional and individual rights must be defined?

4. How should religious discrimination in employment be understood in American labor law and in well-formed personnel administrative practice in religiously affiliated higher education? How might such a concept be more fully incorporated into the system of American law? into the employment policies and procedures of religiously affiliated colleges and universities? How should religiously discriminatory policies and procedures in personnel administration be organized so as to assure "due process" in employment decisions?

5. What is the constitutional and statutory basis of governmental jurisdiction in determining the merit of claims of employment discrimination in religiously affiliated institutions of higher education, and what are the limits and conditions of such jurisdiction?

6. What forms of legal reasoning have courts followed - - and what forms may they be expected to follow in the foreseeable future - - in reaching decisions concerning the rights of institutions and individuals, respectively, in the exercise of religious preference in employment decisions at religiously affiliated institutions of higher education?

INTRODUCTION

7. How might differing understandings of institutional mission among religiously affiliated institutions of higher education affect the determination of their legal rights and responsibilities in employment policies and practices?

8. What are the kinds of limitations which should be placed by law on the right to exercise religious discrimination in employment in religious organizations and in religiously affiliated institutions of higher education? What is to be said of the constitutionality of an "unbounded exemption" for religiously affiliated colleges and universities which would allow them to exercise religious preference for all faculty and staff positions? When might courts find that institutional use of religious preference is really a mask to disguise discriminatory intent in some other respect?

9. What is the scope of the bona fide occupational qualification under the law of nondiscrimination in employment, and how does this exemption affect the exercise of religious and valuational preference in employment decisions in independent and religiously affiliated colleges and universities?

10. How should the tradition of academic freedom in American higher education affect the exercise of religious and valuational preference in employment decisions in independent and religiously affiliated colleges and universities?

11. What are the important trends in federal and state law affecting the exercise of religious and valuational preference in educational employment in an increasingly pluralistic society?

12. What statutory language is most functional for defining the right of religiously preferential hiring in religiously affiliated higher education, while at the same time strengthening the legal prohibition of forms of discrimination which are educationally and socially inappropriate?

INTRODUCTION

NOTES TO INTRODUCTION

1. William A. Kaplin, "Law on the Campus 1960-1985: Years of Growth and Challenge," Journal of College and University Law, Volume 12, 1985.

2. Philip R. Moots and Edward McGlynn Gaffney, Jr., Church and Campus: Legal Issues in Religiously Affiliated Higher Education, University of Notre Dame Press, 1979, p. 71.

3. Ibid., p. 35.

4. Data taken from Edward McGlynn Gaffney, Jr., and Philip R. Moots, Government and Campus: Federal Regulation of Religiously Affiliated Higher Education, University of Notre Dame Press, 1982, pp. 35-39.

5. The circuit court decision was later upheld only in part by the Fifth Circuit Court of Appeals. See below, pp. 185-188.

6. Government and Campus, p. 62. See below, pp. 188-189 for the subsequent decision of the Fifth Circuit Court of Appeals in this case.

7. Ibid., p. 63. See below pp. 195-197 for additional comments on this case.

8. Ibid., pp. 64,65.

9. Kent M. Weeks, editor of original edition, and Mark G. Yudof, editor of 1987 revision, Legal Deskbook for Administrators of Independent Colleges and Universities, Mercer University Press for the Center for Constitutional Studies, 1987.

10. Fernand N. Dutile and Edward McGlynn Gaffney, Jr., State and Campus: State Regulation of Religiously Affiliated Higher Education, University of Notre Dame Press, (1984).

CHAPTER ONE

A TAXONOMY OF RELIGIOUSLY AFFILIATED
HIGHER EDUCATION

Religiously affiliated institutions of higher education in the United States represent a rich variety of mission, scope of programs, size, organization, and sponsorship. There are no easy generalizations which will cover the broad range of employment policies and practices which are to be found in the midst of all this institutional diversity.

From time to time researchers have sought to develop a taxonomy which would permit classification of religiously affiliated higher education for purposes of analytical description, but their effort has been frustrated by the immense diversity of the system. Yet some scheme of classification is essential for our purpose, since the law of higher education inevitably makes use of classifications, definitions, and descriptive generalizations. Our research must begin, therefore, with some broad characterizations of the system of religiously affiliated institutions of higher education, with special reference to their employment policies and practices.

We have identified approximately 1100 accredited institutions of post-secondary education in the United States which we would classify as religiously affiliated. We use the term in a broad sense (following the practice of most studies of church-related higher education) to include all those institutions which have some orientation to or association with religious values, purposes, or traditions. The church relationship of some of these institutions has been attenuated over the years, and many of these would now classify themselves simply as independent, rather than as religiously affiliated. Their historic ties to a religious organization or tradition, however, have exercised a formative influence on their development and continue to be a factor in their understanding of institutional mission and their approach to educational and administrative decision making.

Of these 1100 institutions we classify about 570 as general baccalaureate institutions. An additional 80 or so are baccalaureate institutions with a significant array of graduate and graduate professional programs, although they remain largely undergraduate institutions. About 40 are comprehensive universities. About 175 institutions are theological seminaries or schools of divinity, some of these being organized as schools or departments within colleges or universities. There are also about 65 rabbinical schools, and another 90 or so are Bible colleges or Bible institutes. About 65 are two-year junior colleges, and there are about 15 other very small two-year Catholic institutions (we call them seminary-colleges) organized primarily for the foundational training of religious.

It is obvious that within this diverse mix of institutions there is a wide variety of ways in which religious and valuational factors are considered in educational program design, in student admission, and in appointments to the faculty, administration, and staff. In institutions engaged in theological education and professional preparation of religious workers, religious and moral criteria play a significantly differ role in employment decisions than they do in university programs in professional education or in engineering or business technologies. Values-related factors play significantly different roles in faculty appointments at institutions emphasizing a teaching mission than at those with a strong research emphasis.

Many religiously affiliated colleges and universities view their religious belief systems and historic religious associations as decisively determinative for their mission concepts and for educational and administrative policy. In such institutions the right to recruit and retain faculty, administrative, and support personnel who share the institution's religious and moral values is at the heart of the institution's educational distinctiveness. In others where the religious affiliation is more nominal than real, educational policy and employment policy are often not materially different from what they would be in public institutions. It is clear, therefore, that our research is

20

required to identify some general models of the ways in which religious beliefs and values are considered in employment decisions at religiously affiliated institutions of higher education before we can speak realistically about the present state of the law affecting the operations and policies of such institutions.

1.   Some Models of Religiously Preferential Hiring

The right of an academy of learning to place moral as well as professional conditions on the privilege of participating in its life is a long and firmly established tradition of the higher learning. This right arises from the system of values which are inherent in the functions of scholarship and teaching. Among the ideals of the academy are such classic virtues as honesty, respect for truth, justice (fairness), reasonableness, freedom, collegiality, commitment to the educational and personal development of students, etc. An academy of learning cannot function without such qualities, and it is entirely appropriate for an academic institution to require that those who participate in its common life should be capable of accomodating their academic and communal pursuits to the requirements of such values and ideals.

Our particular question in this study concerns the additional requirement of religious qualifications for academic, administrative, and/or staff employees of institutions of higher education which have a religiously oriented mission and/or organizational relationship. The examination of this issue in the particular setting of American law demands recognition of the variety of religious orientations and church relationships which are apparent among these institutions.

In the most comprehensive study of church-related higher education ever conducted, the Danforth Commission on Church Colleges and Universities surveyed about 800 institutions which maintained some kind of church relationship or religious orientation or were founded under religious sponsorship. The Commission sought a basis for a classification of types and degrees of church relationship in six different factors which it considered determinative: ownership, composition of the board of control, financial support, acceptance of denominational standards or use of denominational name, educational aims, and selection of faculty and administrative personnel. Using these criteria the Commission identified four major institutional types:

> The Defender-of-the-Faith College.
> The Non-affirming College.
> The Free Christian College.
> The Church-related University.[1]

The Commission's taxonomy was controversial in both its language and its methodology. The Commission ostensibly followed an empirical method in developing its classifications, but the language it chose in identifying the various types of church relationship was hardly neutral. Furthermore, the Commission's criteria failed to include a number of taxonomic factors of a more functional and operational nature: for example, the degree of separatism in the controlling denomination or rule of faith, the manner in which a theological criterion is employed in faculty and administrative appointments, the use of a religious or ethical test in student admission, the nature of institutional controls over student behavior, the frequency and character of campus worship activities, the scope of the curricular requirement in religion, etc. Factors like these are at least as significant in identifying forms of religious orientation and church relationship as are the formal and organizational factors emphasized in the Danforth methodology (and, incidentally, in most other studies of church-related higher education as well.) Most informed observers, however, will recognize something approximating the Danforth classifications as appropriate groupings for American colleges and universities with religious origins or orientations.

Merrimon Cunninggim has distinguished the following models of church-relatedness:

TAXONOMY OF HIGHER EDUCATION

1) The **Embodying College**, which explicitly seeks to be the mirror or reflection of its supporting church, sound in both faith and observance;
2) The **Proclaiming College**, which joyously confesses its affiliation with its sponsoring church body and shares in the witness of its religious tradition as an academic partner, while valuing pluralism in the collegiate community and maintaining its distinctiveness as a community of learning;
3) The **Consonant College**, which emphasizes its independence and de-emphasizes its church-relatedness, while at the same time remaining committed to the tradition of its related church and viewing its role as that of a supportive ally of the church's values.[2]

Cunninggim views each of these collegiate models as satisfying two essential requirements of a genuinely church-related college or university; viz. it "puts forth some sort of claim to being connected with a church, and, second, supports that claim with some sort of observable action that makes the claim credible." His classification scheme seeks to recognize a wide variety of forms in which church-related institutions might act supportively of a religious tradition or association, and different degrees of intensity and priority in their commitments to such supportive action.

In the pursuit of its mission as supportive of the religious values and traditions of its supporting church, a college or university may make strategic use of religious and valuational criteria in employment decisions. In institutions in which the religious purpose is central and controlling in a comprehensive sense, such criteria might be used in all or most employment decisions. In some institutions a rigorous and comprehensive evaluation of religious orientation and perspective might be required in faculty appointments, though not in non-academic appointments. In other institutions such tests might be used selectively in faculty appointments: e.g., in departments of philosophy, theology, or religion, or in faculty appointments with tenure. In other institutions such tests might be limited to major

23

leadership positions: e.g. trustees, the president, and senior administrative officers. In other institutions applicants for faculty and administrative positions might be asked to indicate their general awareness of and sympathy with the religious traditions and values with which the institution is identified and to promise to do nothing to interfere with or to undermine the pursuit of such values. The range of diversity in the interpretation and application of religious criteria in employment policies among religiously affiliated institutions of higher education is immense.

Our study of the exercise of religious preference in employment decisions in religiously affiliated higher education makes use of four major categories of institutions:

> Pervasively Religious Institutions.
> Religiously Supportive Institutions.
> Nominally Church-related Institutions.
> Independent Institutions with Historic Religious Ties.

A. Pervasively Religious Institutions

A significant number of religiously affiliated institutions view themselves as pervaded by a religious purpose and belief. In such institutions the use of valuational criteria in faculty and staff appointments, and even in student admissions, takes on a determinate form, arising from the concept of education as pervaded by a religious concern.

The concept of an educational process centered on religious faith represents an honorable tradition, which has made important contributions both to American education and to American culture. Howard Lowry has expressed the concept in his definition of religiously affiliated higher education as "a study of all of life for the discovery of divine truth," as a process of teaching/learning in which religion is not "a fragment or phase of the educational process, but its permeating factor and its inner unity."[3] D. Elton Trueblood has contended that what distinguishes a Christian college from other types of educational institution is "the penetration of the total college life by the central

24

Christian convictions."[4]   And Nels F.S. Ferre has proposed a concept of a religiously oriented college as "a fellowship of inquiry under God." In such a college, as Ferre conceives it, theological study is "avowedly the center of the curriculum," and "academic life centers in the total life of the Christian community." Such a college, says Ferre, accepts it as its vocation "to find for the world, and to help the world to do, the will of God."[5]

The idea of education as permeated by a religious purpose need not be construed in narrowly sectarian terms, as the above-mentioned writers would be particularly concerned to argue. Nor are the purposes of pervasively religious institutions of higher education necessarily understood narrowly in terms of preparation for ministerial professions. In a religiously pervaded liberal arts college, the aims of education center on the integration of all of learning in relation to ultimate values and religious beliefs which are viewed as potentially controlling for human life.

In pervasively religious institutions of higher education, the selection of participants who can contribute to the achievement of a religiously-based integration of experience is of critical importance to the success of the enterprise. Some pervasively religious colleges follow a creedal or denominational test in such a process of selection; others pursue a more flexible approach such as that advocated by Ferre. In many pervasively religious institutions the ideal of education requires that all members of the community, including all students and staff, should be able to meet the religious and valuational requirements of participation in the quest for a religiously integrated common life.

Church-related schools of professional preparation for church vocations present special requirements for employment policy and practice. Such institutions have historically viewed admission to professional study as closely related to recruitment for the church's vocations and have often established specific personal and theological requirements for both faculty appointments and student admission.   Criteria have included not only creedal confessions, but also personal character, moral behavior, marital status, etc.

Some institutions of theological education, however, are distinctly non-sectarian and non-creedal in orientation, and exhibit many of the distinctive characteristics of university-level study. In many the theological tests for faculty appointments have become much less precise and much less important in recent years. American courts have generally been reluctant to become involved in the evaluation of policies and operations of churches affecting their ministers or in the affairs of institutions of professional preparation affecting church vocations. But as the curricula of seminaries and Bible colleges develop stronger emphasis on the "academic study of religion" and become less focused on professional preparation, they take on more and more of the characteristics of church-related colleges and universities generally and may become more subject to new legal classifications.

The law recognizes the right of sectarianism in education. Institutions with a sectarian purpose or institutions seeking to propagate or inculcate a specific set of religious tenets are protected in the exercise of employment policies and practices designed to achieve their aims. By no means all of the pervasively religious colleges and universities would accept the characterization of their purpose as sectarian or doctrinaire, however. Many would emphasize the distinction between education and indoctrination and would pursue the integration of religious perspectives in the life of learning without reference to any particular sectarian definition. Such institutions have at times discovered that their distinctive understanding of a free and inclusive program of higher learning pervaded by a religious consciousness and purpose is not expressly identified as a model of educational operations recognized and protected by the law.

We estimate that something like 375 accredited institutions of post-secondary education (about a third of the 1100 religiously affiliated institutions we have identified) fall into the classification of "pervasively religious institutions." We include in this group all the Bible colleges and Bible institutes, all the Roman Catholic "seminary-colleges," most of the rabbinical schools and colleges of Hebrew studies, and about three-quarters of the theological seminaries and schools of divinity. We also place in this category about 65 or 70 baccalaureate colleges (about 12 percent of the total), a few baccalaureate institutions with a significant program of graduate and graduate professional programs, and a small number of junior colleges.

Not all of these institutions, of course, are formally owned or directly controlled by a church or religious organization. Many are listed by the U.S. Department of Education (on the basis of information provided by the institutions themselves) simply as "independent" and are not identified as affiliated with any religious group or tradition. The law of higher education has sometimes naively assumed that the identifying characteristics of a "pervasively religious" institution of higher education are necessarily formal or organizational. The critical question, however, concerns not organization under some type of ecclesiastical hierarchy or denominational constituency, but the purposes, programs, policies, and operations of the institution in its pursuit of a concept of faith, learning, and life.

B. Religiously Supportive Institutions

Our second category of religiously affiliated institutions of higher education is more difficult to characterize. A very large number of American colleges and universities view their educational purposes as being strongly influenced by a religious association and/or guided by a religious purpose, even though they would not share the aspiration of making religious concerns and beliefs of central importance in the life of the campus. This understanding takes a number of forms among different institutions and groups of institutions. Although not a pervasive factor in all aspects of campus life and administrative policy, the religious factor plays a major role in employment decisions at such institutions, and they require much the same kinds of legal protection in their exercise of religious preference in employment decisions as do pervasively religious and explicitly sectarian institutions.

Institutions which fall into this second category typically seek a greater degree of campus diversity than would be accepted in pervasively religious institutions. The diversity is usually viewed as desirable from the point of view of broadening the experience of faculty and students and facilitating a more dialectical educational process. Nevertheless, these institutions would stress the importance of a "critical mass" of personnel who are sufficiently oriented toward the religious purposes and heritage of the institution to assure the viability of the educational mission. There would probably be little agreement among these institutions concerning the precise point on the continuum of diversity-homogeneity where this "critical mass" is found, but all would agree that there is some point where personnel decisions affect institutional values. At that point religious preference enters into employment decisions in a manner suited to the theological perspectives and traditions of the institution.

We do not place in this category institutions which exercise religious preference in employment decisions only on a very selective basis. An institution which employs a religious test only for the appointment of the president but would never exercise religious preference in faculty appointments is probably functioning not as a "religiously supportive institution," but as a "nominally church-related institution" under our classification scheme. Nevertheless, there are obviously significant differences of degree in religious orientation among the institutions which we place in this second category.

We estimate that about 275 accredited religiously affiliated institutions fall into this class of "religiously supportive institutions," i.e. institutions of strong religious purpose and character where the degree of religious orientation falls short of being central or all-pervasive. We place in this category about 175 general baccalaureate institutions (about a third of the total of religiously affiliated baccalaureate colleges), 10-15 baccalaureate institutions with graduate programs, and about 45 junior colleges (about two-thirds of the total of religiously affiliated junior colleges). We also assign to this group about 30 seminaries and schools of divinity.

Accordingly, we estimate that of the 1100 institutions identified as religiously affiliated, something like 650 (or 60 percent) are either pervasively religious or strongly religious in purpose to such a degree that they may be expected to depend heavily on the right to exercise religious preference in employment decisions in order to carry out their distinctive educational missions.

C. Nominally Church-related Institutions

Our third category of religiously affiliated institutions of higher education corresponds roughly with Cunninggim's "Consonant College." We use our term "nominally church-related" in a non-pejorative sense. Such an institution emphasizes its independence and de-emphasizes its church-relationship, but often it retains a continuing appreciation of and commitment to those aspects of the tradition of its related church which it finds perennially relevant to the values and purposes of higher education as it understands them.

Our "nominally church-related institutions," in other words, are significantly, but not strongly influenced by their respective religious traditions. Such an institution may view its church-relatedness as an important symbol of historic associations, but not as a controlling value in its present educational mission. It may continue to recognize the church affiliation in its name and to accept the participation of the religious organization in the election of trustees, but it does not consider itself fundamentally responsible or accountable to its related church or order, nor does it depend heavily on the church for support. It views its actions as generally consonant with the values of its related church group, but it does not consider the aim of nurturing religious faith as essential to its own educational task. It is not usually antagonistic to the church; rather it thinks of itself, in Cunninggim's phrase, as a friend and an ally.

A nominally church-related college or university may require or prefer that its president maintain good standing with the church, but it will not consider religious qualifications generally important in filling faculty and administrative positions. Religious qualifications will typically enter into employment decisions only as a kind of bona fide occupational qualification for selected positions. In filling the vast majority of its positions, both academic and non-academic, the institution will seek the most competent personnel for the specific function involved. If religious qualifications are considered at all, they will come into focus after other professional factors have been weighed. In many institutions the policy is that religious factors will be given consideration in faculty and staff appointments if other qualifications of competing candidates are roughly equal, but not otherwise. Thus nominally church-related institutions of higher education generally have little at stake in seeking a broad exception to legal prohibitions against religious discrimination in employment decisions; most would say that such discrimination never occurs in their institutions.

We estimate that something like 335 accredited institutions would be classified as "nominally church-related" in this sense. We place in this category about 240 general baccalaureate institutions (slightly more than 40 percent of the total of religiously affiliated baccalaureate schools), about 50 (somewhat more than half) of the baccalaureate schools with graduate programs, about 20 (half) of the comprehensive universities, about 15 religiously affiliated junior colleges, and a few schools of theological education.

D. Independent Institutions with Historic Religious Ties

Finally, we identify a fourth class of institutions which have taken an additional step of separation from their original religious sponsorship and founding. These are institutions which have been identified as church-related for many years, but no longer acknowledge any form or degree of religious affiliation. At one time they had a significant religious affiliation, but they are now entirely independent and are not religiously oriented in any way. In some cases the related church has continued to declare its sponsoring relationship for a number of years after the college or university has ceased to recognize any church relationship.

Many of these institutions possess resources and traditions which are the envy of all of higher education. They are pace-setters in educational effectiveness and administrative competence, as well as in financial strength. We include them among our group of religiously affiliated institutions of higher education partly in recognition of the continuing impact of their initial church relationship on institutional values, partly out of deference to the many years of their previous inclusion in lists of religiously affiliated colleges and universities.

These institutions have much at stake, of course, in the continued strength and viability of the independent sector, and they frequently cooperate with more religiously oriented institutions in the pursuit of common goals. They have no special requirements, however, in the area of the exercise of religious preference in employment decisions. Most would say that religious factors are never taken into consideration in the appointment or promotion of personnel and that they would be no more exempt from the prohibition against religious discrimination than would any other organization.

We have identified about 120 institutions which fall into this class. About 80 of these are general baccalaureate institutions, and about 35 are universities or baccalaureate institutions with graduate programs. A small number are divinity schools attached to independent universities. Many of these institutions have functioned for several generations without any church relationship, but a significant number have made the final separation from the parent religious organizations only within recent memory.

TABLE 2

DISTRIBUTION OF RELIGIOUSLY AFFILIATED INSTITUTIONS OF HIGHER EDUCATION BY DEGREE OF RELIGIOUS ORIENTATION

	Pervas Rel		Strong Rel		Nomin Ch-rel		No Rel Purp		Total	
	No	Pct	No	Pct	No	Pct	No	Pct	No	Pct
Scope of Mission										
BACC	67	11.8	178	31.3	242	42.6	81	14.3	568	100
BAC/GR	7	8.4	12	14.5	47	56.6	17	20.5	83	100
UNIV	0	0.0	4	9.8	21	51.2	16	39.0	41	100
SEM	131	74.4	31	17.6	9	5.1	5	2.8	176	100
RABB	57	89.1	5	7.8	2	3.1	0	0.0	64	100
BIB COL	92	100.	0	0.0	0	0.0	0	0.0	92	100
JUN COL	6	9.2	43	66.2	16	24.6	0	0.0	65	100
SEM-COL	15	100.	0	0.0	0	0.0	0	0.0	15	100
TOTAL	375	34.0	273	24.7	337	30.5	119	10.8	1104	100

Denominational Affiliation

	No	Pct	No	Pct	No	Pct	No	Pct	No	Pct
BAPT	46	39.3	52	44.4	15	12.8	4	3.4	117	100
CONG	3	9.7	10	32.3	12	38.7	6	19.4	31	100
CHRIST	28	50.0	8	14.3	15	26.8	5	8.9	56	100
LUTH	14	25.0	29	51.8	13	23.2	0	0.0	56	100
METH	12	9.1	39	69.6	69	52.3	12	9.1	132	100
PRESB	20	23.0	13	14.9	40	46.0	14	16.1	87	100
CATHLC	55	19.2	78	27.2	141	49.1	13	4.5	287	100
JEWISH	57	89.1	5	7.8	2	3.1	0	0.0	64	100
HOLINES	22	73.3	8	26.7	0	0.0	0	0.0	30	100
PIETIST	19	41.3	10	21.7	10	21.7	7	15.2	46	100
PENTEC	13	100.	0	0.0	0	0.0	0	0.0	13	100
OTHR DN	28	50.0	13	23.2	7	12.5	8	14.3	56	100
INDEP EV	58	98.3	1	1.7	0	0.0	0	0.0	59	100
INDEP	0	0.0	7	10.0	13	18.6	50	71.4	70	100
TOTAL	375	34.0	273	24.7	337	30.5	119	10.8	1104	100

TABLE 2 (continued)

Region	Pervas Rel No Pct	Strong Rel No Pct	Nomin Ch-rel No Pct	No Rel Purp No Pct	Total No Pct
NORTHST	14 26.4	12 22.6	20 37.7	7 13.2	53 100
MID ATL	98 39.7	32 13.0	76 30.8	41 16.6	247 100
SOUTH	93 28.0	100 30.1	107 32.2	32 9.6	332 100
GRT LKS	65 31.7	57 27.8	58 28.3	25 12.2	205 100
PLAINS	53 33.5	51 32.3	47 29.7	7 4.4	158 100
WEST	52 47.7	21 19.3	29 26.6	7 6.4	109 100
TOTAL	375 34.0	273 24.7	337 30.5	119 10.8	1104 100

Enrollment Range

	Pervas Rel No Pct	Strong Rel No Pct	Nomin Ch-rel No Pct	No Rel Purp No Pct	Total No Pct
0-499	279 69.4	86 21.4	31 7.7	6 1.5	402 100
500-999	55 23.3	84 35.6	71 30.1	26 11.0	236 100
1000-1999	52 10.3	63 23.1	133 48.7	9 17.9	273 100
2000-2999	7 8.2	25 29.4	40 47.1	13 15.3	85 100
3000-4999	5 8.3	10 16.7	36 60.0	9 15.0	60 100
5000-9999	1 3.2	3 9.7	17 54.8	10 32.3	31 100
10000 UP	0 0.0	2 11.8	9 52.9	6 35.3	17 100
TOTAL	375 34.0	273 24.7	337 30.5	119 10.8	1104 100

Such models of the exercise of religious and valuational preference in faculty and staff hiring and retention are familiar ones for students of independent higher education in America. Table 2 summarizes the results of our attempt at classification. The table shows the distribution of religiously affiliated institutions not only by mission and scope of program, but also by denomination, by region, and by enrollment. Variations in the distribution by denominational affiliation are, we think, particularly interesting and significant.

Readers who are familiar with previous studies of religiously affiliated higher education will appreciate the complexity of any such endeavor at classification. We recognize the limitations of our own investigation. We have been assiduous in our attempt to obtain reliable documentation to support our classifications, however, and are generally confident in the broad characterization which we have offered.

The institutions which we have identified as pervasively or strongly religious in purpose and orientation represent the entire spectrum of organized religion in America. There is no religious tradition which does not have a major interest in the exercise of religious preference in employment decisions at the institutions of higher education with which it is affiliated. The issue which we address in this project does not concern the protection of the right of a few "sectarian" groups to pursue their respective faiths; it concerns the continued viability of the educational ministries of American religion in every tradition.

To summarize: Of our 1100 accredited religiously affiliated institutions of higher education, approximately 650 (about 60%) are either "pervasively religious" or "strongly oriented to religious purposes and values" and would be expected to exercise religious discrimination in employment decisions on a comprehensive scale. Of this number about 330 are schools organized primarily for the education of clergy and religious; the remaining 320 are universities, baccalaureate colleges and junior colleges.

Among our other categories of "nominally church-related institutions" and "independent institutions with no religious purposes," religious factors would be expected to enter into employment decisions only on a selective basis. Many of these institutions maintain a church relationship which they view as extremely important, however, and some think of themselves, in fact, as religious organizations. Their interest in the right of church-related educational institutions to exercise religious discrimination in employment is less comprehensive and momentous than it is for institutions with a stronger religious orientation, but it is often a powerful and sincere interest nevertheless.

TAXONOMY OF HIGHER EDUCATION

The church relationships of this diverse system of institutions cover an extremely broad spectrum. The complexity of the system simply does not lend itself to the stereotypic language of legal definition. Some church-related institutions function under close management and control by a church or religious order. At the other end of the continuum is a loose structure through which the church participates in some nominal way in selecting members of the board of control. Many of the colleges and universities with the strongest and most pervasive religious orientations are entirely independent of any organizational relationship to any church or religious organization whatever. In some religiously affiliated institutions property is held by the school as an independent corporation; in others property is held by a church or religious organization or by the school and church jointly. Of course, there are all kinds of gradations along this complex continuum of cooperation, interdependence, and control.

2. Some Findings of Our Recent Survey

For purposes of this project we have made a new survey of religiously affiliated institutions of higher education to obtain current information concerning ways in which they exercise religious preference in employment decisions. Our survey updates and expands information assembled in the Center's 1978 survey. The information provided in our questionnaire was supplied by the president of each of the responding institutions (or by someone acting under the president's direct supervision). The results of this survey, which was completed in 1988, are presented in this section.

We received usable responses from slightly more than 300 institutions (or about 28 percent of the total number of religiously affiliated institutions). The distribution of our responses by type of institution and church affiliation is indicated in Table 3. The distribution of institutions corresponds roughly to that of Table 2, indicating that our sample is reasonably representative in terms of these categories.[6]

TABLE 3

RELIGIOUSLY AFFILIATED INSTITUTIONS
BY TYPE AND CHURCH AFFILIATION
INSTITUTIONS RESPONDING TO SURVEY

	Pervas Rel		Strong Rel		Nomin Ch-Rel		No Rel Purp		Total	
	No	Pct	No	Pct	No	Pct	No	Pct	No	Pct
Type of Institution										
BACC	47	22.2	45	21.2	105	49.5	15	7.1	212	100
BAC/GR	3	10.3	9	31.0	16	55.2	1	3.4	29	100
UNIV	0	0.0	4	26.7	7	46.7	4	26.7	15	100
SEM/DV	32	76.2	6	14.3	4	9.5	0	0.0	42	100
BIB COL	11	100.	0	0.0	0	0.0	0	0.0	11	100
TOTAL	93	30.1	64	20.7	132	42.7	20	6.5	309	100
Church Affiliation										
BAPT	13	38.2	15	44.1	6	17.6	0	0.0	34	100
CONG	1	12.5	1	12.5	4	50.0	2	25.0	8	100
CHRIST	6	50.0	1	8.3	5	41.7	0	0.0	12	100
LUTH	9	42.9	3	14.3	9	42.9	0	0.0	21	100
METH	6	16.2	5	13.5	23	62.2	3	8.1	37	100
PRESB	8	28.6	5	17.9	12	42.9	3	10.7	28	100
CATHLC	7	7.4	28	29.5	58	61.1	2	2.1	95	100
PIETIST	7	38.9	3	16.7	6	33.3	2	11.1	18	100
OTHR DN	22	71.0	3	9.7	5	16.1	1	3.2	31	100
INDEP EV	14	100.	0	0.0	0	0.0	0	0.0	14	100
INDEP	0	0.0	0	0.0	4	36.4	7	63.6	11	100
TOTAL	93	30.1	64	20.7	132	42.7	20	6.5	309	100

The presidents were asked to indicate which of the following chararacterizations would most aptly identify their institutions:

Pervasively religious.
Significantly influenced by religious heritage/purpose.
Nominally church-related.
Neither religiously affiliated nor religiously oriented.

The self-characterizations of the responding institutions are summarized in Table 4. A comparison of this table with Table 3 indicates that many responding presidents from our group of "nominally church-related" institutions seem to dislike that label and prefer to identify their institutions as "significantly influenced" by the religious heritage and association of the institution.[7]

The institutions were asked to report the proportion of the Board of Trustees who are elected by the church or religious organization to which the institution is related. The responses are summarized in Table 5. A number of the "pervasively religious" institutions have no church affiliation of any kind, and their boards are self-perpetuating. Although these institutions would report that none of their board members are elected by a church, they all have a selection process which would assure that members elected have a religious standing and belief which are compatible with the heritage and orientation of the institution. In "nominally church-related" and independent institutions, on the other hand, boards with less than 5% elected by a church or religious organization would typically be composed without reference to religious qualifications.

We also asked the institutions to report the proportion of Educational and General Expenditures which would be drawn in a typical year from contributions or subsidies from a church, denomination, or religious organization. The responses are summarized in Table 5. The table indicates clearly that the proportionate dependence on church financial support varies in direct relation to the degree of religious affiliation identified in our model. The degree of financial dependence is much larger, of course, in seminaries, divinity schools, and Bible colleges than in religiously affiliated colleges and universities.

TABLE 4

SELF-CHARACTERIZATION OF
RELIGIOUSLY AFFILIATED INSTITUTIONS
BY TYPE AND CHURCH AFFILIATION

	Pervas Rel		Signif Rel*		Nomin Ch-Rel		No Rel Purp		Total	
	No	Pct	No	Pct	No	Pct	No	Pct	No	Pct
Type of Institution										
BACC	49	23.1	131	61.8	26	12.3	6	2.8	212	100
BAC/GR	6	20.7	21	72.4	1	3.4	1	3.4	29	100
UNIV	1	6.7	11	73.3	1	6.7	2	13.3	15	100
SEM/DV	31	73.8	10	23.8	1	2.4	0	0.0	42	100
BIB COL	10	90.9	1	9.1	0	0.0	0	0.0	11	100
TOTAL	97	31.4	174	56.3	29	9.4	9	2.9	309	100
Church Affiliation										
BAPT	12	35.3	21	61.8	1	2.9	0	0.0	34	100
CONG	2	25.0	2	25.0	3	37.5	1	12.5	8	100
CHRIST	6	50.0	1	8.3	5	41.7	0	0.0	12	100
LUTH	7	33.3	12	57.1	2	9.5	0	0.0	21	100
METH	6	16.2	21	56.8	10	27.0	0	0.0	37	100
PRESB	8	28.6	15	53.6	5	17.9	0	0.0	28	100
CATHLC	11	11.6	83	87.4	0	0.0	1	1.1	95	100
PIETIST	9	50.0	8	44.4	1	5.6	0	0.0	18	100
OTHR DN	23	74.2	6	19.4	2	6.5	0	0.0	31	100
INDEP EV	13	92.9	1	7.1	0	0.0	0	0.0	14	100
INDEP	0	0.0	4	36.4	0	0.0	7	63.6	11	100
TOTAL	97	31.4	174	56.3	29	9.4	9	2.9	309	100

* Note the change in heading from Tables 2 and 3.

Table 5 also reports information obtained from our respondents concerning the way in which title is held to the property and plant facilities of the institution. Most of the institutions in which a church or religious organization

TABLE 5

RELIGIOUSLY AFFILIATED INSTITUTIONS
BY INDICATORS OF ORGANIZATIONAL STRUCTURE
INSTITUTIONS RESPONDING TO SURVEY

	Pervas Rel		Strong Rel		Nomin Ch-Rel		No Rel Purp		Total	
	No	Pct	No	Pct	No	Pct	No	Pct	No	Pct

Percent of Board Elected by Religious Organization

100%	53	57.0	20	31.3	12	9.1	2	10.0	87	28.2
76-99%	3	3.2	0	0.0	1	0.8	0	0.0	4	1.3
51-75%	8	8.6	8	12.5	10	7.6	0	0.0	27	8.4
26-50%	3	3.2	9	14.1	15	11.4	0	0.0	27	8.7
5-25%	2	2.2	11	17.2	33	25.0	1	5.0	47	15.2
0- 5%	24	25.8	16	25.0	61	46.2	17	85.0	118	38.2
TOTAL	93	100	64	100	132	100	20	100	309	100

Percent of E&G Revenue from Church Subsidies/Contributions

95-100%	5	5.4	0	0.0	0	0.0	0	0.0	5	1.6
76-94%	4	4.3	2	3.1	0	0.0	0	0.0	6	1.9
51-75%	11	11.8	3	4.7	0	0.0	0	0.0	14	4.5
26-50%	15	16.1	5	7.8	2	1.5	0	0.0	22	7.1
5-25%	34	36.6	20	31.3	10	7.6	0	0.0	64	20.7
0- 5%	24	25.8	34	53.1	120	90.9	20	100.	198	64.1
TOTAL	93	100	64	100	132	100	20	100	309	100

Title to Property/Plant Held By:

Inst	58	65.2	49	76.6	116	89.2	14	93.3	237	79.5
Church	17	19.1	8	12.5	7	5.4	1	6.7	33	11.1
Jointly	14	15.7	7	10.9	7	5.4	0	0.0	28	9.4
TOTAL	89	100	64	100	130	100	15	100	298	100

holds complete or joint title over campus property are institutions engaged in theological education. In the preponderant majority of religiously affiliated colleges and universities real property is held by the institution as an independent corporation.

TABLE 6

INSTITUTIONS WITH NO RELIGIOUS TESTS FOR EMPLOYMENT BY CLASS OF EMPLOYEE RESPONDING INSTITUTIONS

	Pervas Rel		Strong Rel		Nomin Ch-Rel		No Rel Purp		Total	
	No	Pct	No	Pct	No	Pct	No	Pct	No	Pct
Class of Employee										
PRES	0	0.0	5	7.8	66	50.0	20	100.0	91	29.4
SR OFF	4	4.3	13	20.3	115	87.1	20	100.0	152	49.2
JR OFF	17	18.3	34	53.1	128	97.0	20	100.0	199	64.4
STAFF	40	43.0	43	67.2	131	99.2	20	100.0	234	75.7
FT FAC	3	3.2	26	40.6	128	97.0	20	100.0	177	57.3
TEN FAC	2	2.2	25	39.1	125	94.7	20	100.0	172	55.7
THEO FAC	1	1.1	7	10.9	92	69.7	20	100.0	120	38.8
Percent of Full-time Faculty Professing Religious Faith (Institutions Reporting Range)										
76-100%	88	94.6	53	82.8	53	40.2	2	10.0	196	63.4
51-75%	2	2.2	8	12.5	44	33.3	2	10.0	56	18.1
26-50%	0	0.0	2	3.1	9	6.8	2	10.0	13	4.2
0- 25%	1	1.1	1	1.6	7	5.3	3	15.0	12	3.9
No Knwl	2	2.2	0	0.0	19	14.4	11	55.0	32	10.4
TOTAL	93	100	64	100	132	100	20	100	309	100

TAXONOMY OF HIGHER EDUCATION

The institutions were asked to indicate the classifications of employees for which some kind of religious qualifications would be required for appointment. Table 6 indicates the percent of institutions which make no use of religious tests in appointing specified classes of employees. The table shows that institutions classed in our scheme as "independent with no religious orientation or purpose" make no use of religious tests in employment decisions, and that a majority of nominally church-related institutions make use of religious tests only selectively, as in the case of appointments to the presidency or to the faculty in religion or theology. In our "pervasively religious" and "religiously supportive" categories, on the other hand, religious preference is exercised in employment decisions over the full range of positions, although a significant minority of these institutions never apply religious tests for employment of junior officers and non-academic staff.

Religious tests are used in virtually all faculty appointments in pervasively religious institutions. In about a quarter of our "religiously supportive" institutions, however, no religious tests are used as a matter of policy for either full-time or tenured faculty, although most of these institutions would generally seek faculty who have church associations or would be supportive of the religious mission.

Table 6 also indicates the percentage of full-time faculty whom the president estimates are members of a church or religious organization or would make a profession of religious faith. The data show not only a tendency toward a more religiously oriented faculty in the more religiously oriented institutions, but also the reluctance of the president in less religiously oriented institutions to make any estimate of the religious composition of the faculty and staff (since the institution does not ordinarily inquire into these matters).

We asked the institutions to indicate what forms of religious qualification are required for appointment in those

41

classifications of employees where religious tests are used. We identified the following examples:

Church member.
Creedal standard.
Personal faith.
Church participation.

In "pervasively religious" institutions we found that more than 35% use all four of the above types of qualification in full-time faculty appointments, while about 60% use at least three and about 75% use at least two. Among "religiously supportive" institutions, on the other hand, only one out of six institutions uses two or more of the above forms of religious tests in full-time faculty appointments. In most of the creedally oriented evangelical colleges and universities and in many schools of theological education, the religious qualifications required by policy include personal religious faith and some standard of theological orthodoxy. In many other institutions which use a religious test, however, the requirement does not extend into the area of personal belief, but is defined in terms of some kind of church association or sympathy with the institution's religious mission.

The foregoing profile of religiously affiliated higher education confirms the Center's earlier findings concerning the diversity of this sector of American education. The Center's research reveals some of the difficulties which beset the search for legal definitions and classifications which will be applicable to all this diversity. It will simply not do to measure the degree of religiousness of these institutions by means of formalistic or organizational criteria based on the composition of the board of control, the proportion of educational and general revenues derived from church sources, or the manner in which campus property is owned, etc. Such factors do not necessarily reflect the nature and scope of an institution's orientation to religious purposes or the form of its exercise of religious preference in employment decisions.

On the other hand, to obtain reliable information concerning the religious orientation of such institutions for use by regulatory agencies and courts would be entirely unworkable administratively, and would probably raise serious questions concerning a form of government entanglement in religion which would have a chilling effect on the free exercise of religion among these institutions.

NOTES TO CHAPTER ONE

1. Manning M. Pattillo, Jr., and Donald M. Mackenzie, Church-Sponsored Higher Education in the United States, Washington, D.C., American Council on Education, 1966, pp. 191-197.

2. Merrimon Cunninggim, "Varieties of Church-relatedness in Higher Education," in Robert Rue Parsonage, ed., Church-related Higher Education, Valley Forge, Pa., Judson Press, 1978, pp. 29-42. Cunninggim offers his categories as alternatives to those used in the Danforth study of church-related higher education, some of which he regards as pejorative.

3. Howard Lowry, The Mind's Adventure, Philadelphia, Westminster Press, 1950, p. 104. Lowry was President of The College of Wooster at the time.

4. D. Elton Trueblood, "The Marks of a Christian College," in John Paul von Grueningen, ed., Toward a Christian Philosophy of Education, Philadelphia, Westminster Press, 1957, p. 163. Cf. his The Idea of a College, New York, Harper, 1959. Trueblood had a distinguished career as a teacher and author at Haverford and Earlham Colleges and has exercised a profound influence in Quaker spirituality.

5. Nels F. S. Ferre, Christian Faith and Higher Education, New York, Harper, pp. 121-135. Ferre taught religion and theology at such institutions as Andover Newton Theological School, Vanderbilt University Divinity School, and The College of Wooster.

6. The number of responses from junior colleges, seminary-colleges, and rabbinical schools was too small to allow us to include them in our analysis. Our survey sample shows a somewhat higher proportion of baccalaureate colleges and a somewhat smaller proportion of seminaries and divinity schools than is exhibited in our larger group of religiously affiliated institutions. It is to be noted, however, that several of the responding baccalureate institutions have seminaries organized within them, and their reports are for both the collegiate and the seminary programs.

7. About 85% of the institutions which we would classify as "nominally church-related" (on the basis of information concerning their educational purposes and the way in which they exercise religious preference in employment decisions) describe themselves as "significantly influenced" by the religious heritage of the institution. The proportion of institutions identifying themselves as "significantly influenced" by a religious heritage and purpose is 56.3 percent of the total of responding institutions, as compared with 20.7 percent which we would place in our category of "religiously supportive (strongly religious)." This discrepancy in classification is due primarily to the use of "significantly" and "strongly" as the key descriptors in the respective surveys.

CHAPTER TWO

THE CONCEPT OF RELIGION
IN AMERICAN LAW

Our project involves an investigation of the legal principles which define the public interest in regulating the exercise of religious preference in employment decisions at religiously affiliated institutions of higher education. The law proscribing religious and other forms of discrimination in employment exempts "a religious corporation, association, educational institution, or society" from the general prohibition against discrimination on the basis of religion. Such statutory language calls for a threshold determination of the religiousness of an association, group, or institution in order to determine its eligibility for the exemption if it is challenged. A general investigation of the criteria and procedures for making such a determination is therefore essential to our project. Central to that determination, of course, is the concept of religion in American law.

Judicial decisions directly involving a challenge to the exercise of religious preference in employment decisions at religiously affiliated institutions of higher education are rare. We must seek precedents in cases arising in analogous circumstances. In this chapter we shall examine the concept of religion and of a religious school in American law. In subsequent chapters we shall survey the First Amendment jurisprudence which has grown up around the issue of public aid to religiously affiliated schools. We shall then be in a position to address the more specific legal issues affecting employment decisions at such institutions.

Prof. Douglas Laycock complains of the uncertainty and unpredictability of recent judicial decisions in cases involving church labor relations.[1] He finds that although these cases have often reached defensible results, they have typically not been successful in resolving the fundamental issues. He attributes the uncertainty and vagueness of the principles underlying judicial decision to the failure of the

45

U.S. Supreme Court to develop any coherent theory of the religion clauses of the First Amendment.

Laycock suggests the need to recognize that there are several kinds of rights protected by the Free Exercise Clause, including not only the right of every individual to follow the dictates of his/her religious faith or conscience free from regulation, but also the rights of institutions and organizations in the exercise of their religious beliefs and the pursuit of their religious activities. In the area of church labor relations, Laycock finds, the right of church autonomy is of paramount importance, although at present it tends to be overlooked in American law. Churches and religious organizations, he says, "have a constitutionally protected interest in maintaining their own institutions free of governmental interference." Like Laycock, we see the need for confirmation and clarification of the underlying assumptions and forms of legal reasoning and constitutional interpretation which provide the basis for defining the autonomy of religious and religiously affiliated institutions in the area of employment policy.

1. The Forms of Legal Reasoning

The volume and complexity of the law confound the layman, and its details often exceed the grasp of lawyers and judges as well. The immense expansion of the law has produced in many people a rather cynical view of the legislative and judicial processes, as being essentially subjective and biased. The multiplicity of statutes and the profusion of judicial opinions often obscure the coherence of the principles of justice. Yet coherence and consistency are essential to the fairness and stability which are the basic requirements of any system of justice.

We contend that consistency has essentially the same meaning in law as in logic, and that it is a norm for assessing legal promulgations and judgments. Judges and legislators, too, bear the burden of avoiding self-contradiction and absurdity as they participate in the development of the law. Particular judgments must be based on coherent thought and a coherent system of rules. If the consistency of the rule of law is an elusive ideal, it is nevertheless a goal towards which the legal mind must constantly strive.

Fundamental to the coherence of the legal system is the doctrine of stare decisis, the principle that established precedents must be followed. The doctrine arises from the conviction that judgments may not be arbitrary, that the law must treat all individuals and circumstances equally, that a rule of law which applies in one set of circumstances also applies in another set of similar or coordinate circumstances. Of course, things get complicated when there is a multiplicity of rules in the total system of law and when relevant facts are not precisely similar. One function of legal research is to cull out of the welter of statutory formulations and judicial rules of judgment (ratio decidendi) a framework which can help to explain or justify particular provisions or holdings and to clarify the principles of justice.

The reasoning of courts is probably less pragmatic than the tactics of forensic lawyers might assume, but less analytical than academic commentators might wish. Courts struggle to adhere to the relevant precedents consistently and to consider the confirmed and relevant facts fairly. The imperfection of the results achieved is universally admitted. Yet the legal search for coherence can be traced in the assumptions, rules of decision, and canons of inference which lend order to the emerging body of the law.

The search is complicated by the variety of the models of legal reasoning which divide not only legal scholars, but legislators, judges, and regulative agencies as well. Philip Bobbitt has recently produced a useful typology of the forms of legal and constitutional argument within a dialectical process of legal and constitutional development.[2] He identifies six types of legal argumentation and constitutional interpretation, each of which finds illustration in the advocacy of some highly distinguished legal and judicial minds. His classifications are a useful reminder of the

47

diversity of factors and methodologies which must be taken into consideration in any comprehensive theory of law. Bobbitt offers the following typology of legal and constitutional argument:

Textual approach: emphasizing the analysis of the text of the Constitution or the law.

Historical approach: emphasizing the continuing adaptation of the Constitution and the law to changing social, economic, and political conditions.

Doctrinal approach: emphasizing the promulgation and interpretation of the fundamentals of constitutional or legal doctrine.

Prudential approach: emphasizing the continuing rational consideration of means and ends and the implications of a calculus of benefits as the proper framework for the interpretation and application of the law.

Structural approach: emphasizing the dynamic interplay of the branches of government, the functioning of the federal system, and the relationship between the individual and the state.

Ethical approach: emphasizing the utility of political and legal institutions as means to the achievement of moral ends.

All these types of legal argument and constitutional interpretation, says Bobbitt, are found, as a matter of fact, in the real world of legislative and judicial decisions. Certain judges or legislators will tend, of course, to favor one type of reasoning, others will tend toward another. The arguments are as important, indeed, as the decisions, for the reasoning of legislators and judges provides a basis for subsequent decisions. In law, as in science, explanation is prediction. "Wrongly explaining," says Bobbitt, is as bad as "wrongly deciding."

The search for the principles governing the formation of the law through legislative enactments and regulatory and judicial interpretation, Bobbitt contends, requires careful judgment concerning the forms of legal and constitutional

48

argument which are functional, at any particular time and place, in bringing the law into useful application in human life. He argues, we think convincingly, for acceptance of a diversity of forms of legal argument as critical to the continuing adaptability of the Constitution and of the law to changing circumstances. No single type of legal or constitutional argument, Bobbitt contends, can provide an adequate basis for constitutional interpretation, for a theory of legislation, or for a rationale of judicial review. "No sane judge or law professor can be committed solely to one approach," Bobbitt declares. "Because there are so many facets to any single constitutional problem and many functions performed by a single opinion, the jurist or commentator uses different approaches, as a carpenter uses different tools and often many tools in a single project."[3]

The details of Bobbitt's analysis do not concern us here. Our only point is that simplistic or doctrinaire approaches to the analysis of the law affecting religiously affiliated higher education will not do justice to the immense complexity not only of this system of institutions, but also of the law itself. The process of legislative development and judicial review is inevitably multi-faceted, and its complexity will not permit facile prediction of its course. We must reject the notion, as Bobbitt puts it, that there exists a complete set of legal presuppositions or axioms from which laws and judicial decisions may be deduced, or that the course of legal development can be effectively charted once we have discovered a handful of philosophical theories and empirical regularities which control its fate.

A broad consensus on the legal rights of churches, religious organizations, and religiously affiliated institutions is seen by many analysts as depending on clear constitutional doctrine, understood in terms of a comprehensive ethical or political theory or a general theory of the relation between church and state. Others have serious doubts, however, about either the possibility or the desirability of a systematic or doctrinal approach to legal definition and advocate an "instrumentalist" approach to legal thinking which recognizes a wide range of factors affecting the development of law. We think Bobbitt's recognition of the diversity of the forms of legal reasoning is a useful contribution to the discussion of such issues.

In the analysis which follows we shall attempt an approach to legal reasoning which avoids narrowly doctrinaire or normative standards of interpretation. We are controlled, as we have said, by the notion of the autonomy of religiously affiliated institutions of higher education, but we do not wish to view this concept in abstraction from the corresponding notion of institutional accountability. The separation of church and state is a profoundly important American concept, but the derivation of judicial decisions from this principle requires investigation of a broad array of concerns bearing on the understanding of religion, as well as on the values underlying a pluralistic society. Our approach, then, will be comprehensive, yet realistic; systematic, yet pragmatic; coherent, yet dialectical.

2. The Legal Definition of Religiousness

The definition of religion has presented serious difficulties not only to students of the phenomenology of religion, but also to legislators and judges. The term appears in the language of the law, but its meaning is not always clear. Statutory criteria typically fall far short of a comprehensive definition. The clarification of the legal meaning of "religion" has been left largely to the courts, most of which have, in the words of Prof. Kent Greenawalt, "prudently eschewed theoretical generalizations" in making necessary threshold determinations of religiousness.[4]

The absence of any systematic legal definition of religion is, in part, a reflection of that failure of the Supreme Court to develop any coherent theory of the religion clauses of the Constitution, which Laycock thinks explains the uncertainty of the law of church labor relations. The Court has acted to protect certain rights of both individuals and religious organizations - - to assure, for example, the freedom to carry on "religious activities," to build churches and schools, to conduct worship services,

50

to pray, to proselytize, to define and teach religious doctrines and moral values, to select and train clergy and other leaders, etc. The language of religion has also entered into statutory and judicial protection of various rights of individual conscience, such as refusal to engage in military activities, to accept compulsory medical treatment and innoculations, to accept compulsory public education, to commit Sabbath nonobservance under legal, economic, or social compulsion, etc.[5] But the Court has not articulated an analytical definition, which would explain its determination of such activities as "religious" and as protected under the First Amendment.

At times there has been a tendency for analysts to require any threshold determination of religiousness to be traced to beliefs sincerely and conscientiously held. Thus religious liberty may be understood as a special form of freedom of conscience, which might constrain an adherent of a religion to engage in disputed or illegal activity. The factual determination which controls any finding of religiousness would, in that case, be whether the activities in question are undertaken from sincere religious motivations, or whether they are actually required by religious doctrine.

Laycock maintains that such an approach "reflects a rigid, simplistic, and erroneous view of religion."[6] In his view many activities would properly be called religious even though they are not directly related to religious beliefs or doctrines. Indeed, there are religious traditions which would contend that an emphasis on authoritative doctrines is inconsistent with the nature of true religion. To make the test of religiousness the presence of sincere and conscientious doctrinal belief, says Laycock, misconstrues the essence of religion and invites an impermissible governmental intrusion into the religious life.

Prof. Ira C. Lupu suggests that confusion and uncertainty concerning application of the religion clauses would be reduced if the right of Free Exercise were understood as a special instance of the more general rights of conscience and of association. A Madisonian theory of the general right of conscience, he believes, would assure the free exercise of religion for individuals, and a comprehensive theory of the right of free association would protect religious organizations in their free exercise. He proposes the following principle to govern the free exercise exemptions accorded under the American system to churches and religious bodies:

> A religious organization may use any criteria in choosing its members, and it may always exclude nonmembers from employment positions of associational significance.[7]

Lupu presents his "members only" principle of religious liberty as a particular instance of the rule of associational freedom for any kind of voluntary association. He commends the principle partly because of the difficulty of developing a comprehensive theory of the religion clauses, and partly from a desire for constitutional simplification. He claims that his principle opens up the theoretical analysis of the legal exemption for religious organizations to engage in certain kinds of employment discrimination, and that it confirms the right to the free exercise of religion not only for individuals but also for institutions.

Lupu is convinced that his analysis strengthens the legal protection of the rights of religious organizations to engage in employment discrimination through avoiding what he regards as the impossible problem of determining the degree of religiousness in such organizations or their activities. Under the standard analysis of the Free Exercise Clause, he maintains, any exemption which allows religious organizations to engage in employment discrimination would end up offending against either the Free Exercise or the Establishment Clauses in some respect or other. The autonomy of the church is won at the expense of the Free Exercise rights of individuals. And the legal determination of the threshold question of the religiousness of a particular organization or activity might involve an entanglement of government in religious affairs at the expense of the

Establishment Clause. Lupu contends that the "members only" principle, derived from analysis of the general freedoms of speech, assembly, and association, would avoid such problems by obviating the problems of line-drawing and intrusiveness.

Prof. Bruce N. Bagni thinks that in any case where a purportedly religious organization seeks immunity from the law, a court would unavoidably have to inquire whether or not the organization is, in fact, religious.[8] If religiousness were assumed in all cases where the claim was made, large-scale "discrimination in the name of the Lord" would become legally possible. Bagni recognizes the risk inherent in legally distinguishing the religious from the nonreligious in claims to immunity, but he sees no way to avoid the necessity of such inquiry.

Bagni proposes an "epicenter scheme," under which a court's inquiry would focus not on questions of the sincerity of religious convictions, but on identification of the core "spiritual" activities of religious organizations, which government must constitutionally refrain from regulating, as distinguished from their "secular" activities, which are properly subject to control in the public interest. Bagni sees the epicenter as representing "the purely spiritual life of the church." He views any issues which arise in the epicenter (such as employment policies for clergy, membership policies, modes of worship, etc.) as exclusively the concern of the church or religious organization and as not subject to governmental regulation.

As one moves out from the core, however, a series of increasingly "secular" concerns arise, and at these levels Bagni sees the church becoming subject to secular regulation proportionate to the degree of secularity of its activities and relationships. "A church acting outside the epicenter," says Bagni, "may still enjoy some degree of first amendment protection, but its claims may be evaluated in the light of competing, and perhaps more weighty, general societal interests." Thus Free Exercise rights might protect a racist church, but they do not necessarily insulate a church-related school which pursues a racially discriminatory admissions policy.

Bagni suggests that the issue which should control determination of the Free Exercise basis of racial discrimination in a religiously affiliated school is the degree to which the educational program is pervaded by a religious purpose. He proposes the following test:

> If the court decides that the school is a religious
> school whose dominant purpose is to teach secular and
> religious subjects in a particular religious context, the
> school's admission policy, regardless of its basis or
> scope, must be upheld as an exercise of religious
> associational freedom. . . . If a school found not to be
> predominantly religious interposes a religious objection
> to integration on behalf of its students, its claim shoud
> be denied.[9]

We prefer Greenawalt's approach, which seeks to develop a concept of religion which is sufficiently broad to satisfy the comprehensive requirements of judicial determination under the religion clauses. Such an approach involves what Greenawalt calls an "analogical" process of interpretation, which recognizes that the concept of religion is too complex to permit a definition by analysis of its essence (definition per genus et differentiam). He proposes a Wittgensteinian strategy for clarifying the concept of religion by identifying rules for its usage, in the absence of a definition in terms of essential conditions.

No specification of the essential or defining qualities of religion, Greenawalt contends, will encompass all the instances of beliefs, practices, and organizations which are regarded as religious in modern culture. A more fruitful approach at definition, he suggests, would be to identify instances to which the concept indisputably applies and then to allow for its extension to other, more controversial, areas by determining significant ways in which the new instance is similar to the familiar and accepted instances.

What is involved in this methodology is recognition of religion as a multi-variant, rather than a unitary concept.

Greenawalt claims that there is no single condition that is necessary and sufficient for religion. He endorses William Alston's analysis of "religion-making characteristics," which are neither necessary-and-sufficient conditions for religion nor essential to religion, but are "related in a looser way to the application of the term." When enough of these characteristics are present to a sufficient degree, we have religion. Yet no single criterion or set of criteria is decisive for the applicability of the term. To insist that any one characteristic or set of characteristics must be present, Alston maintains, would introduce a degree of precision that is not to be found in the concept of religion in actual usage. As he puts it, "The best way to explain the concept of religion is to elaborate in detail the relevant features of an ideally clear case of religion and then indicate the respects in which less clear cases can differ from this, without hoping to find any sharp line dividing religion from nonreligion."[10]

As applied in the law, Greenawalt's "analogical method" involves identification of a number of characteristics of individuals, practices, or groups which are indisputably religious. These might include (adapting Alston's formulation): belief in the supernatural and in an afterlife; a general picture of the world as a whole and of the place of the individual therein; a more or less coherent organization of one's life based on the world-view; a distinction between sacred and profane objects, and a system of ritual acts focused on the sacred; a particular perspective on moral obligations as derived from or sanctioned by the divine; "religious" feelings (like awe, the sense of mystery, or adoration) connected in idea with the divine; and a social group and an organization for promoting and perpetuating the shared life and values of the group.

No single element in this set of characteristics, Greenawalt suggests, should be recognized under the law as being essential to religion. Should any feature be absent, a legal finding of religiousness might still be possible. Religions need not be viewed by the law as sharing any single feature in common, Greenawalt maintains, because there is no single feature which is indispensable.

Greenawalt emphasizes that use of the analogical approach in reaching a threshold determination of religiousness in cases involving the religion clauses will require sensitivity to the cause of action. A court would need to attend not only to the legal consequences that flow from the threshold determination of religiousness, but also to the nature of the claim involved. If the claim concerns the permissibility of governmental support of an activity or organization, what the organization does will be more significant than what its members individually believe. If the claim concerns the exercise of individual conscience, the nature of the underlying belief will be critical. Flexibility in the application of the various elements of religion in the formation of a framework for judicial decision has the additional advantage, in Greenawalt's view, of avoiding "a rigid distinction between Free Exercise and Establishment cases that both strains the constitutional language and obscures important differences among cases arising under each clause."[11]

Greenawalt finds that the courts have long applied what amounts to an "analogical approach" in the threshold determination of religiousness. In Washington Ethical Society v. District of Columbia, 249 F.2d 127 (D.C. Cir. 1957), the U.S. Court of Appeals for the District of Columbia decided that the Ethical Society was entitled to tax exemptions made available to churches. The opinion (which was written by Warren Burger before he was elevated to the Supreme Court) determined that the society was a religious corporation or society, even though it propounded no theistic beliefs. The court's decision was based on a finding of a strong similarity between traditional religious aims and practices and those of the Society. The opinion made no attempt, however, to state necessary or sufficient conditions for being a religion or a church. The legal determination was based purely on analogical legal reasoning.

In Fellowship of Humanity v. County of Alameda, 153 Cal. App.2d 673, 315 P.2d 394 (1957), a California court came to a similar determination concerning the eligibility of the nontheistic Fellowship of Humanity for a tax exemption allowed under California law for real property dedicated to "religious worship." The lengthy opinion of the court propounded an expansive view of religious worship, and suggested the possibility that a more narrow construction of the term "religious" for purposes of tax determination might constitute an impermissible discrimination against certain types of religious belief in violation of the First Amendment.

In this opinion the court presumed to offer a brief statement on the conditions which should be viewed as necessary and sufficient for determination of such an exemption, declaring that "religion" includes: "(1) a belief, not necessarily referring to supernatural powers; (2) a cult, involving a gregarious association openly expressing the belief; (3) a system of moral practice directly resulting from an adherence to the belief; and (4) an organization within the cult designed to observe the tenets of belief." The language of this well-intentioned court strikes Greenawalt as a clear indication of the quicksand into which he thinks all such endeavors to define the essence of religion fall.

In 1961 the U.S. Supreme Court declared its acceptance of a broad understanding of religion similar to the one which controlled the Fellowship of Humanity case. In Torcaso v. Watkins, 367 U.S. 488 (1961), the Court struck down a state law requiring office holders to declare a belief in a supreme being, holding that Buddhism, Taoism, Ethical Culture, and Secular Humanism were all religions, despite being non-theistic, and that the state's declared preference for theistic forms of religion violated the Establishment Clause.

THE CONCEPT OF RELIGION

A similar broadening of the concept of religion was involved in United States v. Seeger, 380 U.S. 163 (1965), a conscientious objector case decided under the Universal Military Training and Service Act. The statute exempted from universal conscription any person who was conscientiously opposed to military service by reason of "religious training and belief," but it specifically defined religious belief as "an individual's belief in relation to a Supreme Being involving duties superior to those arising from any human relation, but [not including] essentially political, sociological, or philosophical views or a merely personal moral code."

Seeger, who specifically rejected any belief in or dependence upon a Supreme Being, was found by the Court to be a conscientious objector under the statute within the proper meaning of religion, which the Court construed with the aid of Paul Tillich's concept of religion as centered in an object of "ultimate concern." The Court found that Seeger held a sincere and meaningful belief which satisfied the statutory definition of a religion, since his belief "occupies in the life of its possessor a place parallel to that filled by God of those admittedly qualifying for the exemption." The Court's reasoning is an apt illustration of Greenawalt's analogical approach in the judicial determination of religiousness.[12]

In Welsh v. United States, 398 U.S. 333 (1970), the Court carried its reasoning in Seeger one step further. In submitting his application for exemption as a conscientious objector, Welsh had explicitly acknowledged that his beliefs were not religious but had been derived from his readings in history and sociology and from his view of the disutility and wastefulness of war under modern conditions. In spite of Welsh's explicit declaration to the contrary, four justices found his beliefs to be "religious" under the language of the federal statute, while a fifth (whose vote was necessary for the decision) found it a violation of the Establishment Clause for Congress to differentiate between religious and nonreligious conscientious objectors.

THE CONCEPT OF RELIGION

Like Greenawalt, Prof. Laurence Tribe has endorsed a flexible approach to the legal definition of religion. He is concerned, however, about the rule of "parallelism," articulated by the Supreme Court in Seeger. Definitions by analogy seem to Tribe to be too "pliable" to satisfy the requirement of consistency and predictability in judicial decisions. He contends that the authenticity of claims to protection under the religious liberty clauses should be determined not on the basis of the Seeger majority's concept of religion, but "in terms of the social function of the group or in terms of the role the beliefs assume in the individual's life."[13]

Tribe proposes that courts should follow the general rule: Anything that is "arguably religious" should be considered religious in the Free Exercise Clause; and anything that is "arguably non-religious" should be considered non-religious in the Establishment Clause. The error he wishes to avoid in Free Exercise cases is that of making the definition of religion too narrow to provide adequate protection for heterodox religious beliefs. The error he wishes to avoid in Establishment cases is that of making the definition of religion so broad that it would strike down legislation whose primary purpose is to advance such non-sectarian ideals as human dignity, equality, freedom, and enlightenment. If religion were always defined in terms of whatever ideology might function in the belief system of non-theists in the way the concept of God functions in the belief systems of persons and institutions commonly identified as religious, then, warns Tribe, the Establishment Clause could become "an awful engine of destruction."

Greenawalt objects to Tribe's criterion on the grounds that it requires the term "religion" to be construed in two distinct senses in the Free Exercise and Establishment Clauses, respectively, at the expense of a unitary concept of religious liberty under the First Amendment. Furthermore, he contends, the modifier "arguably" is vague and amorphous. Tribe's formula would seem to identify three categories of the "clearly religious," the "clearly nonreligious," and a probably much larger domain of "arguably religious-arguably non-religious" in between. Greenawalt thinks it would create chaos were the courts to regard everything that falls in the middle classification as religious for the Free Exercise Clause and as non-religious for the Establishment Clause.

Examples of cases in this middle group which, Greenawalt suggests, might pose problems under the Free Exercise Clause might include a group which makes "religious" use of psychedelic drugs, or a Marxist organization; examples which might pose problems under the Establishment Clause might be Christmas carols, the pseudo-scientific (quasi-metaphysical) doctrine of Creationism, and Transcendental Meditation. Many people would argue that the former should not be included under the protections of the Free Exercise Clause and the latter should not be permitted for government support under the Establishment Clause. "Thus," concludes Greenawalt, "the standards of arguably religious and arguably non-religious are not only too vague to provide much guidance, but they yield a crucial intermediate category that is too large for wise interpretation of the religion clauses."[14]

In his much-quoted dissenting opinion in Everson v. Board of Education, 330 U.S. 1 (1947), Justice Wiley Rutledge explicitly rejected any dual construction of the term "religion" in the religion clauses of the First Amendment. The term appears only once in the text, his grammatical analysis noted, and the same meaning governs both prohibitions.

> It does not have two meanings, one narrow to forbid 'an establishment' and another much broader, for securing 'the free exercise thereof.' 'Thereof' brings down 'religion' with its entire and exact content, no more and no less, from the first into the second guaranty, so that Congress and now the states are as broadly restricted concerning the one as they are regarding the other.

THE CONCEPT OF RELIGION

In the Free Exercise Clause, Rutledge remarked, Congress is not restricted to protecting the free exercise merely of creedal forms of religion, or some particular system of religious belief. The Amendment secures the free exercise of all forms of religious expression, creedal and non-creedal, sectarian and nonsectarian. Similarly, in the Establishment Clause, the term "religion" is not used in a formal or technical sense. "The prohibition broadly forbids state support, financial or other, of religion in any guise, form, or degree. It outlaws all use of public funds for religious purposes." Rutledge's formulation occurred in a dissenting opinion, of course, but it expresses an understanding which typically governs judicial construction of the religion clauses.

The Supreme Court has repeatedly declared its opposition to any legal or judicial determination of the doctrinal content of authentic religious belief. Well over a century ago the Court declared, "The law knows no heresy and is committed to the support of no dogma, the establishment of no sect."[15] In Fowler v. Rhode Island, 345 U.S. 67 (1953), the Court was more specific: "It is no business of courts to say that what is a religious practice or activity for one group is not religion under the protection of the First Amendment."

In modern times the threshold determination of religion by American courts has been guided by the principles eloquently articulated by several justices in United States v. Ballard, 322 U.S. 78 (1943). In Ballard the Supreme Court held that a District Court had acted properly in instructing the jury not to consider the question of the truth of defendants' alleged religious beliefs in considering their guilt/innocence in a case concerning use of the mails to defraud. Writing for the majority Justice William O. Douglas noted that the Court had viewed the First Amendment as embracing two concepts: The first, freedom to believe is absolute, he said; the second, freedom to act, cannot be, by the very nature of things. Justice Douglas continued:

THE CONCEPT OF RELIGION

Freedom of thought embraces the right to maintain theories of life and of death and of the hereafter which are rank heresies to the followers of the orthodox faiths. Heresy trials are foreign to our Constitution. Men may believe what they cannot prove. They may not be put to the proof of their religious doctrines or beliefs. . . The religious views espoused by respondents may seem incredible, if not preposterous, to most people. But if these doctrines are subject to trial before a jury charged with finding their truth or falsity, then the same can be done with the religious beliefs of any sect.

The broadening of the concept of religion in American law has been criticized in some quarters as another symptom of the recent erosion of religious liberty. We read no such implication in the above decisions. The constitutional and statutory protections of theistic belief are by no means compromised or weakened when similar protections are extended to sincere and conscientious non-theistic or "heterodox" belief. The principle of religious liberty does not require the legal system to give preference to theistic over non-theistic religions; it requires only that no one should be prohibited or deterred from holding a religious belief or from the free exercise of religion, whatever its doctrinal elements may be.

American law has refused to propound an analytical definition of religion, believing that to do so would embroil it improperly in the definition of the content of orthodox doctrine. The Supreme Court has also been extremely reluctant to allow governmental or judicial assessment of the form or degree of religiousness exhibited or maintained by particular religious or religiously affiliated institutions, on the grounds that any such assessment would involve the government in excessive entanglement in the affairs of religious organizations and would have a chilling effect on their Free Exercise rights. Nevertheless, the Court has been unable to avoid using some kind of classification of religiously affiliated schools in order to determine the applicability of state and federal statutes and to interpret constitutional doctrine.

NOTES TO CHAPTER TWO

1. Douglas Laycock, "Towards a General Theory of the Religion Clauses: The Case of Church Labor Relations and the Right to Church Autonomy," Columbia Law Review, Vol. 81, November, 1981, p. 1373.

2. Philip Bobbitt, Constitutional Fate: Theory of the Constitution, New York, Oxford University Press, 1982.

3. Ibid., p. 124.

4. R. Kent Greenawalt, "Religion as a Concept in Constitutional Law," California Law Review, Vol. 72, September, 1984, p. 753.

5. The examples are listed in Laycock, op.cit., pp. 1388,1389.

6. Ibid., p. 1390.

7. Ira C. Lupu, "Free Exercise Exemption and Religious Institutions: The Case of Employment Discrimination," Boston University Law Review, Vol. 67, May, 1987, p. 431.

8. Bruce N. Bagni, "Discrimination in the Name of the Lord: A Critical Evaluation of Discrimination by Religious Organizations," Columbia Law Review, Vol. 79, 1979, pp. 1514-1549.

9. Ibid., pp. 1540-1543.

10. William P. Alston, "Religion," in Paul Edwards, ed., The Encyclopedia of Philosophy, Vol. 7, New York, The Macmillan Company and The Free Press, 1967, p. 142. Alston's List of "religion-making characteristics" is oriented toward a concept of the supernatural and may be viewed by some as doctrinally too specific to serve as a general model.

Alston handles this concern by allowing that belief in the supernatural might be "whittled away to nothing" in some systems like Buddhism without their ceasing to be "religions."

11. Greenawalt, op. cit., p. 769.

12. Greenawalt finds a Tillichian definition of religion as inadequate as any other when used as a single or defining criterion for religiousness. He contends that it would be difficult to render any account of the concept of "ultimate concern" which would yield the necessary coherence and predictability needed in a legal standard. A "psychological" approach to the definition of "ultimate concern" is no more likely to provide guidance for legal decision than a "metaphysical" approach. Furthermore, Greenawalt contends, analogical reasoning might well find that certain beliefs would satisfy the test of religion even if they did not satisfy the standard of "ultimate concern." Greenawalt's analysis thus goes beyond the requirement that religion should be defined broadly in the law. He requires that the legal determination of religion should proceed apart from the assumption that religion has a definable essence of any kind. Cf. James McBride, "Paul Tillich and the Supreme Court's 'Ultimate Concern' as a Standard in Judicial Interpretation," Journal of Church and State, Vol. 30, Spring, 1988, pp. 245-272.

13. Laurence Tribe, American Constitutional Law, Mineola NY, The Foundation Press, Second Edition, 1988, pp. 1168,1169.

14. Greenawalt, op.cit., pp. 813,814.

15. Watson v. Jones, 80 U.S. (13 Wal) 1, 679, 728 (1871).

CHAPTER THREE

EMPLOYMENT DISCRIMINATION
STATUTES AND REGULATIONS

Federal law places a number of restraints on the employment practices of educational institutions, including those serving in the independent and religiously affiliated sector. Among the major federal statutes are the following:

Civil Rights Act of 1861 (Section 1981)
Civil Rights Act of 1964 and Subsequent
Amendments (esp. Titles VI and VII)
Higher Education Act of 1965 and Subsequent
Amendments (especially Title IX)
Age Discrimination in Employment Act of 1967
Fair Labor Standards Act (including the Wage and
Hour Law and the Equal Pay Act)
Rehabilitation Act of 1972 (especially Section 503)
Civil Rights Restoration Act of 1987

There are also a number of executive orders and regulations of governmental agencies, issued under various provisions of law. These promulgations typically have the force of law, since they are issued under statutory or constitutional authority. Finally, there are the laws promulgated by the several states, of which many are patterned on a federal model, while others reflect distinctive provisions of the constitution and political traditions of the particular state.

In this chapter we present a summary of statutory and regulatory language affecting the exercise of religious preference and/or discrimination in employment decisions at religiously affiliated institutions of higher education. We also present a brief commentary on the meaning of such language. The more extensive analysis of the law, of course, requires a review of judicial interpretation and application, to which we shall turn beginning in the following chapter.

EMPLOYMENT DISCRIMINATION STATUTES

1. Civil Rights Act of 1964

The Civil Rights Act of 1964 was one of the most controversial pieces of social legislation of the Twentieth Century. The margin of legislative support was so close that significant compromises on both substantive provisions and Congressional procedures were required in order to achieve passage of the bill. The result is a law which, with all its limitations and imperfections, has had a profound impact on discriminatory practices in all areas of American life.

Title VI, Nondiscrimination in Federally Assisted Programs

Title VI of the Civil Rights Act declares it to be the policy of the United States that discrimination on the grounds of race, color, or national origin shall not occur in connection with programs and activities receiving Federal financial assistance. Section 601 of Title VI provides that, "No person in the United States shall on the ground of race, color, or national origin, be excluded from participation in, be denied the benefits of, or be subjected to discrimination under any program or activity receiving Federal financial assistance."[1] (Our emphasis.)

The Act authorizes and directs each federal department and agency which is empowered to extend federal financial assistance to any recipient, whether "by way of grant, loan, or contract other than a contract of insurance or guaranty," to effectuate the nondiscrimination provisions of Section 601, by "issuing rules, regulations, or orders of general applicability which shall be consistent with achievement of the objectives of the statute authorizing the financial assistance in connection with which the action is taken."

Thus the nondiscrimination requirement of Title VI applies to any educational program for which federal financial assistance is extended under a law administered under the Department of Education. As examples of such programs the Department lists the following: loans and

66

grants for construction or remodelling of facilities or for acquisition of equipment; educational research; training institutes for elementary or secondary school personnel; student loans and Educational Opportunity grants; grants for acquisition of library resources; direct institutional aid under the Developing Institutions program; grants for cooperative education programs; surplus real and related property disposal for educational purposes, etc. Before authorizing any form of federal assistance, the Department of Education requires an assurance of institutional compliance with the general requirement of nondiscrimination as promulgated in federal law.

The coverage of the statutory proscription against employment discrimination reaches "any program or activity receiving Federal financial assistance." The coverage depends, of course, on the range of application of the term "recipient of federal assistance." Under the definitions explicitly stated in the Act, the term covers not only an institution receiving direct aid, but also any State, any public agency, or any individual to whom federal financial assistance is extended, either directly or through another recipient. The courts have consistently held that recipients of indirect aid fall within the class of "programs receiving Federal financial assistance." However, a regulation promulgated by the Office of Civil Rights of the Department of Education states that the "term does not include any ultimate beneficiary under any such program."[2] Distinguishing between "direct," "indirect," and "ultimate" recipients of federal aid inevitably involves the exercise of judgment in the particular circumstances, and has proved to be one of the more controversial aspects of the administration of the law.

Title VII, Equal Employment Opportunity

Title VII of the Civil Rights Act is addressed to the prohibition of discriminatory employment practices and provides, in part, that:

EMPLOYMENT DISCRIMINATION STATUTES

It shall be an unlawful employment practice for an employer - -

(1) to fail or refuse to hire or to discharge any individual, or otherwise to discriminate against any individual with respect to his compensation, terms, conditions, or privileges of employment, because of such individual's race, color, religion, sex, or national origin; or

(2) to limit, segregate, or classify his employees or applicants for employment in any way which would deprive or tend to deprive any individual of employment opportunities or otherwise adversely affect his status as an employee, because of such individual's race, color, religion, sex, or national origin.[3]

This title prohibits any form of employment discrimination on the basis of religion or sex, as well as discrimination on the basis of race, color, or national origin. As originally enacted the law provided a comprehensive exemption for all educational institutions, both public and independent. The exemption was based on information indicating to Congress that there was not widespread discrimination in academic employment and on Congressional confidence that educational institutions could be counted on to monitor their employment operations in compliance with the general purposes of the Civil Rights Act. In 1972 the original exemption for employment of individuals engaged in educational activities of nonreligious educational institutions was struck out. All nondiscrimination requirements of the Civil Rights Act now apply to nonreligious educational institutions equally with all other employers However, the Act provides a series of exemptions for religiously affiliated educational institutions as noted below.

As originally enacted the law provided (in Section 702):

This title (Title VII) shall not apply to . . . a religious corporation, association or society with respect to the employment of individuals of a particular religion to perform work connected with the carrying on by such corporation, association or society of its religious activities or to an educational institution with respect to the employment of individuals to perform work connected with the educational activities of such institution.

In 1972 this provision was amended (under the Equal Employment Opportunity Act of 1972) to read:

This title shall not apply to a religious corporation, association, educational institution, or society with respect to the employment of individuals of a particular religion to perform work connected with the carrying on by such corporation, association, educational institution, or society of its activities.[4]

In previous research the Center for Constitutional Studies has presented an extensive analysis of the provisions of Title VII in both its original enactment and in the amendments enacted by Congress in 1972, paying special attention to the legislative history.[5] The Center researchers viewed the intention of the 1972 amendments as being

not to affect the ability of religiously affiliated colleges to exercise religious preference in faculty hiring, but to eliminate the (previous) exemption for educational institutions in the area of race and sex discrimination. . . . It is clear to us that religiously affiliated colleges are limited to an exemption from the ban on religious discrimination and that they are legally bound to comply with the strictures of the act concerning employment discrimination based on race, color, sex, or national origin.[6]

The Act includes a definition of "religion" as including "all aspects of religious observation and practice, as well as belief."[7] The primary aim of this definition is to specify the obligation of employers to make reasonable accomodations of an employee's or a prospective employee's religious observance or practice, as long as doing so does not cause undue hardship on the conduct of the employer's business. The statutory definition of "religion" thus functions primarily to specify aspects of individual religious rights which employers are required to accomodate or are prohibited from offending. The Act does not promulgate a definition of religious institutions.

Section 703(e)(1) of the Civil Rights Act allows all employers, employment agencies, and labor organizations to take into account an individual's religion, sex, or national origin (but not his race or color) in those particular instances where one or more of these characteristics is a "bona fide occupational qualification reasonably necessary to the normal operation of [a] particular business or enterprise." Both Congressional intent and judicial interpretation have construed this BFOQ exemption in a strictly limited sense. The law also allows for the exercise of religious preference and discrimination in employment for religious organizations and religiously affiliated educational institutions. The statute provides:

> Notwithstanding any other provision of this title,
> (1) It shall not be an unlawful employment practice for an employer to hire and employ employees, for an employment agency to classify or refer for employment any individual, or for an employer, labor organization, or joint labor-management committee controlling apprenticeship or other training or retraining programs to admit or employ any individual in any such program on the basis of his religion, sex, or national origin in those certain instances where religion, sex, or national origin is a bona fide occupational qualification reasonably necessary to the normal operation of that particular business or enterprise.
> (2) It shall not be an unlawful employment practice for a school, college, university, or other educational institution or institution of learning to hire and employ employees of a particular religion if such school, college, university, or other educational institution or institution of learning is, in whole or substantial part, owned, supported, controlled, or managed by a particular religious corporation, association or society, or if the

curriculum of such school, college, university, or other educational institution or institution of learning is directed toward the propagation of a particular religion.[8]

Moots and Gaffney suggest that the legislative history of the Act "precludes reliance on the BFOQ exception as the legal basis of exercising religious preference with respect to positions not [directly] linked to the religious mission of the college." They conclude that "if colleges should desire to exercise religious preference in all employment positions, the statutory authority for such policy is not the BFOQ exception, Section 703(e)(1), but the exemption provided in Section 702, or the exception provided for some religiously affiliated colleges in Section 703(e)(2)."[9]

Section 703(e)(2), which broadens the allowance for the exercise of religious preference in employment at religiously affiliated colleges and universities, was not affected by the 1972 amendments. It gives statutory authorization to certain religiously affiliated colleges and universities to take into consideration the religious background or orientation of all their employees or prospective employees without violating the civil rights law.

However, the authors note certain factors which complicate the use of this exemption by institutions which depend heavily on public financial assistance. Fulfillment of the first criterion (ownership, support, control, and management) might involve an institution in constitutional questions concerning its eligibility to receive public institutional aid under the Establishment Clause. On the other hand, recent changes in the corporate organization of some institutions may have so modified their organizational relationships with their sponsoring churches as to impair their ability to meet the requirements of this exemption. Fulfillment of the second criterion (orientation of the curriculum) would appear to raise constitutional questions concerning the effect of public financial assistance as constituting governmental support of religion.

EMPLOYMENT DISCRIMINATION STATUTES

To summarize, religious and religiously affiliated organizations are exempted from the Title VII prohibition against religious discrimination in employment in three ways:

1. General Exemption for Religious Organizations

The prohibition against employment discrimination on the basis of religion does not "apply to a religious corporation, association, educational institution, or society with respect to the employment of individuals to perform work connected with the carrying on by such corporation, association, educational institution, or society of its activities."

The language of the original statute limited the scope of the exemption for religious organizations to the carrying on of their "religious activities." In amending this section in 1972 Congress specifically and deliberately removed the qualifier, "religious," as the modifier of "activities." But the amendment then limited the scope of the exemption in another respect by restricting the exemption to "religious" educational institutions. Thus a "religious educational institution" has the same exemption as a "religious corporation, organization, or society," namely an exemption allowing "employment of individuals of a particular religion" to perform any work connected with the carrying on of its activities. The issue for religiously affiliated institutions of higher education then becomes whether they fall within the range of application of the term "religious educational institution."

2. Bona Fide Occupational Qualification

Religious and religiously affiliated organizations are permitted (as is any other employer) to exercise employment discrimination on the basis of religion, sex, or national origin "in those certain instances where religion sex, or national origin is a bona fide occupational qualification reasonably necessary to the normal operation of that particular business or enterprise."

72

The BFOQ exemption is available to any employer, without regard to religion. The basis of the BFOQ exemption is restricted to qualifications in religion, sex, or national origin and does not extend to race or color. Thus the law never recognizes race or color as a bona fide occupational qualification; but it is prepared to allow religion, sex, or national origin as an occupational qualification in those instances where such qualifications are certainly bona fide. Under this exemption an enterprise established for a religious purpose would be protected in its right to employ religiously qualified individuals in those positions in which religion is a bona fide occupational qualification, reasonably necessary to the normal operation of the enterprise, or (in Moots and Gaffney's formulation) in those "positions directly linked to the religious mission of the college."

The statute does not give to a religious organization or religiously affiliated educational institution an autonomous right to specify the positions for which the bona fide occupational qualification exemption applies. If an institution's use of a BFOQ exemption is challenged, the decision whether a religious or sexual qualification is bona fide will be made by the civil courts. If an institution depends on the BFOQ exemption, therefore, it is more susceptible to litigation than if it depends on the broader exemption of Section 703(e)(2). The courts have tended to define the exemption narrowly.

3. Religious Educational Institutions

An educational institution which is, "in whole or in substantial part, owned, supported, controlled, or managed by a particular religious corporation, association, or society" is allowed to employ individuals of a particular religion in any of its positions. The same allowance is made for educational institutions in which "the curriculum . . . is directed toward the propagation of a particular religion."

This exemption authorizes certain religiously affiliated institutions of higher education to exercise religious

73

preference and/or discrimination in employment decisions over the entire range of their operations. One of two qualifications must be satisfied by such an institution: either (1) An organizational relationship to a church or religious organization involving substantial ownership, control, management, or support; or 2) A curriculum directed toward the propagation of a particular religion. The precise meaning of the language specifying these qualifications requires careful analysis.

As we have previously emphasized, religiously affiliated institutions of higher education are related to their sponsoring churches and religious organizations in a variety of ways. In some cases campus property is owned by the supporting church, and close policy control, extensive management authority, and substantial financial support are maintained by the church. At the other end of the spectrum of religious affiliation are nominally church-related institutions, which function essentially as independent corporations. Of course, there are institutions functioning at many points along this continuum. How the language of the 703(e)(2) exemption applies in all this diversity is not entirely clear.

A significant number of pervasively or strongly religious institutions are entirely independent corporations and have never had any kind of organizational relationship with any church or religious group. Such institutions would not qualify for the 703(e)(2) exemption under the criterion of organizational control and would qualify for the exemption only by accepting the probably disconcerting characterization of their curricula as "directed toward the propagation of a particular religion."

As the Supreme Court emphasized in Tilton V. Richardson, 403 U.S. 672 (1971), the degree or form of association between a college or university and its supporting church is not dispositive of the question of its religiousness. The institutions in Tilton were recognized to be clearly religiously affiliated, yet not so pervasively religious that their secular educational functions were

74

inseparable from their religious purposes. The question is whether such institutions may be found sufficiently religious to be eligible for the exemption of Title VII, yet sufficiently secular to allow them to be eligible for direct public aid. We shall need to return to this question later in our investigation.

2. Higher Education Act of 1965

The Higher Education Act does not deal as directly as does the Civil Rights Act with employment policies and practices in institutions of higher education. Nevertheless, a number of the provisions of the Act are relevant to our investigation. Several of these provisions address the question of the conditions under which religiously affiliated institutions may be exempted from the general prohibition against religiously based employment discrimination.

Title VII, Academic Facilities

Title VII of the Higher Education Act deals with Construction, Reconstruction, and Renovation of Academic Facilities and generally carries forward the programs originally created under the Higher Education Facilities Act of 1963. The Title includes a provision restricting federal support to academic facilities used for secular purposes and states: "No project assisted with funds under this subchapter shall ever be used for religious worship or a sectarian activity or for a school or department of divinity."[10]

Among the Higher Education Amendments enacted by Congress in 1986 was a major revision of the section of Title VII dealing with Loans for Construction, Reconstruction, and Renovation of Academic Facilities. The legislation authorized the government to create and participate in a non-governmental, for-profit corporation, the College Construction Loan Insurance Association. Section 752(e)(2) of the Higher Education Amendments of 1986 specifies the requirements which must be satisfied for any federal guarantees or insurance for obligations for academic facilities issued through this agency. The language of the statute, which provides exceptions and conditions for religiously affiliated institutions, includes some significant provisions. The amended section provides as follows:

(e) Nondiscrimination Required - -

(1) The corporation may not carry out any activities with respect to any educational facilities purpose of a participating institution if the institution discriminates on account of race, color, religion (subject to paragraph (2)), national origin, sex (to the extent provided in Title IX of the Education Amendments of 1972), or handicapping condition.

(2) The prohibition with respect to religion shall not apply to an educational institution which is controlled by or which is closely identified with the tenets of a particular religious organization if the application of this section would not be consistent with the religious tenets of such organization.

(3) Each participating organization shall certify to the corporation that the institution does not discriminate as required by the provision of paragraph (1).[11]

The language of this section represents an attempt to reduce uncertainty concerning the conditions under which direct aid to religiously affiliated institutions of higher education may be permitted under this Title. The Act continues to prohibit Federal financial support of facilities used for sectarian educational purposes or for theological education. The language of the statute is important, however, as employing a new criterion for identifying a religious educational institution. An institution may qualify for this exemption either by being controlled by a religious organization or by being "closely identified with the tenets of a particular religious organization" (our emphasis).

Title IX, Discrimination on the Basis of Sex

Title IX of the Higher Education Act (originally enacted in 1965 and extensively amended in 1972) deals with

EMPLOYMENT DISCRIMINATION STATUTES

Discrimination Based on Sex or Blindness in institutions of higher education. The statute provides, in part:

> No person in the United States shall, on the basis of sex, be excluded from participation in, be denied the benefits of, or be subjected to discrimination under any education program or activity receiving Federal financial assistance.[12]

This prohibition against any form of discrimination on the basis of sex is explicitly limited in this Act to educational institutions receiving federal financial assistance. The Act further stipulates that the prohibition applies only to institutions of vocational education, professional education, and graduate higher education, and to public institutions of undergraduate education. The Act exempts public educational institutions with a traditional and continuing policy of admitting only students of one sex.

More significant for our purpose is the Title's exemption for "educational institutions of religious organizations with contrary religious tenets," viz.:

> This section shall not apply to an educational institution which is controlled by a religious organization if the application of this subsection would not be consistent with the religious tenets of such organization.

The exemption above is provided for the purpose of allowing the exercise of religious conscience and belief in what has become a highly controversial area of human behavior and public policy. There are a number of ways in which the religious concerns of a religiously affiliated institution of higher education might come into conflict with its adherence to certain provisions of Title IX and related federal regulations. For example, religiously derived convictions about sexual morality, pregnancy, parenthood, and abortion may run counter to a statutory or regulatory requirement stated in or inferred from Title IX. Title IX thus seeks to accomodate religion-based institutional policies respecting human sexuality which are inconsistent with specific provisions of the Title.

An amendment to Title IX, enacted as the Pregnancy Discrimination Act of 1978, prohibits any educational discrimination on the basis of pregnancy, childbirth, or related medical conditions, and requires that women affected by pregnancy, childbirth, or related medical conditions must be treated in the same way as other persons "for all employment purposes." The Equal Pay Act, enacted as an amendment to the Fair Employment Standards Act, requires that equal pay be given to male and female employees when their work requires substantially equal skill, effort, and responsibility and is performed under similar working conditions. These amendments make no provision for exemptions for religiously oriented employers.

Other Provisions of the Higher Education Act

The Higher Education Act contains a paragraph prohibiting discrimination in any federally assisted study, project, or contract, but explicitly authorizing research into the nature, causes, and effects of discrimination. The paragraph provides:

> Institutions of higher education receiving Federal financial assistance may not use such financial assistance whether directly or indirectly to undertake any study or project or fulfill the terms of any contract containing an express or implied provision that any person or persons of a particular race, religion, sex, or national origin be barred from performing such study, project, or contract, except no institution shall be barred from conducting objective studies or projects concerning the nature, effects, or prevention of discrimination, or have its curriculum restricted on the subject of discrimination, against any such person.[13]

The Basic Adult Education Title of the Higher Education Act includes a paragraph prohibiting grants for sectarian instruction. The language of this paragraph expands somewhat on the definitions employed in other statutory prohibitions against sectarian application of federal aid. The paragraph provides:

> No grant may be made under this chapter for any educational program, activity, or service related to sectarian instruction or religious worship, or provided by a school or department of divinity. For purposes of this section, the term 'school or department of divinity' means an institution or a department or branch of an institution whose program is specifically for the education of students to prepare them to become ministers of religion or to enter upon some other religious vocation, or to prepare them to teach theological subjects.[14]

3. Civil Rights Restoration Act of 1987

In Grove City v. Bell, 465 U.S. 555 (1984), the U.S. Supreme Court ruled that student receipt of federal assistance constituted a jurisdictional basis for regulation of independent educational institutions under Title IX, even though the institution in which the student matriculates receives no direct federal aid. The Court also ruled, however, that the "program or activity" which thus comes under federal regulation in Title IX is limited to the individual program receiving federal assistance and does not extend to all programs of the institution.

The Grove City decision was focused on the question whether receipt of Basic Educational Opportunity Grants (BEOG's) by a college's students triggers coverage of the entire institution under the nondiscrimination requirements of Title IX, irrespective of whether the college itself had solicited or received any federal funding. Following the Grove City decision Congress labored to pass legislation designed to compensate for that part of the court's decision which limits the scope of the Title IX prohibition against sex discrimination to specific programs within an educational institution receiving federal funding. After several years of debate the Congress finally enacted Public Law 100-259

EMPLOYMENT DISCRIMINATION STATUTES

[S.557], The Civil Rights Restoration Act of 1987. The Act provides for a number of amendments to Title IX, as well as to the Rehabilitation Act and the Civil Rights Act, for the purpose of "restor[ing] the prior consistent and long-standing executive branch interpretation and broad institution-wide application of these laws as . . . administered" prior to <u>Grove City</u>.

The Act introduced a new definition of a "program or activity" into each of the amended laws concerned with the proscription of discriminatory policies or practices. The new language was designed to assure institution-wide coverage of nondiscrimination provisions of the respective laws in any institution which receives federal assistance. The amended laws now stipulate that "for purposes of this title (section) the term 'program or activity' and 'program' mean all of the operations of . . . (2)(A) a college, university, or other postsecondary institution, or a public system of higher education."

In the course of the prolonged debate concerning the Civil Rights Restoration Act Congress received considerable testimony, urging revision of the religious exemption in Title IX of the Higher Education Act, which allows educational institutions which are "controlled by a religious organization" to claim exemption if there is "a conflict with particular tenets of the controlling religious organization." It was contended that this language does not protect the religious integrity of many religiously affiliated and religiously oriented institutions and fails to recognize changes in the organization of many church-related institutions which have occurred in recent years.

The National Association of Independent Colleges and Universities, in testimony before the Congress, called for revision of the exemption paragraph to provide language which would be clearer and more inclusive of those religiously oriented institutions which might have concerns in the area of sex-related admissions, employment, or student discipline. The NAICU proposal would have changed the definition of "programs" covered by the language of the exemption to read as follows:

> Such term ["program" or "activity"] does not include any operation of an entity which is controlled by or which is closely identified with the tenets of a religious organization if the application of Section 901 to such operation would not be consistent with the religious tenets of such organization.[15]

Former Executive Director of the Center for Constitutional Studies, Edward McGlynn Gaffney, Jr., in testimony before the Congress, suggested the following language:

> This section shall not apply to an educational institution which is an integral part of the religious mission of a church, or which, although not part of such mission, is religious in purpose and character, and for whom application of this subsection would not be consistent with religious tenets, convictions, practices or ministry of such institution.

Such proposed changes in the religious exemption were not accepted in the amendments finally enacted in the Civil Rights Restoration Act. The Congress took the view that new revisions to the exemption ran the risk of so loosening the language of the exemption as to open a "giant loophole" in the religious exemption, which would "lead to widespread sex discrimination in education." The Congress was also persuaded by the contention of the Department of Education that the existing statutory language was providing adequately for granting the exemptions for which religiously affiliated educational institutions were asking. The Congress noted that "the Office of Civil Rights has never denied a request for religious exemption" and "no requests for religious exemption are pending at this time."[16]

The Senate Report on the legislative history of the Civil Rights Restoration Act observed that the two most frequently cited reasons for requests for religious exemptions from religiously affiliated institutions under Title IX involved religious beliefs requiring sex discrimination for ministerial training, and differential treatment of pregnant students and employees, particularly if unmarried. A number of institutions also voiced concerns about the possibility that Title IX prohibitions might require institutional policies on hiring, student admission, and student discipline to take no notice of whether or not an individual may have had an abortion, in opposition to a strongly held religious institutional conviction concerning the immorality of abortion. The Congress rejected recommendations from the higher education community for changes in the language of the Title IX exemption for religiously affiliated educational institutions. However, the Congress included in the Civil Rights Restoration Act a provision specifically exempting institutions from performing or condoning abortions contrary to their religious convictions.

4. Executive Order 11246

In the aftermath of the Civil Rights legislation of the 1960's, the entire federal government has been mobilized in a comprehensive program of implementation, to assure that all vestiges of discrimination on the basis of race, color, national origin, religion, or sex are removed from national affairs. A series of Executive Orders have been issued to add impetus to the implementation of the nondiscrimination policies throughout the federal government. Executive Order 11246, issued by President Lyndon B. Johnson on September 24, 1965 (and frequently amended), extended the nondiscrimination requirements of federal law to all contractors with whom the government conducts business. The Order provides that any Government contractor or contracting agency, unless exempted,

> will not discriminate against any employee or applicant for employment because of race, color, religion, sex, or national origin. The contractor will take affirmative action to ensure that applicants are employed, and are treated during employment, without regard to their race, color, religion, sex, or national origin. Such action

shall include, but not be limited to the following:
employment, upgrading, demotion, or transfer;
recruitment or recruitment advertising; layoff or
termination; rates of pay or other forms of
compensation; and selection for training, including
apprenticeship. . .

The contractor will, in all solicitation or
advertisements for employees placed by or in behalf of
contractor, state that all qualified applicants will
receive consideration for employment without regard to
race, color, religion, sex, or national origin.[17]

The Executive Order's prohibition against religious
discrimination provides no exemptions for religiously
oriented contractors such as are allowed in legislative
enactments. Federal contractors are prohibited, without
qualifications or exemptions, from exercising any form of
religious preference in employment decisions. The Order
applies, however, only to institutions and agencies with
substantial federal government contracts. Smaller religiously
affiliated colleges and universities are unlikely to be
affected. The scope of the prohibitions covers all activities,
services, and products provided under the federal contract.

For a number of years religiously affiliated universities
have complained that the orders issued by the Executive
Branch on the subject of nondiscrimination in federally
assisted programs differ significantly from the provisions of
federal law, apparently ignoring, and possible opposing, an
important freedom of religiously affiliated institutions which
has been acknowledged by Congress. Furthermore, the
sanctions, available to an administrative agency of
government without judicial process, permit a peremptory
denial, withdrawal, or termination of contracts upon a
finding by the agency that discrimination has occurred. It
is true, of course, that no one can claim a right to a
federal contract. But there is cause for much misgiving in
the opportunity for use of executive discretion in the
issuance/cancellation of federal contracts not only to assure
prompt delivery of service for federal funds, but also to
achieve broader social objectives. As one higher education

representative commented in testimony before the Department of Labor:

> Executive discretion is rightly free to supervise accomplishment of contractual obligations. But when this same power is made into a weapon to create and impose public policy, then it intrudes upon the rights and freedoms of the people. It should be exercised only within limits imposed by the legislature, subject to judicial review. When large sectors of institutional life become financially dependent upon federal contracts, at public invitation and for the public good, then this contractual relationship must not be abused to afford the government a new and uncontrollable power to manipulate society as it pleases. . . . We recommend that the Department refrain from imposing upon federal contractors . . . restrictions or requirements that would not be countenanced by the Constitution or the law.[18]

5. Federal Regulations

The regulations and rulings of several federal administrative agencies must also be taken into consideration in understanding the law of nondiscrimination in employment. Chief among these agencies are the Equal Employment Opportunity Commission (EEOC), the Office of Federal Contract Compliance Programs (OFCCP), and the Internal Revenue Service (IRS). Regulations of the Office of Civil Rights of the Department of Education are also important.

The EEOC "Guidelines on Discrimination Because of Religion," issued under the authority of Title VII of the Civil Rights Act, are focused on the responsibility of employers to "reasonably accomodate" the religious beliefs and practices of employees. The guidelines also seek to clarify the definition of the "religious" nature of a belief or practice as suggested by the standard developed in the Supreme Court decisions in United States v. Seeger, 380 U.S. 163 (1965) and Welsh v. United States, 398 U.S. 333 (1970).[19] All employers are required under the Guidelines to make reasonable accomodation to the religious needs of their employees, so long as the purposes of the enterprise are not compromised.

The EEOC guidelines do not refer to the exemptions for religious discrimination in employment provided under Title VII for religious organizations and religiously affiliated educational institutions. No reference is made in the guidelines to EEOC rulings or interpretations of these exemptions or to the judicial decisions bearing on the question of EEOC jurisdiction over such organizations and institutions.

The OFCCP is charged with the responsibility of enforcing Executive Order 11246, and is authorized to employ the sanctions of possible cancellation, suspension, or termination of the federal contract in whole or in part, and/or declaration that the contractor is ineligible for future contracts with the federal government. In a 1975 regulation the OFCCP amended its regulations to conform more closely to the language of the Civil Rights Act. (The Executive Order itself was not amended.) The new regulation provides:

> It shall not be a violation of the equal opportunity clause for a school, college, university, or other educational institution or institution of learning to hire and employ employees of a particular religion if such school, college, university, or other educational institution or institution of learning is, in whole or in substantial part, owned, supported, controlled, or managed by a particular religion or by a particular religious corporation, association, or society, or if the curriculum of such school, college, university, or other educational institution or institution of learning is directed toward the propagation of the particular religion. The primary thrust of this provision is directed at religiously oriented church-related colleges and universities and should be so interpreted.[20]

85

EMPLOYMENT DISCRIMINATION STATUTES

The IRS has not issued rulings adversely affecting the ability of religiously affiliated institutions to exercise religious preference in employment decisions, with one exception. The exception concerns regulations denying tax-exempt status to schools which discriminate on racial grounds. Some institutions claim a religious basis for the exercise of such discrimination, but the IRS, with the support of the U.S. Supreme Court, has construed racially discriminatory employment or admissions policies at educational institutions as contrary to public policy and thus as constituting sufficient reason for refusing tax-exempt status.[21]

As an earlier Center publication has pointed out, the Internal Revenue Code employs language which is intended to clarify the criteria for identifying institutions which should be entitled to a statutory exemption on religious grounds.[22] The code recognizes exemption for an organization which functions as an "integrated auxiliary" of a church, describing it as "operated, supervised, or controlled by or in connection with a religious organization."[23] In a recent regulation the IRS used the terms "religiously affiliated" and "religiously associated" in characterizing such "integrated auxiliaries." The regulation explains:

> The term 'affiliated' means either controlled by or associated with a church or with a convention or association of churches. For example, an organization, a majority of whose officers or directors are appointed by a church's governing board or by officials of a church, is controlled by a church. . . . An organization is associated with a church . . . if it shares common religious bonds and convictions with that church.

Regulations of the Office of Civil Rights of the Department of Education (OCR) explicitly provide for the exercise by religiously affiliated institutions of the statutory exemption from the general prohibitions against religious and sex discrimination. The Assurance of Compliance form which institutions are required to file with the Department of Education contains instructions for claiming a religious exemption as a religiously "controlled" institution, under the stipulation that:

> An application or recipient will normally be considered to be controlled by a religious organization if one or more of the following conditions prevail:
> (1) It is a school or department of divinity; or
> (2) It requires its faculty, students, or employees to be members of, or otherwise espouse a personal belief in, the religion of the organization by which it claims to be controlled; or
> (3) Its charter and catalog, or other official publication, contains explicit statement that it is controlled by a religious organization or an organ thereof or is committed to the doctrines of a particular religion, and the members of the governing body are appointed by the controlling religious organization or an organ thereof, and it receives a significant amount of financial support from the controlling religious organization or an organ thereof.

OCR regulations spelling out prohibited forms of sex discrimination in student admissions and employment at institutions of higher education are quite extensive. Under authority of Title IX the OCR regulations include such prohibitions as the following:

> No person shall, on the basis of sex, be denied admission, or be subjected to discrimination in admission, by any recipient to which this subpart applies. . .
> In determining whether a person satisfies any policy or criterion for admission . . . a recipient to which this subpart applies: (1) shall not apply any rule concerning the actual or potential parental, family, or marital status of a student or applicant which treats persons differently on the basis of sex; (2) shall not discriminate against or exclude any person on the basis of pregnancy, childbirth, termination of pregnancy, or

87

recovery therefrom, or establish or follow any rule or practice which so discriminates or excludes. . .

A recipient shall treat disabilities related to pregnancy, childbirth, false pregnancy, termination of pregnancy and recovery therefrom in the same manner and under the same policies as any other temporary disability . . . (and shall provide for) a leave of absence for so long a period of time as is deemed medically necessary by the student's physician, at the conclusion of which the student shall be reinstated to the status which she held when the leave began. . . .

No person shall, on the basis of sex, be denied the benfits of, or be subjected to discrimination in employment, or recruitment, consideration, or selection therefor, whether full-time or part-time, under any education program or activity operated by a recipient which receives or benefits from Federal financial assistance. . . .

A recipient may take action otherwise prohibited by this subpart provided it is shown that sex is a bona fide occupational qualification for that action, such that consideration of sex is essential to successful operation of the employment function concerned.[24]

The OCR regulations provide that such prohibitions do not apply to "an educational institution which is controlled by a religious organization to the extent application of this part would not be consistent with the religious tenets of such organization." An educational institution seeking exemption from the requirement of nondiscrimination on the basis of sex must submit an application for such exemption, including "a statement by the highest ranking official of the institution, identifying the provisions of this part which conflict with a specific tenet of the religious organization."[25]

6. State Nondiscrimination Statutes

Most states have statutes which prohibit employers from discriminating against employees or prospective employees on the basis of religion. Exceptions are typically provided, however, to accomodate the constitutional principle of religious liberty. The exceptions are typically patterned after the language of the Civil Rights Act of 1964.

A survey of state laws affecting the exercise of religious preference in employment decisions in religiously affiliated higher education is beyond the scope of the present study. However, we wish to report a few examples which we regard as significant.

Model Anti-Discrimination Act

In 1966 the National Conference of Commissioners on Uniform State Laws approved the Uniform Law Commissioners' Model Anti-Discrimination Act. Chapter Three of this Act deals with nondiscrimination in employment. Section 302 defines discriminatory practices in language virtually identical to that of Section 703(a) of the Civil Rights Act. Section 308 recognizes the exemption provided in Section 702 of the 1964 version of the federal statute. The Model Act also provides for a BFOQ exception which parallels that of the federal statute. Section 309 (2) of the Model Act provides a significant variant from the federal Section 703 (e)(2) by omitting any reference to the curriculum of the school as a criterion of eligibility for the exception: This section of the Model Act provides that it is

> not a discriminatory practice for a religious educational institution or an educational organization operated, supervised, or controlled by a religious institution or organization to limit employment or give preference to members of the same religion.

State civil rights statutes often follow the lead of the Model Act and are basically similar to the federal statute, but there are some significant differences from state to state. Several states, in an explicit departure from the language of the Model Act, provide for a quite broad freedom of choice in the definition of the religious basis of discrimination in employment, providing that a religiously affiliated college may use religious criteria in employment decisions if those decisions are "calculated to promote religious principles."[26]

New York

The New York State Human Rights Law proscribes employment discrimination on the basis of race, color,. national origin, sex, or religion, but provides a broad exemption for religious institutions:

> Nothing contained in this section shall be construed to bar any religious or denominational institution or organization, or any organization operated for charitable or educational purposes, which is operated, supervised, or controlled by or in connection with a religious organization, from limiting employment . . . to or giving preference to persons of the same religion or denomination or from making such selection as is calculated by such organization to promote the religious principles for which it is established or maintained.[27]

Institutions which qualify for the exemption may exercise religious preference in employment "to persons of the same religion or denomination," or "make such selection as is calculated by such organization to promote the religious principles for which it is established or maintained." This broad exemption (with its emphasis on the institution's right to determine what employment decisions are calculated to promote its religious principles) is limited to charitable or educational organizations "operated, supervised, or controlled by or in connection with a religious organization." To qualify for the exemption, however, a college may have to sacrifice its eligibility for state funding, to its severe disadvantage in the competitive market of higher education.

The State of New York has one of the more comprehensive of state programs of financial aid to independent higher education. The state provides substantial capitation support, funds for special programs, and construction grants for nonpublic as well as public colleges and universities, provided that the institution meets certain eligibility requirements based on state law and the constitutions of the United States and the State of New York.

The New York State Constitution is somewhat more explicit than is the U.S. Constitution in prohibiting the use of public property or money to aid schools controlled by religious groups, providing (in the so-called Blaine Amendment)[28] that,

> Neither the state nor any subdivision thereof shall use its property or any public money, or authorize or permit either to be used, directly or indirectly, in aid or maintenance, other than for examination or inspection, of any school or institution of learning wholly or in part under the control or direction of any religious denomination, or in which any denominational tenet or doctrine is taught, but the legislature may provide for the transportation of children to and from any school or institution of learning.[29]

The determination of the eligibility of religiously affiliated colleges and universities for direct grants from public funds is made by the State Education Department on the basis of information which the institutions supply to the Commissioner of Education. The Commissioner asks for information "concerning the purposes, policies, and governance of the institution and concerning its faculty, student body, curricula, and programs," with special reference to denominational connections which might affect the admission of students or the appointment of faculty and to the importance of religion in the curriculum and in campus life.

In requesting information to be used in determining institutional eligibility for state aid, the Commissioner of Education poses such questions as the following:

(1) What are the stated purposes of the institution, as set forth in its charter or legislative authority?

(2) Is the institution wholly or in part under the control or direction of any religious denomination?
(3) Does the institution receive financial assistance from any religious body?
(4) Do the policies of the institution with respect to the selection of members of its governing board, its administrative officers or its faculty provide that the faith or creed of a candidate shall be relevant in any way to his selection?
(5) Do the policies of the institution with respect to the admission of students provide that the faith or creed of an applicant shall be relevant in any way to his admissibility to the institution?
(6) Is any denominational tenet or doctrine taught in the institution? If the answer is affirmative, please provide full information concerning the nature and extent of such instruction and indicate whether it is mandatory or optional.
(7) Does the institution award any degree or degrees in the field of religion? Does the institution include within its structure, or is it affiliated with any seminary or schools of theology?
(8) What is the place of religion in the programs of the institution?

If the answer to any of these questions is affirmative, the Commissioner requests the institution to supply information concerning the particulars.

Both state officials and the courts have sought to interpret the Blaine Amendment broadly, so as to enable a religiously affiliated college or university to qualify for state aid. In College of New Rochelle v. Nyquist, 37 A.D. 461, 326 N.Y.S. 2d at 771 (1971), a New York court ruled that a college founded by a Catholic religious order, operated under "Catholic auspices," and "devoted to the Christian tradition in its uniqueness and complexity" was eligible to receive direct state aid without violating the state constitution. The court explained that the Blaine Amendment must be construed:

to proscribe State aid where the affiliated religious denomination controls or directs the institution towards a religious end; where the institution is controlled to a degree so as to enable the religious authorities to propagate and advance - - or at least to attempt to do so - - their religion. Mere affiliation or a sharing of administrative control by a denomination will not, in and of itself, bring the institution within the proscription of the statute; such a situation cannot be said to have caused religion to 'pervade' the atmosphere of the College as to effectuate religious control or direction by a religious denomination.

In the mid-1960's Governor Nelson Rockefeller appointed the Select (Bundy) Committee on the Future of Private and Independent Higher Education in the State of New York to address the financial crisis then being faced by independent colleges and universities in the state. In 1968 the Committee issued its recommendations, which were based on a finding that there was a pressing need for strong public financing of higher education in the state through direct assistance to both public and private institutions. To overcome the constitutional obstacle to direct aid to religiously affiliated colleges and universities, the Committee bravely recommended the repeal of the New York State Constitution, Article XI(3) as it applies to higher education, and urged a program of direct grants to denominational institutions, provided that they were primarily devoted to education, rather than to religion. The Committee declared:

> We are far from concluding that all religious institutions should have state assistance. On the contrary, we would oppose any assistance to institutions whose central purpose is the teaching of religious belief. We suggest that each institution applying for state funds be examined as a whole to determine if it is primarily a religious institution or primarily an institution of higher education. Clearly, no seminary should have state help, in our view. We do not favor aid to those which are mainly concerned with the indoctrination of their own faithful. Nor should there

be state assistance to any institution which discriminates in its admission on religious grounds, any more than there should be aid to any which discriminates on grounds of color or race.

But we firmly reject the wider argument that all institutions of higher education having any religious connection should be ineligible. We think this kind of rigidity flies in the face of both logic and experience. History demonstrates that there is no automatic connection between the presence or absence of religious affiliation and the presence or absence of those qualities which make a college or university a major instrument of public service. There are secular institutions which are narrow and restrictive in their conception of their task; there are religiious institutions which stretch outward to all men and to all human concerns.[30]

The proposal for a constitutional amendment was never taken up. But the legislature proceeded to enact a comprehensive new program of state aid both to public institutions of higher education and to qualifying independent institutions. The dilemma thus presented to a college or university with a strong religious orientation was deep. As Timothy S. Healy, then President of Fordham University, put it, if a church-related college or university is precluded by its religiousness from participation in the new state programs, than it has only two choices: "either accept its second-class citizenship and die by strangling in its growth - - a process, given the financial pressures of the 1960's, likely to be more painful than prolonged; or seek with all deliberate speed to incorporate itself into some public or other private system which could guarantee its future only by completely denying its past."[31]

The course of action taken by a number of religiously affiliated institutions in New York has been to modify their organizational relationships, their educational purposes and programs, and their admission and employment policies to whatever extent necessary to establish their eligibility for direct state aid. We find it significant that in the 1990 edition of the Higher Education Directory only three New York colleges and universities (not including seminaries and rabbinical schools) now identify themselves as having a religious affiliation. All the others, including a large number with strong religious traditions and associations, now label themselves as "Independent-Nonprofit" institutions.

Washington

The Washington Anti-Discrimination Law prohibits discriminatory employment practices based on race, color, national origin, creed, sex, marital status, or sensory, mental, or physical handicap.[32] The provisions of the law are enforced by the State Human Rights Commission.

The statute permits an employer to base employment decisions on one of the protected characteristics if it constitutes a bona fide occupational qualification for the position. The State Human Rights Commission recognizes a BFOQ in conditions: (1) where the qualification is essential to, or will contribute to the accomplishment of the purposes for which the person is hired; or (2) where the qualification must be considered in order to correct a condition of unequal employment opportunity.[33]

Religious or sectarian organizations are not considered to be employers for purposes of the Anti-Discrimination Law. The Human Rights Commission states that in determining whether an institution of higher education should be so classified, it "looks to the question of the institution and considers it to be religious or sectarian if it has a religious orientation and mission." Institutions classified as religious or sectarian organizations are regarded as totally exempt from the law. The Commission declares that "they are free to discriminate on the basis of handicap, sex, age, et cetera, as well as creed."[34]

95

NOTES TO CHAPTER THREE

1. 42 U.S.C. 2000d.

2. 34 CFR, Part 100.

3. 42 U.S.C. 2000e-2(a).

4. 42 U.S.C. 2000e-1.

5. See Philip R. Moots and Edward McGlynn Gaffney, Jr., Church and Campus: Legal Issues in Religiously Affiliated Higher Education, op.cit., pp. 39-54; Edward McGlynn Gaffney, Jr. and Philip R. Moots, Government and Campus: Federal Regulation of Religiously Affiliated Higher Education, op.cit., pp. 44-49.

6. Government and Campus, p.47.

7. 42 USC 2000e (Title VII, Section 701).

8. 42 U.S.C. 2000e-2(e)

9. Church and Campus, p. 51.

10. 20 U.S.C. 1132e(c).

11. 20 U.S.C. 1132f-1(e).

12. 20 U.S.C. 1681(a).

13. 20 U.S.C. 1142

14. 20 U.S.C. 1210.

15. NAICU hoped that such language would be accepted by Congress, since it had been used in the Higher Education Amendment on Academic Facilities enacted in 1986. See above p. 76.

16. Although this was a factually true statement at the time it was made, the Congress failed to observe that some institutions had waited for as long as ten years before the Office of Civil Rights took any action on their applications.

17. Executive Order 11246 (30 F.R. 12319). The order has been amended several times: Executive Order 11375, October 13, 1967 (32 F.R. 14303); Executive Order 11478, August 8, 1969 (34 F.R. 12985); Executive Order 12086, October 5, 1978 (43 F.R. 45601).

18. Statement by James Burtchaell, then Provost of The University of Notre Dame, in an appearance before the U.S. Department of Labor on behalf of the College and University Department of the National Catholic Educational Association, October 1, 1975.

19. The Commission's interpretation of the responsibility to accomodate and its understanding of the meaning of "religious" were accepted by Congress after considerable debate and were subsequently incorporated in a 1972 amendment to Title VII. (Pub. L. 92-261, Title VII, Sect. 701; 42 U.S.C. 2000e (j)).

20. 41 C.F.R. 60-1.5(a)(5); cf. 41 C.F.R. 60-50.1(2).

21. Internal Revenue Code 501 (c)(3); Rev. Rul. 71-447; Rev. Proc. 75-50, Sect.4.07, 1975-2 C.B. 587. Cf. Bob Jones v. United States, 461 U.S. 367 (1983); see below pp. 197-202.

22. Government and Campus, p. 78.

23. I.R.C. 6033(a).

24. 34 CFR 106.21-106.61. The Office of Civil Rights has not yet issued new regulations pursuant to provisions of the Civil Rights Restoration Act of 1987.

25. 34 CFR 106.12.

26. Such states are Arizona, Hawaii, Illinois, Massachusetts, New York, Ohio, and Pennsylvania.

27. N.Y. Exec. Law 296.11

28. Adopted by the New York Constitutional Convention in 1894, following the unsuccessful effort by Senator James G. Blaine to obtain passage of a similar amendment to the Federal Constitution.

29. New York Constitution, Art. 11, Para. 3.

30. Report of Select (Bundy) Committee on the Future of Private and Independent Higher Education in New York State (1968), p. 49.

31. Timothy S. Healy, S.J., in his Introduction to Walter Gellhorn and R. Kent Greenawalt, The Sectarian College and the Public Purse: Fordham - - A Case Study, Dobbs Ferry NY, Oceana Publications, 1970, pp. viii,ix.

32. Wash. Rev. Code Ann. 49.60.

33. Wash. Rev. Code Ann. 162.16.

34. Letter from Morton M. Tytler, Senior Assistant Attorney General, as reported in Fernand N. Dutile and Edward McGlynn Gaffney, Jr., State and Campus: State Regulation of Religiously Affiliated Higher Education, University of Notre Dame Press, 1984, pp. 371,372. We shall later consider the Washington statute in connection with the case of Seattle Pacific University v. Orin C. Church (1986), see below pp. 235-239.

CHAPTER FOUR

SECULAR AND RELIGIOUS FUNCTIONS
IN ESTABLISHMENT CLAUSE JURISPRUDENCE
(1) AID TO ELEMENTARY AND SECONDARY SCHOOLS

In both statutory and judicial determinations, the law affecting the exercise of religious preference in employment decisions in religiously affiliated institutions of higher education requires some means of distinguishing between religious and non-religious beliefs or activities, between religious (or religiously affiliated) institutions and non-religious institutions. We shall find an examination of the development of the Supreme Court's Establishment Clause jurisprudence useful in clarifying the Court's analysis of religion in its institutional application.

We focus on the Establishment Clause rather than the Free Exercise Clause, because it is here that the Court has been most active in determining the rights of religious, and religiously affiliated, organizations. The Court's doctrine of Free Exercise has tended to focus on individual, rather than institutional, rights and is also less fully developed than is its Establishment Clause jurisprudence.[1]

1. Higher Education, Yes; Pre-collegiate Education, No

During the Kennedy and Johnson administrations there was a comprehensive national debate on educational policy. It was a time of major overhaul of the higher education system in the interest of making the system more adequate for modern conditions. As public institutions grew rapidly in both size and scope, there was a corresponding concern about the maintenance of strength in the independent sector, not only because of the perceived importance of pluralism in American education and society, but also because of the distinctive missions and resources of independent colleges and universities. Since most of the independent institutions are religiously affiliated, the design of a comprehensive national policy for the support of higher education raised difficult questions of church-state relations.

AID TO PAROCHIAL SCHOOLS

All the national higher education associations joined with government in the search for an effective and coherent national policy in education. The policy sought was one which would strengthen the system of public education, while at the same time encouraging the development of the independent institutions within the context of constitutional principle. The key legislative components of the federal program which emerged included the Higher Education Facilities Act (1963), the Higher Education Act (1965), and the Elementary and Secondary Education Act (1965), which were added to the student aid programs previously provided under the National Defense Education Act (1958). These components, combined with the thrust of the new civil rights legislation, have defined the legal framework for the development of higher education law in recent years.

For the independent and religiously affiliated sector, the program depended primarily on student aid as a means of supporting individuals who elected to attend independent and religiously affiliated institutions. However some programs of direct institutional support were developed as well.

One of the early contributions to the national debate on educational policy was a memorandum prepared in 1961 by Alanson W. Willcox, General Counsel to the Department of Health, Education, and Welfare, on The Impact of the First Amendment to the Constitution Upon Federal Aid to Education.[2] The memorandum was controlled by the assumption that any use of public funds to advance religion, to finance religious groups, or to support religious institutions is forbidden by the First Amendment. Willcox contended, however, that legislation designed to further the education and welfare of youth without regard to religious affiliation or lack thereof might be constitutional, even if it affords incidental benefit to church schools. He cited as a precedent the police and fire services provided at public expense for the protection of pupils at religiously affiliated schools. He noted that the line between direct support and incidental benefits was, of course, difficult to draw, remarking that it was easier to predict what the First Amendment forbids than what it allows.

Willcox began with the U.S. Supreme Court's decision in Everson v. Board of Education, 330 U.S. 1 (1947), which had unambiguously declared, "No tax in any amount, large or small, can be levied to support any religious activities or institutions, whatever they may be called, or whatever form they may adopt to teach or practice religion." Neither a state nor the Federal Government, said Justice Hugo Black, writing for the Court, may pass laws which aid a single religion, aid all religions, or prefer one religion over another. Neither a state nor the Federal Government "can, openly or secretly, participate in the affairs of any religious organizations or groups and vice versa." Such a construction of the "wall of separation" between church and state did not prevent the Everson Court from upholding a program of state reimbursement of transportation costs incurred by children in attending parochial schools.

Willcox predicted, however, that the Supreme Court would find it more difficult to uphold federal aid to parochial elementary and secondary schools than to sustain public support of religiously affiliated higher education. The constitutional principle, he maintained, is the same for all religiously affiliated educational institutions at either level. But he saw dramatic differences in the factual circumstances surrounding education at the two levels which, he predicted, would lead to far different results in the Court's differentiation between permissible and impermissible aid. Among the important circumstantial differences he noted the following:

1) Higher education has historically placed greater emphasis on the role of private institutions, the majority of which happen to have had a religious origin.
2) Primary schooling has long been recognized as essential for every child, and secondary education is rapidly coming to be so viewed. Higher education,

however, has always been viewed as a matter of individual decision.

3) The typical college student is mature enough to understand the significance of sectarian as compared to secular teaching and to apply critical standards in reaching his/her own decisions in matters of religious belief.

4) There is a substantial national interest in maintaining the system of private colleges and universities, since without them public institutions would be unable to cope with the numbers of students seeking higher education. Furthermore, exclusive dependence on the public institutions would lead to an emphasis on fields of study deemed directly useful to the national defense and welfare, to the detriment of a balanced higher education curriculum.

Because of these differences, Willcox predicted, federal aid to higher education is much less likely to encounter constitutional difficulty than aid to primary and secondary schools. Speaking for the Kennedy administration, he recommended federal support of higher education through such programs as scholarships and student loans, "cost of education" allowances ("capitation grants") paid directly to institutions, and subsidies and loans to institutions for certain kinds of facilities. Such higher education programs, he was confident, would encounter no constitutional difficulties if Congress wished to enact them. However, his Department recommended against any form of institutional aid to religiously affiliated elementary and secondary schools, on the grounds that such aid would probably not pass the test of constitutionality.

Willcox's rationale involved several highly controversial distinctions. His generalizations about the factual differences between elementary/secondary education and higher education struck many of his contemporaries as quite arbitrary, and they appear even more questionable when viewed from the distance of twenty-five or thirty years.

Furthermore, his analysis of the constitutionality of institutional aid depends on an elusive differentiation between religious and secular functions of education. Nevertheless, a number of the assumptions articulated in Willcox's memorandum can be traced both in the educational legislation of the 1960's and in judicial decisions of recent years.

A quite different point of view was presented in a memorandum on The Constitutionality of the Inclusion of Church-Related Schools in Federal Aid to Education, prepared by William R. Consedine, Director of the Legal Department of the National Catholic Welfare Conference in response to Willcox's analysis.[3] Consedine's memorandum refused to acknowledge that there were significant differences between religiously affiliated education at the pre-collegiate and post-secondary levels. He contended that it was in the national interest to have an excellent program of education at all levels and that the only question for government was the question what institutions are competent to provide such excellence. He proposed a strategic plan of federal aid to education at all levels, both public and private, both secular and religious (though not including proprietary institutions organized for profit).

Consedine's recommendations were based on the argument that non-public and religiously affiliated schools, too, perform a public function which, by its nature, is deserving of public support. There exists no constitutional bar, he contended, to aid to education in religiously affiliated schools in a degree proportionate to the value of the public function which they perform.

Furthermore, Consedine argued, every parent or child has a constitutional right to choose a religiously affiliated school as the institution in which the child's education will be acquired, as long as that school meets reasonable state requirements of educational quality. Accordingly, Consedine's memorandum argued, it is in the public interest, and it is a basic obligation of government, to assure the continued availability of the educational choice afforded by the system of religiously affiliated schools. He warned that massive spending for public education, without a corresponding program of support for religiously affiliated education, would in time result in a weakening of church-related schools, many of which would be forced to close. In that case, he said, the educational choice protected by the Supreme Court in Pierce v. Society of Sisters, 268 U.S. 510 (1928), would be effectively destroyed.

The Catholic Welfare Conference memorandum called for legislation aimed at the promotion and improvement of the education required for the general welfare, including the concerns not only of prosperity and defense, but also of culture. Achieving this purpose, Consedine emphasized, would require improving educational opportunities in both the public and the private, non-profit sectors.

Consedine rejected the contention that the American tradition of elementary and secondary education had been a tradition of non-religion or irreligion. On the contrary, he contended, American education, even in the public sector, has always been hospitable to religious values and religiously based moral training. Religiously affiliated schools, on the other hand, have always played a major role in secular education, and they constitute an important foundation on which the future development of American education may be built.

Both the HEW and Catholic Welfare Conference memos depend on the differentiation between the secular and religious activities of schools. Neither advocates the use of public funds to support religious activities or sectarian teaching. Consedine agreed that Everson prohibited tax levies to support any religious activities or institutions, but he noted that the majority carefully avoided any language which would prohibit aid to "education in secular subjects given in church-related schools." The Court, he contended, has not stated a doctrine of the absolute separation of church and state. On the contrary, it has allowed for certain forms of church-state cooperation in addressing human needs in the public interest.

Consedine construed _Everson_ as declaring the following principles:

1) Government may support the education of citizens in various ways.
2) 'Education of citizens' may take place in church-related schools.
3) Government may not support a religion or a church, as such, but so long as its program confers directly and substantially a benefit to citizen education, that program is constitutionally unobjectionable, although benefit is at the same time incidentally conferred upon a religion or a church.

It is a doctrine which has been widely accepted in circles of religiously affiliated education, although it has by no means been consistently followed in the decisions of American courts. The underlying assumption that it is possible to distinguish between the secular benefits and the sectarian functions of religiously affiliated education is one which our project must examine with some care.

2. Some Representative Elementary/Secondary School Cases

In a long line of cases emerging from _Everson_ the Supreme Court has sought to discriminate between permissible and impermissible forms of church-state cooperation in education and to identify constitutional and unconstitutional forms of state support of religiously affiliated schools. In these decisions the Court has sought to remain within the framework of the two principles of _Everson_: 1) No form of public support of religion in any guise is permitted under the Constitution; 2) A program of public aid which in some manner indirectly or incidentally aids an institution with a religious affiliation does not necessarily violate the Establishment Clause. The Court has

105

chosen to accept the sometimes frustrating responsibility of seeking to demarcate the lines separating forms of aid to religiously affiliated education which may be approved under the First Amendment and those which must be struck down. Whatever is to be said about the social utility of this line of decisions, it is rarely commended for its consistency and predictability.

In Everson v. Board of Education, 330 U.S. 1 (1947), the Court said "Yes" to state reimbursement to parents for the cost of transporting their children to attend sectarian elementary and secondary schools, holding that New Jersey's authorization of such reimbursements was for a public purpose. The Everson Court barely reached agreement (in a 5-4 decision), and even the majority opinion admitted that its decision on school transportation "approaches the verge of impermissible action." Justice Hugo L. Black explained, in delivering the majority opinion, that the Court's decision was not intended to prohibit any state from enacting legislation which would restrict public-subsidized transportation services to students attending public schools if it desired to do so. The Court only wished to declare that a state is permitted under the Constitution to extend the benefits of public welfare legislation to all citizens without regard to their religious beliefs or associations.

In McCullom v. Board of Education, 333 U.S. 203 (1948), on the other hand, the Court struck down, by an 8-1 majority, a state's use of its machinery for compulsory school attendance to enable sectarian groups to give religious instruction to public school pupils on a "released time" basis in public school buildings. In his concurring opinion Justice Felix Frankfurter noted that the decision of the Court "did not imply indifference to the basic role of religion in the life of the people, nor rejection of religious education as a means of fostering it." The claims of religion, Frankfurter wrote, "are not minimized by refusing to make the public schools agencies for their assertion." Frankfurter saw the McCullom decision as meaning simply that "the public school must keep scrupulously free from entanglement in the strife of sects" and as requiring "strict confinement of the State to instruction other than religious, leaving to the individual's church and home, indoctrination in the faith of his choice."

The distinction between permissible and impermissible aid to parochial schools was pursued in a series of decisions following Everson and McCullom. In Zorach v. Clauson, 343 U.S. 306 (1952), the Court authorized released time for religious instruction away from the public school, declaring that to refuse to cooperate in this way with religious groups would manifest a constitutionally impermissible hostility to religion. In Board of Education v. Allen, 392 U.S. 236 (1968), it upheld a program of textbook loans made directly to parochial school students. But in Meek v. Pittenger, 421 U.S. 349 (1975), it prohibited a state program involving loans of non-textbook instructional materials and equipment to parochial schools and invalidated a program of auxiliary remedial, counseling, and psychological services to parochial school students conducted by public employees on parochial school property.

In Lemon v. Kurtzman, 403 U.S. 602 (1971), the Court invalidated a Rhode Island program of state salary supplements to teachers engaged in the teaching of secular subjects in nonpublic schools, and struck down a Pennsylvania program under which the state purchased certain "secular educational services" from nonpublic schools, directly reimbursing those schools for teachers' salaries, textbooks, and instructional materials. Later in Aguilar v. Felton, 473 U.S. 402 (1985), the Court struck down a similar program in the New York City schools, despite a special attempt by the public schools to assure that there was no religious instruction in such publicly funded classes.

In Wolman v. Walter, 433 U.S. 229 (1977), the Court invalidated a state program of providing non-textbook instructional materials and equipment directly to parochial school students but upheld a state program of standardized testing, scoring, diagnostic, and remedial services for nonpublic schools at neutral sites. And in Committee for Public Education and Religious Liberty v. Regan, 433 U.S. 229 (1977), the Court upheld reimbursements to parochial schools for certain testing, recordkeeping, and reporting services, emphasizing that schools could not divert these cash payments to religious purposes.

In Committee for Public Education and Religious Liberty v. Nyquist, 413 U.S. 756 (1973), the Court invalidated a state program of tuition reimbursements and tax credits for parents of students in nonpublic schools, and grants for maintenance and repair of facilities and equipment for nonpublic schools. But in Mueller v. Allen, 463 U.S. 388 (1982), it approved a program of state income tax deductions for expenses incurred in providing tuition, textbooks, and transportation for children attending an elementary or secondary school, either public or private.

In each of these decisions the constitutional question was decided through the Court's determination of questions of fact concerning the degree of religiousness involved in the activity or association facilitated by public funds. The Court's flexibility in interpreting the religion clauses results, as Justice Lewis Powell once observed,[4] in a certain untidiness in its decisions. It might have been analytically cleaner, Powell admitted, if the Court had accepted the broadest implications of the principle (advocated by some members of the Court) that "substantial aid to the educational function of [sectarian] schools . . . necessarily results in aid to the enterprise as a whole." But consistent application of that rule, said Powell, would have doomed the "persistent desire of a number of states to find proper means of helping sectarian education." Thankfully, he said, the Court had not thought such a harsh result was required by the Constitution. Few people, indeed, would consider such a result to be in the public interest. Powell wrote:

Our decisions have sought to establish principles that preserve the cherished safeguard of the Establishment Clause without resort to blind absolutism.

If this endeavor means a loss of some analytical tidiness, then that too is entirely tolerable.

Board of Education v. Allen (1968)

In Board of Education v. Allen, 392 U.S. 236 (1968), the Court used the Everson precedent to approve a program under which public funds were used to purchase textbooks to be loaned to students in religiously affiliated elementary and secondary schools. The initiative in the selection of such textbooks under the challenged program rested with officials of the parochial school, who submitted requests for "the books desired," subject to the approval of state authorities as provided in the state law. The Court found by a 5-4 majority that "secular and religious teachings were not necessarily so intertwined" as to make it impossible to separate the state's loan of textbooks to students from the teaching of religion in the parochial schools which such students might happen to attend.

Justice William O. Douglas, strongly dissenting from the majority, saw the facts in Allen as decisively different from those in Everson.

There is nothing ideological about a bus. . . The textbook goes to the very heart of education in a parochial school. It is the chief, although not solitary, instrumentality for propagating a particular religious creed or faith. How can we possibly approve such state aid to a religion?

Justice Black, who had written the Everson opinion, agreed, saying that the Establishment Clause barred any state from using funds levied from all its citizens to purchase any books which will be used by sectarian schools. Douglas contemplated with consternation the prospect of a battle over control of the decision as to what textbooks are "secular" or "religious." He endorsed the lower court's declaration that there is no reliable standard for distinguishing secular from religious textbooks, and noted

Justice Robert H. Jackson's comment in <u>McCullom</u> that it will often be difficult to say "where the secular ends and the sectarian begins."

Douglas saw the Constitutional conflict as inherent in the nature of religious schools, which he declared were established for the express purpose of providing "an education oriented to the dogma of the particular faith." He found such an understanding of the aims of education among religiously affiliated colleges and universities as well as in parochial schools.[5] The religious orientation of parochial schools and colleges seemed to Justice Douglas to make it impossible for states to become involved in any way in the teaching/learning process in such schools without violation of Constitutional principle. The majority of the Court, however, saw no constitutional conflict in the statutes challenged in <u>Allen</u>.

Lemon v. Kurtzman (1971)

The landmark case of <u>Lemon v. Kurtzman</u>, 403 U.S. 601 (1971), concerned a challenge to two state programs, one in Rhode Island involving salary subsidies paid by the state directly to teachers engaged in teaching secular subjects at nonpublic schools, and one in Pennsylvania authorizing the state Superintendent of Public Instruction to "purchase" certain "secular educational services" from nonpublic schools through direct reimbursements to such nonpublic schools for the direct costs of teacher salaries, textbooks, and other instructional materials. In both states the overwhelming preponderance of the nonpublic schools were Roman Catholic parochial schools. The complainants, challenging the constitutionality of the operating statutes, alleged that the church-affiliated schools who benefited from the programs were controlled by religious organizations and conducted their educational operations for the express purpose of promoting a particular religious faith.

In finding these programs unconstitutional the Court reached the same degree of unanimity as it had in

McCullom, with only one justice (White) dissenting. The Court determined that the very nature of the purposes of church-related elementary and secondary schools in the teaching of religion made it impossible for states to provide subsidies to faculty salaries in such schools in a manner which would restrict such support to the secular function of education. The Court found that the state programs in question necessarily involved an excessive government entanglement in religion because of the character and purposes of the institutions that were benefited.

Chief Justice Warren Burger, writing the opinion of the Court, declared that the Court could agree in the abstract with the legislatures of the two states that "secular and religious education are identifiable and separable." But he denied that the distinction could be maintained operationally in the programs which had been created. Allen had allowed that a state program for loaning textbooks to parochial school children could successfully distinguish secular from sectarian books, with the result that furnishing "secular" textbooks to parochial school children did not necessarily foster the teaching of religion in violation of the Establishment Clause. But in Lemon Burger declared that "teachers have a sustantially different ideological character from books" (just as Douglas had declared in Allen that books are different from buses). The conflict of the secular and religious functions inheres in the situation of the parochial school classroom, he maintained, for "inevitably some of a teacher's responsibilities hover on the border between secular and religious orientation."

The question on which the decision of the Court depended was not whether religious instruction had, in fact, been injected into the "secular" courses to which state funding was restricted; nor whether parochial school teachers could be expected to succeed in their conscientious attempts to segregate their religious beliefs from their secular educational functions for purposes of participating in the state subsidies; nor whether the state could be depended upon to successfully monitor and guarantee the effective separation of the secular and sectarian functions of education in the continuing operation of the program. The comingling of the secular and the religious, said Burger, "inheres in the educational situation" of the parochial school, despite the good will and professional responsibility of both the schools and the state. "We conclude that the cumulative impact of the entire relationship arising under the statutes in each State involves excessive entanglement between government and religion."

The Lemon opinion promulgated a three-pronged test which has underlain the Establishment Clause jurisprudence of the Court in recent years. The Court viewed the Establishment Clause as designed to guard against three evils: "sponsorship, financial support, and active involvement of the sovereign in religious activity."[6] Addressing these concerns, Lemon gleaned from earlier Supreme Court precedents three tests of a constitutionally permissible program of public aid to a religious or religiously affiliated organization:

1) First, the statute must have a secular legislative purpose.
2) Second, its principal or primary effect must be one that neither advances nor inhibits religion.
3) Finally, the statute must not foster 'an excessive government entanglement with religion.'

The Court added a further requirement that operation of the statute must not contribute to "political divisiveness along religious lines." The Court saw the First Amendment as particularly intended to protect not so much against the "strife of sects" as against the alignment of political positions with religious faiths. It is to be expected that religious groups should from time to time take strong positions on public issues, said the Court, and their right to do so must be protected. But a statute which intensifies political fragmentation and divisiveness on religious lines would involve the government in a form and degree of entanglement which the Lemon Court judged to be inconsistent with the Establishment Clause.

In its recent Establishment decisions the Court has followed the rule that if any one of these tests is not met, federal aid is impermissible. The reasoning of the Court in applying its three-part test has been essentially that of the Willcox memorandum. The Lemon Court contended that the Constitutional principle involved is unitary: "Under our system the choice has been made that government is to be excluded from the area of religious instruction . . . The Constitution decrees that religion must be a private matter for the individual, family, and the institutions of private choice, and that while some involvement and entanglement are inevitable, lines must be drawn." But in drawing these lines the Court has accepted the burden of taking into consideration the factual circumstances affecting the relation between religious and secular factors in particular cases, and has propounded a diversity of constructions of the unitary constitutional principle.

A number of commentators have complained of the incoherence of the three-part test of Lemon.[7] Justice Sandra O'Connor has been particularly critical of the "entanglement" part of the test. She writes, in her dissenting opinion in Aguilar v. Felton, "To a great extent the anomalous results in our Establishment Clause cases are 'attributable to [the] entanglement prong.'"[8] However, the Court continues to depend heavily on Lemon in case after case, and there is no sign of its imminent demise.

The Court has sought to prevent its three-fold test from being construed as a touchstone of Establishment. Lemon itself declared that "the line of separation (between church and state), far from being a 'wall,' is a blurred, indistinct, and variable barrier depending on all the circumstances of a particular relationship," and acknowledged that the Court could "only dimly perceive the lines of demarcation in this extraordinarily sensitive area of constitutional law."[9] Later in Lynch v. Donnelly, 465 U.S.

668, at 678 (1984), Chief Justice Burger, writing the majority opinion upholding use of religious symbols in a municipal Christmas display, remarked that the Court had consistently declined to take a rigid, absolutist view of the Establishment Clause. Burger quoted the opinion of the Court in Walz v. Tax Commission, 397 U.S. 668 (1970), which had declared "the Court's refusal to construe the Religion Clauses with a literalness that would undermine the ultimate constitutional objective as illuminated by history." (Burger's italics.) The purpose of the Religion Clauses, in the Walz Court's view, is "to state an objective, not to write a statute."

On the day that Lemon was decided (8-1) the Supreme Court also delivered its (5-4) opinion in Tilton v. Richardson, 403 U.S. 672 (1971), which affirmed the constitutionality of the federal Higher Education Facilities Act of 1963. (We shall later examine this opinion at some length.[10]) In that opinion, which was also delivered by Chief Justice Burger, the Court declared that direct aid to religiously affiliated colleges and universities is not necessarily a violation of the Establishment Clause. In Lemon, however, the Court had held that state purchase of secular educational services from parochial elementary and secondary schools unavoidably violates the Establishment Clause.

Several justices found the Court's reasoning in Tilton inconsistent with that of Lemon. Justices William Brennan and Byron White expressed that assessment in their concurring and dissenting opinions in Lemon. Justice Douglas, who had concurred in Lemon, declared in Tilton (with the concurrence of Justices Black and Marshall) that he was dissenting "out of a feeling of despair that the respect which through history has been accorded the First Amendment is this day lost."[11]

Justice White, who dissented in Lemon and concurred in Tilton, saw no significant difference in factual circumstances between the two cases. In his dissenting opinion in Lemon

114

he declared his agreement with the decision in Tilton "that the Federal Government may finance the separate secular function carried on in a parochial setting" at the higher education level; but he found it arbitrary for the Court to determine in Lemon that it was impossible to separate the secular and the sectarian functions of education at the elementary and secondary education level. If Lemon is correctly decided, Tilton is wrongly decided, White maintained, and if Tilton is correctly decided, Lemon is wrongly decided. For his part he would allow both the pre-collegiate and the post-secondary programs, provided that there is a showing on the facts that institutional support does not really go to religious instruction.[12]

The decision of the Court in Lemon, White contended, creates an insoluble paradox for religiously affiliated schools:

> The State cannot finance secular instruction if it permits religion to be taught in the same classroom; but if it exacts a promise that religion will not be so taught - - a promise the school and its teachers are quite willing and able on this record to give - - and enforces it, it is then entangled in the 'no entanglement' aspect of the Court's Establishment Clause jurisprudence.
> Why the federal program in the Tilton case is not embroiled in the same difficulty is never adequately explained. (Lemon at 668)

Justice William Brennan took a similar view of the relationship between Lemon and Tilton, but differed from White in coming to a separationist conclusion. In his concurring opinion in Lemon Brennan reaffirmed his conviction that "general subsidies of religious activities would, of course, constitute impermissible state involvement with religion" (Quoting his concurring opinion in Walz, 397 U.S. at 690). However, the Court has recognized, he observed, that both parochial schools and sectarian universities provide both a secular and a sectarian education. Whether these two functions can be distinguished in the case of direct institutional aid is the point of debate. Brennan doubted that the distinction is viable in any sectarian setting, whether pre-collegiate or post-secondary, since integration of secular and religious education "is both the theory and the strength of the religious school." He argued:

> I emphasize that a sectarian university is the equivalent in the realm of higher education of the Catholic elementary schools in Rhode Island; it is an educational institution in which the propagation and advancement of a particular religion are a primary function of the institution. I do not believe that construction grants to such a sectarian institution are permissible. The reason is . . . that the secular education is provided within the environment of religion; the institution is dedicated to two goals, secular education and religious instruction. When aid flows directly to the institution, both functions benefit.

Brennan saw no significant difference between the Federal Government's requiring a sectarian university not to teach any religious subjects or to hold any religious activities in a building paid for with federal funds (Tilton), and Rhode Island's requiring a parochial school teacher not to teach religion while engaged in secular education paid for with state funds (Lemon). Both prohibitions are required by the neutrality of government in religion. The problem in both cases is the feasibility of keeping the secular and the sectarian aspects of education functionally separate. If a university chooses to be sectarian, he argued, it ought not to receive construction grants from the federal government. And if parochial schools are inherently sectarian, as the facts in Lemon attest, then they ought not to receive any form of institutional aid from the state.

The perspective of the Lemon-Tilton majorities, however, was essentially that of the HEW Memorandum of ten years earlier: Institutional aid to religiously affiliated

116

elementary and secondary schools is generally impermissible, but institutional aid to religiously affiliated colleges and universities may be permissible. The differences between the two levels of education appeared decisive for Chief Justice Burger, as he explained in his Tilton opinion:

1) Precollegiate church schools are guided by the aim of assuring future adherents to a particular religious faith "by having control of their total education at an early age" (Walz, at 671). College students are more mature, less impressionable, and less susceptible to religious indoctrination.

2) By their very nature, collegiate and postgraduate courses present only limited opportunities for sectarian influences by virtue of their own internal disciplines.

3) Many church-related colleges and universities are characterized by a high degree of academic freedom and seek to evoke free and critical responses from their students.

In the case of the particular colleges involved in the challenge to the federal program in Tilton, there was no showing, said the Court, that any of them departed from this general pattern of education. They do not restrict student admission or faculty appointments through a religious test. They do not require students to attend religious services. Although students are required to take theology courses, such courses are "taught according to the academic requirements of the subject matter and the teacher's concept of professional standards;" and such courses cover a broad range of human experience and are not restricted to a particular religious tradition. The schools make no attempt to indoctrinate or proselytize and have well-established policies and precedents in academic freedom. "In short," concluded the Chief Justice, "the evidence shows institutions with admittedly religious functions but whose predominant higher education mission is to provide their students with a secular education" (Tilton at 687).

In <u>Lemon,</u> on the other hand, the Chief Justice accepted the determination of the lower court that the parochial schools which were involved in state purchase of "secular" education were "an integral part of the religious mission of the Catholic Church" and exhibited a set of characteristics which made them inherently "a powerful vehicle for transmitting the Catholic faith to the next generation." The process of "inculcating religious doctrines" in such schools is enhanced, the Court contended, by "the impressionable age of the pupils, in primary schools, particularly." In view of the circumstances and environment in which parochial elementary and secondary education is conducted, the Court determined that "parochial schools involve substantial religious activity and purpose" and that they have a "substantial religious character," which gives rise in the programs challenged "to entangling church-state relationships of the kind the Religion Clauses sought to avoid."

In <u>Lemon</u> the Court contended that state supervision and monitoring of the supported educational activities in the interest of assuring their "secular" character would involve the government in excessive entanglement in the affairs of the schools. A "comprehensive, discriminating, and continuing surveillance" would be required, said the Court, to ensure that the state restrictions on teaching functions were, in fact, obeyed. The contacts required would necessarily involve "excessive and enduring entanglement between church and state" and would have a chilling effect on the Free Exercise rights of the parochial schools. However, the determinations required in the federal construction grants to religiously affiliated colleges and universities seemed to the Court to involve no such entanglement.

The courts have consistently been reluctant to become involved, or to allow other agencies of government to become involved, in the entanglements of determining the degree of religiousness of schools. However, such reluctance did not prevent the Supreme Court from finding in <u>Lemon</u> that parochial schools <u>as a class</u> were ineligible under the First Amendment for state institutional aid for secular education functions, and in <u>Tilton</u> that religiously affiliated colleges and universities <u>as a class</u> were eligible for federal construction grants for secular education functions. The Court's determination is significant for our present inquiry in its implication that if religiously affiliated colleges and universities as a class are more eligible for state financial support than religiously affiliated elementary and secondary schools on account of their less pervasive religious character, they would appear to be correspondingly less eligible on constitutional and statutory grounds for religious exemptions for religiously discriminatory employment practices.

In the line of Establishment decisions in elementary and secondary education following <u>Lemon,</u> the Supreme Court has tended toward a more separationist posture. The Court has continued to follow its earlier precedents in allowing educational support for individuals under social welfare legislation, even when such support indirectly benefited religiously affiliated schools (<u>Everson</u>); and it has continued to allow state textbook loans to parochial school children under proper controls to assure the secular character of such books (<u>Allen</u>). But the Court has been reluctant to accomodate new forms of church-state cooperation in elementary and secondary education.

Committee for Public Education and Religious Liberty v. Nyquist (1973)

In <u>Committee for Public Education and Religious Liberty v. Nyquist</u>, 413 U.S. 756 (1973), the Supreme Court struck down three financial aid programs for nonpublic elementary and secondary schools established under a series of 1972 amendments to a New York statute. The programs included: 1) Direct institutional grants for maintenance and repair of facilities and equipment; 2) Tuition reimbursements for parents of children attending nonpublic elementary and secondary schools; and 3) Income tax deductions for parents for each child attending a nonpublic elementary or secondary school. The Court found that all three programs violated the Establishment Clause.

The New York statute was carefully drafted so as to emphasize its purposes of insuring the health, safety, and welfare of students attending nonpublic schools which serve a high concentration of low-income families, and of enhancing the accessibility of alternative educational systems for students of such families. The specific provisions of the legislation were designed to restrict benefits to economically disadvantaged families. Of slightly more than 2,000 nonpublic schools in the state, something less than 14% were estimated to be capable of satisfying the eligibility standards of the program. The New York legislature clearly regarded the program as consistent with the provisions of the state constitution on religious liberty. The U.S. Supreme Court, however, found the program inconsistent with its own Establishment criteria. The majority was 6-3, with Burger, Rehnquist, and White dissenting.

The Nyquist Court accepted a profile, prepared by the lower court, of sectarian, nonpublic schools which might qualify for aid, characterizing them as schools which:

(a) impose religious restrictions on admissions; (b) require attendance of pupils at religious activities; (c) require obedience by students to the doctrines and dogmas of a particular faith; (d) require pupils to attend instruction in the theology or doctrine of a particular faith; (e) are an integral part of the religious mission of the church sponsoring it; (f) have as a substantial purpose the inculcation of religious values; (g) impose religious restrictions on faculty appointments; and (h) impose religious restrictions on what or how the faculty may teach.

The Court accepted the trial court's finding that approximately 85% of the nonpublic schools in the state are church-related and that almost all of the institutions which

120

would be qualified to receive the maintenance and repair grants "are related to the Roman Catholic Church or teach Catholic religious doctrine to some degree." The issue thus presented to the Court was whether, "because of the substantially religious character of the intended beneficiaries, each of the State's three enactments offended the Establishment Clause."

Writing for the Court, Justice Powell declared that, as far as the first test of Lemon is concerned, the state statute had a clearly secular legislative purpose. The "primary effects" test, however, was declared not to have been satisfied by any of the three programs. With respect to the third test the Court added the dictum that "apart from any administrative entanglement of the State in particular religious programs, assistance of the sort involved here carries grave potential for entanglement in the broader sense of continuing and expanding political strife over aid to religion."

The Court found that the maintenance and repair grants had the effect of subsidizing and advancing the religious mission of sectarian schools and violated Lemon's second test. The grant program failed to restrict such grants from being used for facilities in which religious activities might take place. Applying its Tilton precedent, the Court declared that "if tax-raised funds may not be granted to institutions of higher education where the possibility exists that they may be used to construct facilities used for sectarian activities 20 years hence, a fortiori they may not be distributed to elementary and secondary schools for the maintenance and repair of facilities without any limitations on their use." The principle governing this reasoning, as stated by Powell, is: "In the absence of an effective means of guaranteeing that state [institutional] aid derived from public funds will be used exclusively for secular, neutral, and nonideological purposes, it is clear from our cases that direct aid in whatever form is invalid."

Powell admitted that the tuition reimbursement and tax credit programs involved benefits to individuals rather than to institutions and that laws providing such benefits had been upheld in Everson and Allen. But the Court contended that the New York reimbursement and tax credit programs are designed, in part, for the purpose of relieving parents of their financial burdens "sufficiently to assure that they continue to have the option to send their children to religion-oriented schools." Thus the effect of the aid, even when distributed directly to parents and only indirectly to schools, is "to provide desired financial support for nonpublic, sectarian institutions."[13]   Such aid, said the Court, is impermissible under the Establishment Clause.

Mueller v. Allen (1983)

Ten years later the Court upheld a Minnesota statute which allowed state taxpayers to deduct expenses incurred in providing tuition, textbooks, and transportation for their children attending an elementary or secondary school. The tax benefits for textbook purchases were subject to a determination by state officials that particular textbooks qualify as "secular." The Minnesota statute, the Court held (by a majority of 5-4), is neutral on its face and in its application and does not have the primary effect of either advancing or inhibiting religion.

The Minnesota tax deduction plan differed from the New York program struck down in Nyquist in being available to all parents, whether their children attend public, private nonsectarian, or private sectarian schools. Powell, who had written the Nyquist opinion striking down tax credits in New York, now concurred in upholding the Minnesota program. Justice William Rehnquist, who wrote the Mueller opinion, continued to argue for the applicability of Everson, Allen, and Walz as precedents for a program of indirect support.

Justice Thurgood Marshall wrote a dissenting opinion (in which the remnants of the Nyquist majority joined), in

122

which he denied that there was any significant difference between the New York and Minnesota tax deduction/tax credit schemes. The neutrality of the Establishment Clause, he contended, forbids not only the tax benefits struck down in Nyquist, but also the tax deduction involved here. "Indirect assistance in the form of financial aid to parents for tuition payments is . . . impermissible," said Marshall, "because it is not 'subject to . . . restrictions' which 'guarantee the separation between secular and religious functions and . . . ensure that State financial aid supports only the former.'"

Rehnquist, on the other hand, found it entirely possible to reconcile the Mueller and Nyquist decisions, emphasizing that the Minnesota benefits were available to all citizens of the state, regardless of their religious affiliation or lack thereof. He found the Minnesota benefits more analogous to the transportation reimbursements upheld in Everson, to the textbook benefits upheld in Allen, and to the G.I. Bill, than to the tuition and tax credit programs struck down in Nyquist. "The historic purposes of the [Establishment] Clause," he reasoned, "simply do not encompass the sort of attenuated financial benefit, ultimately controlled by the private choices of individual parents, that eventually flows to parochial schools from the neutrally available tax benefit at issue in this case."

Aguilar v. Felton (1985)

A brief word may be added concerning the Court's 1985 decision in Aguilar v. Felton, 473 U.S. 402 (1985), and its companion case, School District of City of Grand Rapids v. Ball, 473 U.S.) 382 (1985). Both cases were decided by a narrow 5-4 majority.

In Aguilar a challenge was brought against New York City's use of federal funds under Title I of the Elementary and Secondary Education Act to place public school teachers and other professional personnel in religious and other private schools serving large numbers of disadvantaged

123

children, to provide remedial instruction and clinical and guidance services. It was accepted that the program was intended not to strengthen the schools in which such services were offered, but to enhance the welfare of the participating students. By a 5-4 majority, however, the Supreme Court decided that the program failed to pass its Establishment Clause tests as propounded in Lemon.

New York City had made a special effort to avoid the constitutional objection by creating a rigorous monitoring system for preventing any possible intrusion of a religious content into publicly funded classes conducted in religious schools. But the Court found that, even if successful, such monitoring would not eliminate the excessive entanglement of church and state which is inherently involved in the program. "Even where state aid to parochial institutions does not have the primary effect of advancing religion," said Justice Brennan in writing the opinion of the Court, "the provision of such aid may nevertheless violate the Establishment Clause owing to the interaction of church and state in the administration of that aid." The program in question, he declared, is impermissible because it would require "a permanent and pervasive state presence in the sectarian schools receiving aid."

The Aguilar decision was controlled by the understanding that the recipient institutions were essentially like those in Nyquist, which "have as a substantial purpose the inculcation of religious values," and those in Meek v. Pittenger, 421 U.S. 349 (1975), in which "education is an integral part of the dominant sectarian mission and in which an atmosphere dedicated to the advancement of religious belief is constantly maintained." As evidence of such an orientation and involvement the Court noted that such schools receive funds and report back to their affiliated church, require attendance at religious exercises, begin the school day or class period with prayer, grant preference in admission to members of the sponsoring denomination, and (in the case of the Catholic schools, which constitute the vast majority of the aided schools) are under the general supervison and control of the local parish. Under these circumstances, the Court declared, violation of the Establishment Clause is inherent in the funded program. Brennan wrote:

> Despite the well-intentioned efforts taken by the City of New York, the program remains constitutionally flawed owing to the nature of the aid, to the institution receiving the aid, and to the constitutional principles that they implicate - - that neither the State nor the Federal Government shall promote or hinder a particular faith or faith generally through the advancement of benefits or through the excessive entanglement of church and state in the administration of these benefits."

Justice Sandra O'Connor (joined by Justice Rehnquist) strongly dissented. The Court's holding, she said, greatly exaggerates the supervision necessary to prevent public school teachers from bringing religion into their classes, once they set foot in parochial schools. The actual experience of New York over fourteen years indicates, she contended, that the administrative arrangements for assuring the non-sectarian character of the cooperative program are effective. The District Court determined that, in fact, not one instance of religious indoctrination under the program had been identified, and concluded that "the result feared in other cases" had not materialized in this case. "In light of the ample record," O'Connor said, "an objective observer of the implementation of the Title I program in New York would hardly view it as endorsing the tenets of the participating parochial schools."

The explanation of this record, said Justice O'Connor, is not hard to find: Public school teachers are professionals, who know how to respect regulations and are most unlikely to begin inculcating religion under the influence of the sectarian environment of the parochial schools where they teach. The Court's abstract theory of the risk of sectarianism, she pointed out, flies in the face of the record of how the New York program has actually been working. The tragic fact, she complained, is that the Court's theoretical and counter-factual hypothesis concerning the risk of possible sectarian effects only deprives impoverished schoolchildren of the real benefits which Congress intended they should have, namely help in overcoming their learning deficits.

The Court's difficulty, she argued, arises from its misuse of the "entanglement" test. She agreed that "pervasive institutional involvement of church and state" is a condition to be avoided under the First Amendment. But, she argued, there are clearly forms of cooperation between the state and sectarian organizations which can be conducted without entanglement. "If a statute lacks a purpose or effect of advancing or endorsing religion, I would not invalidate it merely because it requires some ongoing cooperation between church and state or some state supervision to ensure that state funds do not advance religion."

Justice Rehnquist agreed. Recalling the "Catch-22" dilemma noted by Justice White in Lemon, he saw the decision in Aguilar as presenting the following anomaly: "Aid must be supervised to ensure that there is no entanglement, but the supervision itself is held to cause an entanglement." The decision, he argued, strikes down nondiscriminatory, nonsectarian aid to educationally deprived children from low-income families. Rehnquist wrote:

> The Establishment Clause does not prohibit such sorely needed assistance; we have indeed traveled far afield from the concerns which prompted the adoption of the First Amendment when we rely on gossamer abstractions to invalidate a law which obviously meets an entirely secular need.

AID TO PAROCHIAL SCHOOLS

School District of City of Grand Rapids v. Ball (1985)

The companion case, School District of City of Grand Rapids v. Ball, 473 U.S. 382 (1985), involved the school district's Shared Time and Community Education programs, which provided classes at public expense in classrooms located in and leased from nonpublic schools. The cooperative arrangement was challenged by six taxpayers as violating the Establishment Clause. By a 5-4 majority the Supreme Court struck down the programs.

Forty of the forty-one schools at which the programs were operated were religiously affiliated.[14] The lower court determined "without hesitation" that these schools were "sectarian" in the sense that "a substantial portion of their functions are subsumed in the religious mission," that their purpose is "to assure future adherents to a particular faith," and that their essential aim is "to provide an integrated secular and religious education." The Shared Time teachers were full-time employees of the public schools, although a significant proportion of these teachers had previously taught in nonpublic schools. A significant proportion of the Community Education teachers were currently full-time teachers in the religiously affiliated schools.

Justice Brennan, again writing for the Court, identified three possible ways in which the challenged public school programs, operating in such "pervasively sectarian" schools, might impermissibly advance religion:

1) First, the teachers participating in the programs may become involved in intentionally or inadvertently inculcating particular religious tenets or beliefs.
2) Second, the programs may provide a crucial symbolic link between government and religion, thereby enlisting - - at least in the eyes of impressionable youngsters - - the powers of government to the support of the religious denomination operating the school.

3) Third, the programs may have the effect of directly promoting religion by impermissibly providing a subsidy to the primary religious mission of the institutions affected, and may in effect subsidize the religious functions of the schools by taking over a substantial portion of their responsibility for teaching secular subjects.

The Court determined that the challenged programs impermissibly advanced religion in all three ways. Although the purpose of the school district's program was admittedly secular, its effect was found to be religious. In determining that the program presented the risk that public school teachers might "become involved in intentionally or inadvertently inculcating particular religious tenets or beliefs," the Court admitted that the record showed no evidence of specific incidents of religious indoctrination, However, "the absence of proof is not dispositive," the Court contended, for the "sectarian" nature and purposes of the schools are sufficient for a finding of the risk of involvement of the state in sectarian concerns.

Brennan's opinion dwelt at considerable length on the second form of involvement noted above, viz. the "symbolic union of government and religion in one sectarian enterprise." Whether this union is real or perceived was immaterial to the Court. An important concern of Lemon's "effects" test is "whether the symbolic union of church and state effected by the challenged governmental action is sufficiently likely to be perceived by adherents of the controlling denomination as an endorsement, and by the nonadherents as a disapproval, of their individual religious choices." Brennan contended that this issue is particularly significant in a program involving young children in their formative years. "The symbolism of a union between church and state is most likely to influence children of tender years, whose experience is limited and whose beliefs consequently are the function of environment as much as of free and voluntary choice."

3. Summary

Looking back on this complex array of decisions and arguments, we may note several principles which give a certain coherence and predictability to the Supreme Court's Establishment Clause jurisprudence affecting public aid to religiously affiliated elementary and secondary education. The Court is fundamentally guided by the principle that neither the states nor the federal government may support or participate in any educational programs connected with religiously affiliated institutions, unless the secular function of education can be separated from the sectarian function in the operation of the program. As Justice Powell put it in his majority opinion in Nyquist (at 780): "In the absence of an effective means of guaranteeing that the state aid derived from public funds will be used for secular, neutral, and nonideological purposes, it is clear from our cases that direct aid in whatever form is invalid."

Writing for the majority in Grand Rapids (at 392), Justice Brennan noted that, with only one exception, the Court's decisions since Everson (1947) had consistently struck down any direct payments of public dollars to religiously affiliated institutions of elementary and secondary education.[15] The Court has allowed certain forms of "indirect aid" (such as transportation reimbursements and secular textbooks), where any indirect support of religiously affiliated schools is mediated by the decisions of students or their parents and is not the direct, primary, or intended result of state action. Furthermore, the Court has upheld certain kinds of "general welfare services" for children which may be provided by states without regard for the recipients' religious affiliation or lack of it.

But the Court has struck down state schemes providing for tuition grants, tuition tax benefits, loans of non-text instructional materials, reimbursements for maintenance and repair, and payments or reimbursements for faculty salaries, when it has perceived such programs as involving "direct and substantial" aid to a religious institution or a "direct

and substantial advancement of the sectarian enterprise."
The Court has recognized that the terms, "direct and
substantial" or "indirect and incidental," are not precisely
defined, but it regards this as an inherent limitation of
legal interpretation. As the Court said in Zorach v.
Clauson, "The problem, like many problems in constitutional
law, is one of degree."

The Court has refused to propound an analytical
definition of religion, believing that to do so would embroil
it improperly in determining the content of orthodox
doctrine. The Court has also been extremely reluctant to
allow governmental or judicial assessment of the form or
degree of religiousness exhibited or maintained by particular
religious or religiously affiliated schools, on the grounds
that any such assessment would involve the government in
excessive entanglement in the internal affairs of religious
organizations and would have a chilling effect on their Free
Exercise rights. Nevertheless, the Court has been unable to
avoid using some broad definitions and classifications for
religiously affiliated schools in its judicial decision making.

Thus the Court has held that determination of the
permissibility of particular forms of state and federal aid to
religiously affiliated educational institutions must take into
consideration significant differences in the forms and
degrees of religiousness exhibited in different groups of
institutions. The Court has tended to view such
religiousness as more likely to be pervasive and inseparable
from secular educational functions in the case of religiously
affiliated elementary and secondary schools than it is in the
case of religiously affiliated colleges and universities. And
it has generally determined that the substantial religious
character of religiously affiliated elementary and secondary
schools as a class typically gives rise to entangling church-
state relationships in any program of direct state or federal
aid to such institutions.

The Court's decisions in the last twenty-five years have
generally followed the lines predicted by Alanson Willcox in

his 1961 HEW memorandum. Direct aid and most forms of indirect aid to religiously affiliated elementary and secondary education are likely to encounter constitutional difficulty. We turn now to an account of the Court's rather different inclination at the higher education level.

NOTES TO CHAPTER 4

1. We do not go as far as Lupu, however, who declares that only the Establishment Clause, and not the Free Exercise Clause, can provide the basis for determination of the autonomy claims of religious institutions. Ira C. Lupu, "Free Exercise Exemption and Religious Institutions: The Case of Employment Discrimination," Boston University Law Review, Vol. 67, No. 3, May, 1987, pp. 422-442. We believe that religious institutions as well as individuals have a Free Exercise claim to autonomy.

2. The memorandum was widely circulated both inside the government and in the education community. It appeared in Gerogetown Law Journal, Vol. 50, 1961-62, pp. 351-396.

3. The memorandum was also published in the issue of the Georgetown Law Journal as noted in note 2 above.

4. In his opinion concurring only in the judgment in Wolman v. Walter, 433 U.S. at 262 (1977).

5. Douglas quoted as a statement of "the Roman Catholic position" on public and parochial education a formulation by Monsignor John A. Ryan which appears in A. Stokes, Church and State in the United States, 1954, p. 654. As an example at the higher education level Douglas cited an administrative communication in a Catholic university, declaring that, "The primacy of the spiritual is the reason for a Christian university" and that "the classroom that is not a temple is a den." The memorandum respectfully requested the faculty to indicate what they were doing "to make your particular courses theocentric." Douglas also noted the example of a communication concerning a change in organizational

structure at a Presbyterian-affiliated college, in which the administration reassured its correspondents that, "The college wishes to change only its legal relationship to the synod and not its purposes" and promised that it would consult with the synod before making any change in the institutional statement of purpose, which continued to define the college as "Presbyterian-related." Board of Education v. Allen at 262-264. Douglas marshalled a similar argument in his concurring opinion in Lemon v. Kurtzman, 403 U.S. at 635-40 (1971).

6.   Walz v. Tax Commission, 397 U.S. 664,668 (1970).

7.   See, for example, Kenneth Mitchell Cox, "The Lemon Test Soured: The Supreme Court's New Establishment Clause Analysis," Vanderbilt Law Review, Vol. 37, October, 1984, pp. 1175-1203.

8.   Aguilar v. Felton, 473.U.S. at 431,(1985). Her quotation is from Choper, "The Religion Clauses of the First Amendment: Reconciling the Conflict," University of Pittsburgh Law Review, Vol. 41, 1980, pp.673,681. Cf. her dissenting opinion in Lynch v. Donnelly, 465 U.S. 668 (1984).

9.   403 U.S. 612-614 (1970).

10.   See below, pp. 140-144.

11.   Tilton v. Richardson, 403 U.S. at 697 (1971).

12.   As examples of facts which would lead him to determine that federal or state support violated the Establishment Clause, White cited evidence "that any of the involved schools restricted entry on racial or religious grounds or required all students gaining admission to receive instruction in the tenets of a particular faith." Lemon v. Kurtzman, 403 U.S. at 671, n.2, White, dissenting.

13.   Powell's opinion rejected appellees' contention that the
Lemon test required a showing that subsidizing religion was
a primary or principle effect of the challenged program.
The Court was not required, he said, to make "metaphysical"
or "ultimate" judgments concerning a rank ordering of
consequences, nor was it prevented by its own precedents
from considering remote or incidental effects which may be
advantageous to religious institutions (Nyquist, at 783, n.39).
Justices Burger and Rehnquist concurred in the Court's
holding that the maintenance and repair grants were an
impermissible direct aid to religion, but contended that the
Court's precedents in Everson, Allen, and Walz required it
to uphold the tuition reimbursements and tax credits.
Justice White thought the statute should not be struck down
on the face, believing that in the case of any qualifying
schools which were not sectarian under the Court's
"profile," the primary effect of the statute would not be to
advance religion.

14.   Twenty-eight are Roman Catholic, seven are Christian
Reformed, three are Lutheran, one is Seventh Day Adventist,
and one is Baptist.

15.   The exception is Committee for Public Education and
Religious Liberty v. Regan, 444 U.S. 646 (1980), which
permitted public subsidy for certain recordkeeping and
testing services performed by nonpublic schools, but required
by state law.

CHAPTER FIVE

SECULAR AND RELIGIOUS FUNCTIONS
IN ESTABLISHMENT CLAUSE JURISPRUDENCE
(2) AID TO HIGHER EDUCATION

In recent Establishment Clause cases challenging the eligibility of religiously affiliated colleges and universities for state and federal support, the Supreme Court has sought to follow the same assumptions and reasoning as have guided its decisions in the foregoing elementary and secondary school cases. The higher education opinions are full of citations of the elementary and secondary case precedents. But the Court's Establishment Clause jurisprudence has reached strikingly different results in the case of religiously affiliated higher education. Many commentators, and some Supreme Court justices, have contended, indeed, that the two systems of cases are simply inconsistent.

1. Some Higher Education Facilities Cases

During the debate over national educational policy in the Kennedy and Johnson administrations, serious questions were raised concerning the constitutionality of any form of direct public aid to religiously affiliated colleges and universities. Many educational leaders and constitutional scholars strongly recommended that any programs of public support in such institutions should be limited to student aid programs. In the Higher Education Facilities Act of 1963,[1] however, the Congress took a different view, and authorized grants and loans for the construction or renovation of facilities at accredited institutions of higher education, including religiously affiliated colleges and universities, subject to the stipulation that federal aid could not be used for sectarian worship or instruction.

The Act represented a federal response to the demand for expansion of college and university facilities to meet sharply increasing enrollments in higher education. The Act provided for construction of a wide variety of "academic facilities," but expressly excluded

> any facility used or to be used for sectarian instruction or as a place for religious worship, or any facility which . . . is used or to be used primarily in connection with any part of the program of a school or department of divinity.

The Act provided that the United States retains a 20-year interest in any facilities constructed with federal funds, and that if during this period the applicant violates the statutory conditions, the United States is entitled to recover an amount equal to the proportion of the present value of the facility that the federal grant bore to the original cost of the facility. In administering the program the U.S. Commissioner of Education requires applicants to provide assurances that these restrictions and exclusions will be respected. Several states enacted similar programs under state funding.

A number of religiously affiliated institutions immediately applied for and received grants. Challenges to the constitutionality of such programs were quickly brought and began to make their way through the courts. In addressing these challenges, courts found it necessary to distinguish several different forms and degrees of religiousness among institutions of higher learning. The methodologies and findings of the courts are important to our analysis of the legal basis for the regulation of employment policy in religiously affiliated higher education.

Horace Mann League v. Board of Public Works of Maryland (1966)

One of the earliest challenges was presented in Horace Mann League et al. v. Board of Public Works of Maryland, 220 A.2d 51 (1966), in which the Court of Appeals of Maryland upheld the constitutionality of a state program of direct grants to private colleges and universities for construction of buildings, but held that the eligibility of any particular institution for such aid would require a determination that the institution was, in fact, not sectarian. Of the four colleges whose grants were challenged in the suit, the court found that only one was constitutionally entitled to aid. The decision was appealed to the U.S. Supreme Court, which refused certiorari on one appeal and approved a motion to dismiss in another.[2]

The colleges whose receipt of state construction grants was challenged were: Hood College, a liberal arts college for women, then enrolling about 650 students, which is affiliated with the United Church of Christ; Western Maryland College, a coeducational liberal arts college related to the United Methodist Church;[3] the College of Notre Dame of Maryland, a liberal arts college for women, founded by the School Sisters of Notre Dame and related to the Roman Catholic Church; and St. Joseph College, a liberal arts college founded, supported, owned, and governed by the Daughters of Charity of St. Vincent de Paul and strongly oriented in its curriculum toward a Catholic philosophy of education.[4]

The Horace Mann League and several individual taxpayers[5] brought a bill of complaint, challenging the validity, under the federal and state constitutions, of four Maryland statutes, under which the four colleges had received a total of $2.5 million for the construction of buildings. Relying on such U.S. Supreme Court decisions as Everson, Schempp, and McGowan, the court formulated the following test to be applied in determining the constitutionality of the challenged programs:

1. No tax, in any amount, large or small, can be levied to support any religious activities or institutions, whatever they may be called or whatever form they may adopt to teach or practice religions.
2. If the primary purpose [as contradistinguished from an incidental one] of the state action is to promote religion, that action is in violation of the First Amendment.

3. If [the operative effect] of the statute furthers
    both secular and religious ends, an examination of
    the means used is necessary to determine whether
    the state could reasonably have attained the secular
    end by means which do not further the promotion
    of religion.

Under this test the court was required to make a
number of factual determinations in each case. The key
determination concerned whether the institution receiving
state funds is religious or sectarian. The court identified
six factors as determining the religious character of the
colleges in question:

(1) The stated purposes of the college;
(2) The college personnel, which includes the governing
board, the administrative officers, the faculty, and the
student body (with considerable stress being laid on the
substantiality of religious control over the governing
board as a criterion of whether a college is sectarian);
(3) The college's relationship with religious
organizations and groups, which relationship includes the
extent of ownership, financial assistance, the college's
memberships and affiliations, religious purposes, and
miscellaneous aspects of the college's relationship with
its sponsoring church;
(4) The place of religion in the college's program,
which includes the extent of religious manifestation in
the physical surroundings, the character and extent of
religious observance sponsored or encouraged by the
college, the required participation for any or all
students, the extent to which the college sponsors or
encourages religious activity of sects different from that
of the college's own church, and the place of religion
in the curriculum and in extra-curricular programs;
(5) The result or 'outcome' of the college program,
such as accreditation and the nature and character of
the activities of the alumni;
(6) The work and image of the college in the
community.

Using these criteria, the court considered the factual record to determine whether the recipient institutions were so religious or sectarian that the award of construction grants would violate the Establishment Clause. After a lengthy description of the mission, organization, and operations of Hood College, the court saw no constitutional objection to its receiving state funds. The court described the college as "church-related" but not sectarian. It saw its stated purposes in relation to religion as "not of a fervent, intense, or passionate nature, but . . . based largely upon its historical background." It found that the organizational and financial relationships to the United Church of Christ are nominal and non-controlling. It determined that religion does not occupy a "dominant place" in the College's program, and that the college is not viewed by the surrounding community as "religiously slanted." Accordingly, said the court, "We hold that the primary purpose of the grant here involved was not to aid or support religion; . . . and its operative effect is not to aid religion . . . but to promote the educational facilities for women. Consequently the Bill does not violate the First Amendment."

In the case of Western Maryland College, however, the court found the institution "sectarian in a legal sense under the First Amendment," although it granted that such classification "is a rather elusive matter." The court construed the stated purposes of the college as having "a distinctly religious flavor." It noted that under the charter one more than one-third of the governing board must be Methodist ministers, and that the current board consisted of 27 Methodists in a membership of 40, with virtually all the remainder being Protestants. Care is taken, the court reported, to obtain a faculty committed to the Christian philosophy of life, and an atheist would not be employed. The college declares that it "makes no bones about the fact that our philosophy at Western Maryland is a Christian philosophy;" and it makes a conscious effort to integrate religion, and specifically Christianity, with the curriculum and extracurricular life, although the Methodist orientation of the college's religious heritage tends to deemphasize doctrinal formulation in religious instruction. Given these facts, the court felt impelled to conclude that, even if the purpose of the Bill was not to promote religion, the award of a construction grant to Western Maryland College would have the operative effect of advancing religion in a way which violates the Establishment Clause.

In the case of the two Catholic colleges, the court reached the same judgment as in the case of Western Maryland College. It found that Notre Dame's purposes are "deeply and intensely religious," and that the stated purposes of St. Joseph "seem to be even more strongly religious than Notre Dame's." Both institutions were found to be permeated by Catholicity. Both governing boards, said the court, are controlled by the sponsoring religious order, which also controls financial assets and operations. Almost all students are Catholic, and most faculty are priests or nuns. Notre Dame declares that the institution's "whole life is lived in the Catholic atmosphere," and that the college "harmonizes [its entire] program with the philosophy and theology of the Catholic Church." The court held that both colleges were "sectarian in a legal sense" and that neither could constitutionally receive the grant made to it.

The court viewed the Maryland Constitution as more tolerant than the U.S. Constitution respecting tax subsidies of religion. Its holding in Horace Mann was that even though the grants might violate the First Amendment of the Federal Constitution, they did not violate any provision of the Maryland constitution. The court observed that "all of the states, except Maryland and Vermont, have explicit provisions prohibiting the appropriation of public money to schools controlled by religious organizations,"[6] and remarked that "had the people of Maryland desired to change its practice relative to such grants, it certainly would be likely that they would have made similar provisions after so many states had done so." The court noted that Maryland courts had never held grants made for a public purpose to educational institutions impermissible under the state constitution, even when those institutions were controlled by a religious order. And it declared that it saw "no reason to hold otherwise now."

The refusal of the U.S. Supreme Court to grant certiorari had the effect of limiting the impact of the Horace Mann decision to the State of Maryland. The reasoning of this state court decision is by no means an isolated instance, however. Many other courts, both state and federal, might well follow similar reasoning in holding that an institution falling within our classifications as "pervasively religious" or "strongly religious" is too religious or sectarian to be allowed to receive direct state aid under the U.S. Constitution.

Tilton v. Richardson (1971)

In Tilton v. Richardson, 403 U.S. 672 (1971), which is the companion case to Lemon v. Kurtzman, the U.S. Supreme Court considered a challenge to the eligibility of several church-related colleges and universities to receive construction grants under the Higher Education Facilities Act of 1963. The challenge, raised by a group of taxpayers, concerned federal construction grants made to four Catholic colleges and universities in Connecticut: 1) Sacred Heart University for a library building; 2) Annhurst College (subsequently closed) for a music, drama, and arts building; 3) Fairfield University for a science building and a library building; and 4) Albertus Magnus College for a language laboratory. The factual discovery showed that none of the four colleges had violated the statutory restrictions of the Act, that the buildings had been used solely for nonreligious purposes and had no religious symbols in them, that "there is no evidence that religion seeps into the use of any of these buildings," and that "these buildings are indistinguishable from a typical state university facility."

The challenge was based not on any evidence contradicting these factual determinations, but on the argument (as the Court's opinion summarized it) "that government may not subsidize any activities of an institution of higher education that in some of its programs teaches religious doctrines." The Court construed this argument as depending on the contention that "religion so permeates the secular education provided by church-related colleges and universities that their religious and secular functions are in fact inseparable." The Court found no basis for such an assumption in the case of these four colleges, and a 5-4 majority gave its judgment that the federal construction grants do not inevitably advance religion.

Chief Justice Burger, writing for the Court (as he had in Lemon), identified four questions which the Court considered: 1) Does the Act have a secular legislative purpose? 2) Is the primary effect of the Act to advance or inhibit religion? 3) Does the administration of the Act foster an excessive government entanglement with religion? 4) Does the implementation of the Act inhibit the free exercise of religion? The Court answered each of these questions in the negative and upheld the federal program. However, it struck down the provision limiting the federal interest in the structure to twenty years and permitting religious use of the facility thereafter, declaring that such a provision trespassed against the Religion Clauses.[7]

A major factor affecting the majority's decision to uphold was the nature of the grant as they understood it. The terms and conditions of the grant were viewed as reducing the risk of excessive entanglement.

1) The facilities constructed with federal funds are religiously "secular, neutral, and nonideological" and are made available under the Act to all students regardless of the affiliation of the school they attend.
2) The adherence of the recipient institution to the restrictions against nonsecular use of the facility can be readily determined through periodic inspections.
3) The grant involves a one-time, single-purpose contact, involving no continual financial relationships or dependencies, no annual audits, no government analysis of institutional expenditures on secular as distinguished from religious activities.

4) There is less potential for divisive religious-based fragmentation in the political area as a result of the construction grants.

The argument of appellants against permitting such grants was based on a "composite profile" of the "typical sectarian" institution of higher education," which: (a) imposes religious restrictions on admissions, (b) requires attendance at religious activities, (c) compels obedience to the doctrines and dogmas of the faith, (d) requires instruction in theology and doctrine, and (e) does everything it can to propagate a particular religion. The Court admitted that there might be some colleges in the American system of post-secondary education which fit the pattern of the "composite profile." It found no evidence, however, that the four Connecticut colleges instantiated the "composite profile," and it refused to strike down an Act of Congress on the basis of a hypothetical construct.

The "composite profile" presented by appellants reads much like the profile of sectarian, nonpublic schools accepted by the Supreme Court two years later in Nyquist as the factual foundation for its determination that maintenance and repair grants for such schools violated the Establishment Clause.[8] In Nyquist the Court admitted that not all religiously affiliated schools which qualified for the state grants in question satisfied the description of the profile, but it refused to admit factual evidence concerning the separability of secular and sectarian functions in the instance of particular institutions. In Tilton, on the other hand, the Court moved quickly to conclude that appellants' "composite profile" was purely "hypothetical," that the profile was not typical of institutions of higher education generally, and that the U.S. Commissioner of Education could be depended on to deny eligibility to any institutions which, in fact, possess the "profile" characteristics.

The critical issue in both Lemon and Tilton is whether or not the secular function of education can be separated from the sectarian function in religiously affiliated schools. The Court's Establishment decisions in elementary and secondary education indicate a strong tendency to suppose that such separation is difficult, if not impossible, at that level. Tilton, on the other hand, assumes that the separation is relatively easy and widespread at the higher education level.

Burger's opinion cited a number of considerations which led the Court to a different result in Tilton than was reached in the decision delivered the same day in Lemon:

1) We are not dealing here with religious instruction offered to impressionable children, but with investigation of religious subjects under conditions of disciplinary scholarship and academic freedom involving sceptical undergraduates.

2) All four institutions subscribe to the 1940 Statement of Principles on Academic Freedom and Tenure endorsed by the American Associaton of University Professors and the Association of American Colleges.

3) Although several institutional documents presented as evidence include statements of religious restrictions on what may be taught, other evidence showed that these restrictions are not in fact enforced and that the schools are characterized by an atmosphere of academic freedom rather than religious indoctrination.

The majority found in these circumstances a sufficient reason for judging these institutions not sectarian, in the sense in which the parochial schools of Lemon were sectarian. The minority took a different view. In his dissenting opinion Justice Douglas (joined by Justices Black and Marshall) followed his customary practice of treating all "parochial" schools as alike, whether functioning at the pre-collegiate or post-secondary level. It is a sectarian purpose, he declared, that makes a parochial school viable. In a parochial school "religious teaching and secular teaching are so enmeshed that only the strictest supervision and surveillance would insure compliance." In such schools prayer and worship may occur in classrooms as well as in chapels. Religious worship may take place in a music recital hall. A course in the History of Methodism might be taught in a federally financed classroom. "How can the Government know what is taught in a federally financed building," Douglas asked, "without a continuous auditing of classroom instruction? Yet both the Free Exercise Clause and academic freedom are violated when the Government agent must be present to determine whether the course content is satisfactory."

Furthermore, argued Douglas, it is impossible in religiously affiliated schools to prevent the flow of public funds to the support of sectarian purposes. The fact that no religious observances take place in federally financed buildings does not prevent required religious observances from taking place in other buildings. Money saved from one area of an institutional budget is available to be used elsewhere, and when a college has a rent-free building for non-sectarian use it can divert available resources to construction of a building for sectarian use. Douglas found the majority's decision in Tilton "unbelievable" and a cause for despair. The holding of the majority took a different view.

Hunt v. McNair (1973)

In Hunt v. McNair, 413 U.S. 734 (1973), the Supreme Court considered a challenge to a South Carolina statute establishing a state Educational Facilities Authority, to assist institutions of higher education in the construction, financing, and refinancing of projects, primarily through the issuance of revenue bonds. The case arose from a taxpayer's claim that a proposed financing transaction involving the issuance of revenue bonds for the benefit of the Baptist College of Charleston violated the Establishment Clause. By a 6-3 majority the Court upheld the program as satisfying the three-part Lemon test.

The benefits of the South Carolina program were available to all institutions of higher education in the state, whether or not they have a religious affiliation. The

144

governing statute included a provision requiring assurances that no facility built or financed through the Authority "shall be used for sectarian instruction or as a place of worship, or in connection with any part of a program of a school or department of divinity of any religious denomination." The Authority had the right of inspection to assure that such covenants are carried out. Since all of the expenses of the Authority must be paid from revenues from the various projects in which it participates, no general revenues are used to support any project.

Justice Powell, writing for the Court, noted that the Court had consistently rejected the recurring argument (advanced, for example, by Justice Douglas in his dissenting opinion in Tilton) that "all aid is forbidden because aid to one aspect of an institution frees it to spend its other resources on religious ends." The Court's decisions on aid, Powell said, are dependent, rather, on the question whether the recipient institution is so "pervasively sectarian" that the secular and religious functions are inseparable.

In a formulation which added a new refinement to the Court's "primary effects" test, Powell declared, "Aid normally may be thought to have the primary effect of advancing religion when it flows to an institution in which religion is so pervasive that a substantial portion of its functions are subsumed in the religious mission or when it funds a specifically religious activity in an otherwise substantially secular setting." Neither condition was satisfied, he contended, in this case. No claim had been made that the Baptist College of Charleston had violated or was about to violate the prohibition against use of Authority-financed facilities for religious purposes. And the Court found no evidence that the college was any more an instrument of religious indoctrination than were the colleges and universities in Tilton.

Justice Powell took note of the possibility, left open in Tilton, that some colleges and universities were so pervasively sectarian as to be judged ineligible for aid. He stated that both the Court opinion in Lemon and the plurality opinion in Tilton "are grounded in the proposition that the degree of entanglement arising from the inspection of facilities as to use varies in large measure with the extent to which religion permeates the institution." The Court's finding of excessive entanglement in Lemon relied on "the substantial religious character of these church-related schools." In the case of Baptist College, however, there is no showing, said Powell, that the college places special emphasis on the Baptist denomination or on any other sectarian type of education. Both the faculty and the student body are open to persons of any (or no) religious affiliation. Hence, he said, there is no finding of a religiously permeated educational institution.

It was accepted as fact that the members of the college's Board of Trustees are elected by the South Carolina Baptist Convention, that the approval of the Convention is required for major financial transactions, and that the charter of the college may be amended only by the Convention. The Court specifically declared, however, that "formal denominational control over a liberal arts college does not render all aid to the institution a violation of the Establishment Clause." Powell saw the question as turning on whether the college's operations were "oriented significantly towards religious rather than secular education." Finding that they were not so oriented, he saw no Establishment.

In his dissenting opinion (in which Douglas and Marshall joined), Justice Brennan summarized his own (not the Court's) test for impermissible involvement of a state with a religiously affiliated school: Those involvements are foreclosed under the First Amendment, he said, which: "(a) serve the essentially religious activities of religious institutions; (b) employ the organs of government for essentially religious purposes; or (c) use essentially religious means to serve governmental ends, where secular means would suffice." Under his own test Brennan would judge the State's proposed plan of assistance to the Baptist college in violation of the Establishment Clause.

This plan, he maintained, "involves the State in a degree of policing far exceeding that called for by the statutes struck down in <u>Lemon</u>. . . . For it seems inescapable that the content of courses taught in facilities financed under the agreement must be closely monitored by the State Authority in discharge of its duty to ensure that the facilities are not being used for sectarian instruction." The case seemed to him to present a clear and undeniable instance of the involvement of the state in the essentially religious activities of religious institutions, and employment of the organs of government for essentially religious purposes.

2. A Non-categorical Grant Case

Roemer v. Board of Public Works of Maryland (1976)

In <u>Roemer v. Board of Public Works of Maryland</u>, 426 U.S. 736 (1976), the Court took a further step in authorizing public aid to religiously affiliated colleges and universities. A Maryland statute, enacted in 1971, authorized direct annual noncategorical grants to any private institution within the state (including any religiously affiliated institution) that meets certain general eligibility requirements. A qualifying institution must be one that "maintains one or more associate of arts or baccalaureate degree programs, and refrains from awarding only seminarian or theological degrees." The grant is based on the number of students enrolled. Students enrolled in seminarian or theological academic programs are not counted in the student enrollment figures used for computing the amount of the payment. A recipient institution may put the funds to whatever use it wishes, with a single exception: "None of the moneys payable under this subtitle shall be utilized by the institutions for sectarian purposes."

Under the Maryland statute an application must be accompanied by an affidavit of the institution's chief executive officer that the funds will not be used for sectarian purposes and by a description of the specific nonsectarian uses that are planned. The institution must file an annual "Utilization of Funds Report," describing and itemizing the use of state funds, and the chief executive officer must file his own "Post-expenditure Affidavit," stating that the funds have not been put to sectarian use. The recipient institution is further required to segregate state funds in a "special revenue account" and to identify aided nonsectarian expenditures separately in its budget, and must maintain sufficient documentation to permit independent verification that the funds were in fact spent for nonsectarian purposes.

In 1971 $1.7 million were disbursed to 17 private institutions, five of which were religiously affiliated. The recipient colleges were Western Maryland College (a Methodist-affiliated institution originally named in the suit but later dismissed as a defendant-appellee), and four Catholic institutions: the College of Notre Dame, Mount Saint Mary's College, Saint Joseph College, and Loyola College.[9]

A suit was brought by four individual taxpayers, who challenged the statute as violative of the First Amendment and claimed that the four named colleges, all of which were affiliated with the Roman Catholic Church, were constitutionally ineligible for the state aid. The Supreme Court affirmed a lower court ruling that the named colleges were not "pervasively sectarian," despite their formal church affiliation, that the aid was in fact extended only to the "secular side" of education at the schools, and that excessive entanglement in assuring that funds are applied only to secular functions of education does not necessarily result from the fact that the payments are annual. By a narrow 5-4 majority the Court found no violation of the Establishment Clause.[10]

In delivering the opinion of the Court Justice Harry Blackmun presented a clear summary of the development of the Court's Establishment criteria from Everson to Meek. (Other parts of his opinion, as we shall see, are rather less coherent.) Seeing little need for further refinement of the principles governing public aid to religiously affiliated schools, Blackmun affirmed, "Our purpose is not to unsettle those principles, so recently affirmed, or to expand upon them substantially, but merely to insure that they are faithfully applied in this case."

Blackmun read the new "primary effects" test in Hunt as requiring: "(1) that no state aid at all go to institutions that are so 'pervasively sectarian' that secular activities cannot be separated from secular ones, and (2) that if secular activities can be separated out, they alone must be funded." If not a "substantial advance" upon the Court's Establishment doctrine, that is certainly a helpful clarification.

To determine whether an institution is so "pervasively sectarian" that it may receive no direct state aid of any kind, Blackmun declared, it is necessary to paint a general picture of the institution, composed of many elements. He noted that thousands of pages of records had been compiled from which such a profile of the colleges named in this suit might be drawn. He acknowledged that, given all these data, the summary which the Court was accepting from the lower court might be controverted in certain respects. But he refused to engage in "second-guessing" the District Court's findings. "The general picture that the District Court has painted of the appellee institutions," Blackmun concluded, "is similar in almost all respects to that of the church-affiliated colleges considered in Tilton and Hunt."

The District Court's factual findings concerning the role of religion in these campuses may be taken as a loose working statement of criteria which the Supreme Court would accept for identifying a religiously affiliated, but not pervasively religious, college or university. We take the trouble to quote it verbatim:

"(a) Despite their formal affiliation with the Roman Catholic Church, the colleges are 'characterized by a high degree of institutional autonomy.' None of the four receives funds from, or makes reports to, the Catholic Church. The Church is represented on their governing boards, but, as with Mount Saint Mary's, 'no instance of entry of Church considerations into college decisions was shown.'

(b) The colleges employ Roman Catholic chaplains and hold Roman Catholic religious exercises on campus. Attendance at such is not required; the encouragement of spiritual development is only 'one secondary objective' of each college; and 'at none of these institutions does this encouragement go beyond providing the opportunity or occasions for religious experience.' It was the District Court's finding that 'religious indoctrination is not a substantial purpose or activity of any of these defendants.'

(c) Mandatory religion or theology courses are taught at each of the colleges, primarily by Roman Catholic clerics, but these only supplement a curriculum covering 'the spectrum of a liberal arts program.' Nontheology courses are taught in an 'atmosphere of intellectual freedom' and without 'religious pressures.' Each college subscribes to, and abides by, the 1940 Statement of Principles on Academic Freedom of the American Association of University Professors.

(d) Some classes are begun with prayer. The percentage of classes in which this is done varies with the college, from a 'minuscule' percentage at Loyola and Mount Saint Mary's to a majority at Saint Joseph. There is no 'actual college policy' of encouraging the practice. 'It is treated as a facet of the instructor's academic freedom.' Classroom prayers were therefore regarded by the District Court as 'peripheral to the subject of religious permeation,' as were the facts that some instructors wear clerical garb and some classrooms have religious symbols. . . .

(e) The District Court found that, apart from the theology departments, faculty hiring decisions are not made on a religious basis. At two of the colleges, Notre Dame and Mount Saint Mary's, no inquiry at all is made into an applicant's religion. Religious preference is to be noted on Loyola's application form, but the purpose is to allow full appreciation of the applicant's background. Loyola also attempts to employ

each year two members of a particular religious order
which once staffed a college recently merged into
Loyola. Budgetary considerations lead the colleges
generally to favor members of religious orders, who
often receive less than full salary. Still, the District
Court found that 'academic quality' was the principal
hiring criterion, and that any 'hiring bias,' or 'effort by
any defendant to stack its faculty with members of a
particular religious group,' would have been noticed by
other faculty members, who had never been heard to
complain.

(f) The great majority of students at each of the
colleges are Roman Catholic, but the District Court
concluded from a 'thorough analysis of the student
admission and recruiting criteria' that the student
bodies 'are chosen without regard to religion.'"

In his dissenting opinion Justice Potter Stewart took a
quite different view of the facts concerning theology
courses at the four colleges, which he saw as indicating a
fundamental difference in religiousness between these
institutions and the Connecticut colleges of Tilton. In
Tilton the parties had mutually stipulated that theology
courses at the institutions in question were taught
"according to the academic subjects and the teacher's
concept of professional standards," that these courses
"covered a range of human religious experiences and were
not limited to courses about the Roman Catholic religion,"
and that the schools introduced evidence "that they made no
attempt to indoctrinate students or to proselytize." These
stipulations, he said, which had been viewed by the Court as
important to its determination that the Tilton institutions
were eligible for direct aid from public funds, differed
fundamentally from the situation in the parochial schools in
Lemon, which had been judged not to be so eligible.

In the Maryland colleges, as contrasted to the
Connecticut colleges in Tilton, the District Court was unable
to determine that compulsory religion courses were taught
as an academic discipline. Indeed, the District Court found
that the courses were designed, in part, to achieve the

objective of fostering the spiritual development of students, that the staffing of theology departments mainly by clerics was a "congenial means" of furthering that objective, and that, despite the academic freedom accorded to theology professors, there was nothing to compel the conclusion "that courses in religion and theology at the five colleges have no overtones of indoctrination." Accordingly, Stewart denied that there was no constitutionally significant difference between the colleges of Roemer and those of Tilton, and he expressed his agreement with the dissenting member of the three-judge lower court that the challenged act "in these instances does in truth offend the Constitution by its provision of funds, in that it exposes State money for use in advancing religion, no matter the vigilance to avoid it."

The problem of theology instruction in the recipient colleges had led the District Court to require the Council of Higher Education, which administers the grants, to take steps to insure that no public funds would be used to support religion or theology programs. By the time of the Supreme Court's decision the Council had complied, and this compliance was specifically pointed out in the majority opinion. The majority of the Court viewed the problem as mainly one of identifying any religious function (like a worship service) to which state funds must not be allowed to flow. Stewart, however, viewed it as a problem affecting the determination of whether or not the recipient institutions satisfied the Court's test of eligibility for support. At the very least, he saw a change in the criteria for such eligibility from Tilton to Roemer.

Several other criteria employed by the Roemer Court in developing its profile of a religiously affiliated, but not pervasively religious, college or university might well be challenged as dubious indicators of religiousness. Many pervasively religious institutions could satisfy the Court's tests of a secular institution. For example, although the Court construed a denominationally mixed student body as a mark of non-pervasiveness, it would be hard to find a pervasively religious college or university nowadays which restricts student admission to a particular denomination.

Furthermore, practically all colleges and universities, even the most pervasively religious, would satisfy the Court's standard of renouncing indoctrination as a method of instruction for the formation of religious faith.

Similarly, most religiously oriented institutions which make frequent use of prayers at the beginning of classes, business meetings, or school events and who seek campus-wide participation in campus worship services, would emphasize in their policy statements the voluntary nature of the participation they seek. As for organizational closeness, the Court itself has consistently taken the view that the nature of formal relationships between a school and its sponsoring or supporting church is not dispositive of the question of the degree of religiousness in the institution. The Court's profile thus has an element of subjectivity and arbitrariness which will be confusing to many educators in religiously affiliated higher education, anxious to know the conditions under which their programs might be judged eligible or ineligible for public financial aid.

The fact is that the Court was both incapable of and not interested in drawing rigorous and analytical distinctions between different degrees of religiousness in religiously affiliated colleges and universities. Its estimate of the difference between religiously pervasive parochial elementary and secondary schools, on the one hand, and religiously affiliated, but not pervasively religious, colleges and universities, on the other, appears to have been strongly intuitive. And the Court seemed at times to be more concerned with how these institutions appear to the general public or to the local community than with inductively justified classifications.

Once the Court found that the colleges in question were capable of segregating their secular functions from their religious functions, the question became one of establishing administrative procedures which would restrict the flow of funds to the secular functions without requiring an excessive entanglement. Under the restrictions of the Act, funds may be put only to nonsectarian use, and concerning such use the institution must satisfy the Council for Higher Education. The <u>Roemer</u> Court did not feel required either to elaborate a criterion for a "specifically religious activity" or to prescribe a process for program monitoring which would assure that public funds do not flow to such activities. Rather, the majority declared its confidence that state and school officials would make sure that funds are properly used. In fact, the opinion refers frequently to ways in which the regulations of the Council had been changed in response to challenges arising out of this particular litigation.

The Court was prepared to leave it at that. "We must assume," wrote Justice Blackmun, "that the colleges, and the Council, will exercise their delegated control over use of the funds in compliance with the statutory, and therefore the constitutional, mandate." He left open the possibility that should questions arise concerning the flow of public funds to sectarian functions, the courts would be prepared to consider them. He noted, however, that "it has not been the Court's practice, in considering facial challenges to statutes of this kind, to strike them down in anticipation that particular applications may result in unconstitutional use of funds."

Some readers of the Court's Establishment opinions in elementary and secondary education might suggest, however, that the Court has on occasion done just that. Indeed, Justices Rehnquist and O'Connor have contended that the Court has used the "excessive entanglement" criterion to strike down forms of direct aid to parochial schools precisely in anticipation of the presumed difficulty of restricting the flow of funds to nonsectarian purposes, despite specific evidence that no improper use of funds for sectarian purposes had occurred over a period of years.

The Court was assured that excessive entanglement does not necessarily result from the fact that the subsidy is an annual and continuing one, although <u>Tilton</u> had made a special virtue out of a "one-time, single-purpose" arrangement. The Court admitted that the form of aid in

Roemer is different from the form of aid in Tilton, and it admitted that there is greater risk of entanglement in the Maryland annual grants than in the Connecticut construction grants. Nevertheless, it insisted that the case of Roemer is more like Tilton than like Lemon, and it decided accordingly.

As for the "political divisiveness" side of the entanglement test, the Court thought the risk of political fragmentation along religious lines is much less in the case of direct institutional aid to religiously affiliated colleges and universities than in the case of direct aid to parochial elementary and secondary schools. "There is no exact science in gauging the entanglement of church and state," Blackmun sighed as he reached the end of his rationale. The decision of the District Court had placed heavy reliance on the character of the aided institutions and on its finding that these institutions are capable of separating the secular and relgious functions of education. The Supreme Court could not say that such reliance was misplaced, or erroneous.

3. A Student Financial Aid Case

Witters v. Washington Department of Services for the Blind 1986)

In Witters v. Washington Department of Services for the Blind, 106 S.Ct. 748 (1986), the U.S. Supreme Court reached rare unanimity in holding that the First Amendment does not preclude a state from extending financial aid under a vocational rehabilitation assistance program to a legally blind person who wished to study at a Christian college to become a pastor, missionary, or youth director. A Washington statute enacted in 1981 authorized a program to "provide special education and/or training in the professions, business or trades" so as to "assist visually handicapped persons to overcome vocational handicaps and to obtain the maximum degree of self-support and self-care." The petitioner in this case, a student at the Inland Empire School of the Bible in Spokane, applied for financial aid, which was denied by the commission administering the program on the basis of its understanding that "the Washington State constitution forbids the use of public funds to assist an individual in the pursuit of a career in theology or related areas."[11] The administrative ruling was affirmed on appeal and was upheld by the Washington Supreme Court, which relied, however, not on the Washington State Constitution but on the Establishment Clause of the U.S. Constitution.

Justice Thurgood Marshall delivered the unanimous judgment of the U.S. Supreme Court, reversing the judgment of the Washington Supreme Court and declaring that extension of state aid to this applicant "would not advance religion in any manner inconsistent with the Establishment Clause of the First Amendment." The Court was guided, as was the court below, by the three-part test of Lemon, but disagreed with the Washington Supreme Court's finding that the provision of state financial aid to enable someone to become a pastor, missionary, or church youth director violated the "primary effect" test.

In its opinion the Court reaffirmed its previous declarations that a State may not grant aid to a religious school, whether in cash or in kind, where the effect of the aid is "that of a direct subsidy to the religious school" from the State, or where the effect of the aid is that of "promoting a single religion or religion generally." The Court recognized that financial aid may have that effect even when it takes the form of aid to students or to parents. Accordingly, the judicial inquiry must settle on whether or not, in the particular facts of the program under challenge, the form of aid actually results in a state action sponsoring or subsidizing religion.

On consulting the record, the Court determined that the Washington vocational rehabilitation program is "made available generally without regard to the sectarian-nonsectarian, or public-nonpublic nature of the institution benefited . . . and is in no way skewed towards religion." Aid recipients "have full opportunity to expend vocational rehabilitation aid on wholly secular education," and only a "small handful" of the possible careers from which recipients might choose are sectarian. The fact that the aid goes to individuals, rather than to institutions, said the Court, "means that the decision to support religious education is made by the individual, not by the State." Hence the function and effect of the Washington program are hardly to channel state aid to sectarian schools. On the contrary, said the Court, "the link between the State and the school petitioner wishes to attend [is] a highly attenuated one."

In remanding the case for further proceedings, however, the Court addressed only the judgment of the Washington State Supreme Court that the extension of aid violated the U.S. Constitution. The Court allowed that on remand the state court might consider the applicability of the "far stricter" dictates of the Washington state constitution and might reopen the factual record to consider other issues and arguments raised in the lower court proceedings. The Court refused to permit the petitioner to "leapfrog" consideration of those issues and declined to hold "that the Free Exercise Clause requires Washington to extend vocational rehabilitation aid to petitioner regardless of what the state constitution demands or further factual development reveals." In other words, on the question of the applicability of a Free Exercise claim in determining an individual's right to apply vocational rehabilitation aid for a program of ministerial education, the Witters Court refused to express an opinion.

In a concurring opinion, Justice Powell (joined by Chief Justice Burger and Justice Rehnquist and by Justice O'Connor in her separate concurring opinion) complained of the failure of the Court's opinion to mention the precedent of Mueller v. Allen (1983) in its substantive discussion. The omission, said Powell, might mislead lower courts to assume that the Supreme Court found the Mueller case somehow inapplicable in cases such as this one. He contended, however, that, in his judgment at least, Mueller directly supports the judgment reached in Witters.

Mueller sustained a Minnesota program of educational income tax deductions, which provided educational assistance to a class of recipients defined without reference to religion or religious affiliation. Even though such assistance ultimately resulted, through the individual choices of recipients, in a flow of assistance to religiously affiliated schools, the Court upheld the program as involving no Establishment. Powell found the provisions of the Washington and Minnesota aid programs essentially analogous. The state's decision to grant aid is not conditioned, in either case, he said, on whether the individual elects to attend a public or a private school or chooses to study religion or some other subject. Consequently, the state program is neutral as to religion and could not be construed as an establishment of religion.

Witters is significant in its ruling that a program of student assistance, religiously neutral on the face and designed for public welfare purposes, may be applied, within the limits of the Establishment Clause, to enable a student to pursue a program of theological study and ministerial education at an institution of his choice. (Such use of student aid has been prohibited in several states.) The same principle would presumably govern, whether the student elected to attend a Bible college (as in Witters) or a pervasively religious liberal arts college. However, the emphasis in the Washington program on the purposes of vocational rehabilitation might have played a large role in the Court's ruling, and it would be risky to draw conclusions concerning a broad or unlimited application of the Witters precedent in significantly different circumstances.

On remand the Washington Supreme Court affirmed en banc on April 20, 1989 that granting state aid to Witters was prohibited under the constitution of the State of Washington, which provides that "no public money . . . shall be appropriated or applied to any religious instruction," 771 P.2d 1119 (Wash. 1989). The court held, furthermore, that denial of aid to Witters was a violation of neither the Free Exercise Clause of the Federal Constitution nor the

Fourteenth Amendment's Equal Protection Clause. With respect to the Free Exercise issue, the court explained that the student was not being required by the state to violate any tenet of his religious beliefs, and was not being denied benefits because of conduct mandated by religious belief. With respect to the Fourteenth Amendment, the court contended that an individual's interest in receiving aid was required to give way to the state's compelling interest in maintaining strict separation of church and state as set forth in the state constitution. The court reasoned:

> Neither the applicant's freedom to believe nor his freedom to act in a manner consistent with his beliefs is being encroached by the (state constitution's) ban on expenditure of state funds for religious instruction. . . . The denial of tuition for religious instruction is but a refusal of state funds to advance religion in a constitutionally impermissible way; the Commission does not discriminate against the applicant because he is religious, but has refused to use state money to pay for his religious activities.

The court noted that Witters and his attorney had agreed in court that the program in which he had matriculated was a program of "religious education." It seemed to the court that such a program "comes squarely within the express prohibition" of the state constitution, which, it said, "prohibits the taxpayers from being put in the position of paying for the religious instruction of aspirants to the clergy with whose religious views they may disagree."

In an earlier case, Calvary Bible Presbyterian Church v. Board of Regents, 72 Wash 2d 912; 436 P.2d 189 (1967), cert. denied 393 U.S. 960, the Washington Supreme Court had interpreted the term "religious instruction," as used in the state constitution, to mean "instruction that is devotional in nature, and designed to induce faith and belief in the student." The court had no doubt that the state constitution's bans against any appropriation or application of public funds for religious instruction in this sense is

159

absolute. The court said, however, that the constitution does not proscribe "open, free, critical, and scholarly examination of the literature, experiences, and knowledge of mankind." In the Witters case, the court thought that the Bible study and church courses included in his program of studies "necessarily provide indoctrination in the specific beliefs of Christianity."

The court noted that the U.S. Supreme Court had left open the question whether state aid for Witters would violate provisions of the state constitution. In its previous decision in the case the Washington Supreme Court had held the program in violation of the Establishment Clause of the Federal Constitution. It was that decision which the U.S. Supreme Court had reversed. The Washington court now held that the aid violated not the federal, but the state constitution.

In a dissenting opinion (in which two other justices concurred), Judge Utter contended that the majority opinion actually conditions the receipt of vocational rehabilitation funds not on the absence of "religious instruction" as defined by the state constitution, but rather on the absence of a "religious" career goal on the part of the recipient. The state constitution, he argued, does not prohibit application of public funds for vocational training of an individual preparing for a religious career. It prohibits "religious instruction." But the court, he said, has adduced no evidence concerning the manner in which the particular courses taken by Witter are taught. Its conclusion that they are instances of impermissible, rather than permissible study of religious and theological subjects therefore "rests on no more than speculation."

The court assumes, said Judge Utter, that, given Witters' objective of preparing for a church vocation, the courses he takes must be "devotional," "indoctrinative," and designed to "induce faith and belief." But the religious character of the instruction actually given to Witter has not been established by the court. Consequently, he argued, the majority decision effectively discriminates against those applicants for vocational rehabilitation assistance who have chosen to pursue religiously oriented careers in violation of the First Amendment. The decision would thus rule out public student assistance for nonreligious instruction at private religious colleges when the student taking the nonreligious course is intending to prepare for a religious career. Hence "the State's attempt to condition the receipt of vocational rehabilitation assistance on the absence of a 'religious' career goal unconstitutionally abridges the recipient's right under the United States Constitution to freely exercise his faith."

Judge Utter complained that the majority decision fails to provide a "principled analysis," applying its own previously developed methodology for assuring that if the court uses state constitutional grounds, independently of, and possibly in conflict with, the U.S. Constitution, any resulting decision will be be reached for well founded reasons and "not merely by substituting our notion of justice for that of the . . . United States Supreme Court." Utter used the court's own criteria in presenting an extended analysis to confirm his conclusion that public funding of religious instruction is not involved in this case. He also noted that, even if the majority's opinion of the applicability of the state constitution is correct, its decision denying aid would apply only to that portion of the funds for the vocational rehabilitation program coming from the state treasury (namely 20%). The state constitution, he contended, cannot govern the award of the 80% of the program funds coming from federal sources. He concluded:

> The state has constitutional authority to exclude Mr. Witters from the vocational rehabilitation program only for that portion of his training which involves 'religious instruction.' The state has failed to show that any of Mr. Witters' vocational training involves 'religious instruction.' Because the evidence does not indicate that any of Mr. Witters' vocational training will include 'religious instruction,' he is entitled to the full amount of state and federal benefits under the program.

Utter also argued that the state program involved no state action supporting religious instruction. The application of public funds to instruction at a recognized religious institution arises, he contended, as the result of a personal decision by the recipient and is not a decision of the state. The only state action which Utter saw was that of appropriating funds for a neutral vocational rehabilitation program. That, indeed, was the way the U.S. Supreme Court had viewed the aid. The majority of the Washington Supreme Court, however, continues to view the program as constituting an establishment of religion. Whether the U.S. Supreme Court will hear the case again is not known at this writing.

4. Summary

When writing the opinion of the Court in Grand Rapids v. Ball, Justice William Brennan took occasion to comment, "Although Establishment Clause jurisprudence is characterized by few absolutes, the Clause does absolutely prohibit government-financed or government-sponsored indoctrination into the beliefs of a particular religious faith." In the Grand Rapids case the Court found that both the Community Education and the Shared Time programs of the Grand Rapids schools involved substantial risk of state-sponsored indoctrination. Rarely has the Court found indoctrination or inculcation of religious beliefs in college and university education, however, and its Establishment decisions affecting higher education have been correspondingly far more lenient and accomodating than its decisions affecting the pre-collegiate level of education.

The following principles have generally guided the higher education decisions of the Court:

1. Any form of aid to religiously affiliated institutions of higher education, whether direct or indirect, whether in cash or in kind, is impermissible if it has the primary effect of advancing religion or if it results in excessive entanglement of government in

religion. (The Court is unlikely to find a legislative intent to advance religion.)

2. Neither the states nor the federal government may support or participate in the programs of religiously affiliated institutions of higher education unless the secular function of such educational programs can be operationally separated from any sectarian function in such programs.

3. The atmosphere of most colleges and universities is so dominated by the traditions of academic freedom and disciplined scholarship as to readily permit the separation of secular and religious functions and to assure that public funds flow only to the support of the secular purposes for which they are intended.

4. If an institution is so pervasively religious that such separation is not feasible, state or federal aid could not pass the "primary effect" test and would be constitutionally impermissible. Such aid is categorically impermissible in the case of post-secondary institutions whose central mission is theological education and the training of clergy.

5. Under certain conditions student financial assistance may be applied for purposes of theological or ministerial education, but the conditions under which such application may be permissible remain somewhat uncertain.

It is clear that no private or religiously affiliated institution of higher education may receive public aid for sectarian activities. Examples of activities which clearly may not be aided are seminary education for the training of ministers, campus worship, and student religious societies. On the other hand, so long as the institution is not pervasively religious - - so long, that is, as it is possible to separate its secular functions from its religious ones - - it is constitutionally eligible to receive aid directed to its secular activities. It is extremely unlikely that a pervasively religious or sectarian college or university could receive noncategorical public aid, since such an institution could not provide assurance that the "primary effect" of aid would not be to foster religious purposes.

AID TO HIGHER EDUCATION

The judicial precedents indicate that an institution may have a significant religious affiliation and a substantial religious purpose without being judged a "pervasively religious" institution. It is not clear, however, what additional evidence of religiousness would have led some member of the 5-4 Roemer majority to find one of the Maryland colleges sectarian in a legal sense and thus ineligible to receive state aid.

The cases clearly state that where the religiousness of an institution is so pervasive that secular and religious educational functions cannot be separated, courts must find public assistance in violation of the Establishment Clause. The courts therefore need some kind of formula by which the religiousness of colleges and universities may be judicially determined. It is clear that public aid to institutions primarily engaged in theological education or the training of clergy is impermissible. Less clear are the criteria for identifying a sectarian or "pervasively religious" college or university, aid to which would also be impermissible.

It is uncertain whether the descriptors of a "pervasively religious" or "sectarian" college, as presented in several of the Court's Establishment Clause decisions on public aid to religiously affiliated higher education, constitute dicta or law. The formulations tend to be drawn by the lower courts rather than by the Supreme Court justices themselves. Nevertheless, the fact that they now appear in Supreme Court opinions tends to give them new authority.

The major judicial criteria for identifying a sectarian college or university (i.e. one in which the secular and religious functions are so fully integrated that public assistance directed only to the secular is impossible) appear to be the following:

1. An institutional mission involving the comprehensive integration of religious factors in the educational process.

164

2. A religiously selective student admission policy.
3. Comprehensive consideration of religious factors in employment of faculty and staff.
4. Mandatory courses in sectarian religion or theology courses and required attendance at religious activities with a view to fostering adherence to a particular religious faith.
5. Use of indoctrination as a method of instruction; an atmosphere requiring obedience to particular religious doctrines.
6. Close operating control of the educational program by a religious organization.

As we have noted in Chapter Two, any systematic use of such a list of criteria by the judicial system would raise very serious questions. One set of questions would concern the appropriateness of the criteria as indicators of a sectarian character and purpose. Another set would concern the need for flexibility and adaptability in any understanding of religion. The courts may probably be expected to use such criteria selectively and analogically if they use them at all. The potential for misuse is present, however, particularly in lower courts where the formulations presented in the foregoing cases might be viewed as normative.

Our conclusion at the end of this survey of Establishment Clause jurisprudence is that cooperation between church and state in education may be permitted under the First Amendment when federal support and involvement can be limited to secular functions and shielded from religious functions. Correspondingly, one would expect that the government would view its regulatory interest in the operations of religious and religiously affiliated organizations as limited to those secular functions which may be reached by public funding and as not properly extended to their religious functions.

Applied to the area of employment policies and practices, that principle would imply that exemptions which make allowance for religious discrimination in employment

165

would be more readily granted by the government and the courts to institutions so pervasively religious that they are unlikely to qualify for public aid. Furthermore, one would assume that, in the case of institutions where it is possible to separate secular and sectarian functions, the scope of the government's regulatory interest in employment decisions would be limited to those areas of institutional operatons which are reached by public aid. We turn now to the verification of this hypothesis.

NOTES TO CHAPTER 5

1. The Act has been repealed, with the understanding that programs authorized under Title VII of the Higher Education Act (dealing with Construction, Reconstruction, and Renovation of Acdemic Facilities) shall be deemed to be a continuation of the comparable programs authorized under the Higher Education Facilities Act. The original statutory language prohibiting the use of federal funds for the support of religious worship or instruction, also appear in Title VII.

2. Board of Public Works of Maryland v. Horace Mann League, 385 U.S. 97 (November 14, 1966). Justices Harlan and Stewart thought certiorari should be granted. The Association of American Colleges submitted an amicus brief, supporting the petition of the Board of Public Works.

3. The college terminated its formal Methodist affiliation in 1974.

4. St. Joseph College was closed in 1972. Notre Dame, St. Joseph, and Western Maryland were also involved in the Roemer case, which reached the U.S. Supreme Court in 1976. See below, pp. 147-155.

5. The court held that the Horace Mann League, a non-profit educational and charitable corporation organized for the purpose of fostering American public education, lacked standing to challenge the validity of the statutes. The

court proceeded on the determination that the individuals who had joined with the League in bringing the civil action had standing to sue, even though their personal financial stake in the challenged programs was small.

6.   The court cited a note in 50 Yale Law Journal 917 as the source for its information.

7.   This provision of the Act was later amended by Congress.

8.   See above p. 120.

9.   Ten years earlier in the Horace Mann case, the Maryland Court of Appeals had determined that Western Maryland College was "sectarian in a legal sense" and not eligible for a state construction grant. The same determination had been made with respect to the College of Notre Dame and St. Joseph College. See above, pp. 138, 139.

10.   In Horace Mann the Court of Appeals of Maryland had found the College of Notre Dame and St. Joseph College "sectarian in the legal sense" and thus ineligible for state construction grants. The U.S. Supreme Court had refused to grant certiorari in that case. The Court now viewed these colleges (ten years later) as eligible for state noncategorical grants without violation of the Establishment Clause.

11.   The Washington Constitution provides, in part, in Art. I, Para. 11: "No public money or property shall be appropriated to or applied to any religious worship, exercise, or instruction, or the support of any religious establishment;" and in Art. IX, Para 4: "All schools maintained or supported wholly or in part by the public funds shall be forever free from sectarian control or influence."

CHAPTER SIX

EMPLOYMENT DISCRIMINATION
ON THE BASIS OF RACE OR SEX

The right of religious and religiously affiliated organizations to exercise religious preference in employment decisions has been confirmed by several recent judicial decisions. Certain limits of this right have also been clarified. These decisions have been reached on the basis of judicial construction of specific federal and state statutes and on interpretation of the Religion Clauses of the U.S. Constitution.

Several different kinds of determination are involved in these decisions. At one level courts have had to face the question of the conditions under which an action or policy of discrimination should be classified as authentically religious. For a number of religious traditions certain actions which involve employment discrimination on the basis of race or of sex are derived from sincerely and strongly held religious beliefs. The courts have had to determine the conditions under which such forms of discrimination might be protected under a general right of religious autonomy, as opposed to conditions under which a claim for a religious right to discriminate might be merely a pretext behind which an impermissible form of discrimination hides.

Another kind of determination concerns the criterion for determining institutional eligibility for a statutory or constitutional exemption from the general requirement of nondiscrimination in employment. At issue here is the question what are the identifying characteristics of a religious organization, or what are the conditions under which an educational institution affiliated with a religious organization, or an independent, but religiously oriented institution, may be judged eligible for the exemption.

Finally, courts have had to face the question of the scope of the right of religious autonomy under the Constitution. On the one hand, there is the question of how the content of a claim to religious autonomy is to be determined, and whether such determination is to be made only by the religious organization itself, or whether it is a determination which may be made by secular courts. On the other hand, there is the question of how the right of religious autonomy for an institution may be limited by the rights of individuals or by a compelling public or governmental interest.

1.   The Jurisdiction of the N.L.R.B.

N.L.R.B. v. Catholic Bishop of Chicago (1979)

We begin once again with a case affecting religiously affiliated pre-collegiate education. The Supreme Court decision in National Labor Relations Board v. Catholic Bishop of Chicago, 440 U.S. 490 (1979), is an important precedent for the entire theory of church labor relations. Since it was delivered in March, 1979, the decision has frequently been cited in connection with cases involving employment policies and procedures not only in parochial elementary and secondary schools, but also in religiously affiliated institutions of higher education.

The case concerns the jurisdiction of the National Labor Relations Act and of the National Labor Relations Board over the employment policies, procedures, and actions of church-operated schools. The case reached the Supreme Court by way of two separate lower court decisions affecting two parochial school systems, one operated by the Diocese of Chicago and one operated by the Diocese of Fort Wayne-South Bend (IN). In 1974 and 1975 petitions were filed with the National Labor Relations Board by interested union organizations seeking to represent lay teachers in the schools. The NLRB then issued orders, requiring the schools to enter into collective bargaining procedures with the unions. The schools immediately challenged the jurisdiction of the Board, which denied the appeal on the basis of its policy of declining to exercise jurisdiction over religiously sponsored organizations "only when they are completely religious, not just religiously associated."

RACE OR SEX DISCRIMINATION

The schools challenged the Board's orders in petitions to the Court of Appeals for the Seventh Circuit, which denied enforcement of the NLRB orders on two grounds: (1) First, the court held that the NLRB had improperly exercised its discretionary jurisdiction, because the Board's distinction between "completely religious" and "merely religiously associated" failed to provide a workable guide for the exercise of discretion in asserting jurisdiction; and (2) Second, the court held that the Board's jurisdiction was foreclosed by both the Free Exercise and Establishment Clauses, reasoning that by certifying a union as the bargaining agent for lay teachers the Board "would impinge upon the freedom of church authorities to shape and direct teaching in accord with the requirements of their religion."

The U.S. Supreme Court granted certiorari to consider two questions: (a) Whether teachers in schools operated by a church to teach both religious and secular subjects are within the jurisdiction granted by the National Labor Relations Act; and (b) If the Act authorizes such jurisdiction, does its exercise violate the guarantees of the Religion Clauses of the First Amendment? In a 5-4 decision the Court held that "schools operated by a church to teach both religious and secular subjects" are not within the jurisdiction of the Act and that the NLRB was without authority to issue orders to such schools to bargain collectively with a labor organization.

The Court reached this determination on the basis of having found no clear and affirmative Congressional intent that church-operated schools should be within the jurisdiction of the Act and of the NLRB. Absent a clear expression of Congressional intent, the Court refused to construe the National Labor Relations Act "in such a way as would call for the resolution of difficult and sensitive First Amendment questions." That is, the Court found a sufficient basis for delivering its judgment in the case in its construction of the intention of the statute, so that a decision on the constitutional question was unnecessary.

170

RACE OR SEX DISCRIMINATION

The decision in <u>Catholic Bishop</u> was made on a narrow basis and falls short of confirming the respondents' claim of a general Free Exercise right of parochial schools in matters of employment policy. The ruling of the Court was based, not on its constitutional interpretation, but on its construction of the statute defining the authority of the NLRB as not having been clearly intended by Congress to cover parochial schools. The Court noted in dictum, however, that "the Board's exercise of jurisdiction over teachers in church-operated schools would implicate the guarantees of the Religion Clauses." The Court's opinion thus rejected the contention of the NLRB that its claim of broad jurisdiction over church-operated schools did not violate the First Amendment rights of the schools. If the Act had, in fact, granted the challenged jurisdiction over parochial school teachers, the Court stated, the question would have to be addressed whether such jurisdiction was permissible under the Religion Clauses. The Court left no doubt that it saw the exercise of the Board's jurisdiction over such schools as presenting a "significant risk that the First Amendment will be infringed."

Writing for the majority, Chief Justice Warren Burger noted that the Court's recent decisions striking down public aid to parochial schools had been guided by the determination that religious authority necessarily pervades such schools. He emphasized "the critical and unique role of the teacher in fulfilling the mission of a church-operated school," and declared that, "The key role played by teachers in such a school system has been the predicate for our conclusions that governmental aid channeled through teachers creates an impermissible risk of excessive governmental entanglement in the affairs of the church-operated schools." The relationship between church and teacher in a church-operated school, said Burger, is fundamentally different from the employment relationship in a public school or in a nonreligious independent school. "We see no escape from conflicts flowing from the Board's exercise of jurisdiction over teachers in church-operated schools and the consequent serious First Amendment questions that would follow."

171

In his dissenting opinion Justice William Brennan (joined by Justices White, Marshall, and Blackmun), took a totally different view of the intent of the statute. He endorsed the general judicial strategy of construing statutes, where possible, in such a way as to avoid unnecessary constitutional decisions. But in this case he thought it undeniable that the Act was intended by Congress to cover all employers unless expressly excluded, and he noted that Congress had expressly excluded only nonprofit hospitals. The minority of four members of the Court thus took the view that the National Labor Relations Act "includes within its coverage lay teachers employed by church-operated schools," and that in consequence the question of the compatibility of such coverage with the First Amendment needed to be faced. Brennan declared no view on that question, however. His dissent was limited to the declaration "that while the resolution of the constitutional question is not without difficulty, it is irresponsible to avoid it by a cavalier exercise in statutory interpretation which succeeds only in defying Congressional intent."

Barber-Scotia College, NC (1979)

Shortly after the <u>Catholic Bishop</u> decision was delivered two regional panels of the National Labor Relations Board, acting in separate cases, ruled that the status of two religiously affiliated colleges did not preclude the Board from asserting its jurisdiction in formation of a collective bargaining agreement between the institutions and their employees. The claims and actions of the respective regional directors in arranging for elections were confirmed in a Decision on Review and Direction issued by the NLRB in Washington on September 26, 1979.

In <u>245 NLRB No. 48, Barber-Scotia</u> (1979), Barber-Scotia College, a Presbyterian-related liberal arts college in Concord, North Carolina, challenged the jurisdiction of the NLRB in connection with a petition by the Barber-Scotia Professional Association/NEA to be recognized as the representative for certain professional employees of the college. The college contended, on the ground of its being controlled by the United Presbyterian Church, that the Supreme Court decision in Catholic Bishop precluded the Board from asserting jurisdiction. The NLRB held, however, that the college was not "a church-operated school within the meaning of the Catholic Bishop decision." The Board saw Barber-Scotia College as closely resembling the religiously affiliated colleges in Tilton v. Richardson, which had been identified by the Supreme Court as essentially different in educational character from the parochial elementary and secondary schools involved in Lemon v. Kurtzman.

The NLRB decision cited a number of facts which, it contended, supported its finding that Barber-Scotia was not a "church-operated school." The college is operated not by a church, but by an independent board of trustees. Although the college charter, constitution, and bylaws identify the college as controlled and operated by the church, the record, claimed the NLRB, "reveals numerous instances where the College is operated in a manner which does not conform to its charter and bylaws." As examples the Board noted the facts that the college had not received any operating funds from the church since 1977, that it holds title to several pieces of property in its own name, and that "it hires faculty and staff without seeking the church's approval." The Board rejected the college's claim that it was controlled by the church, finding evidence that "the church does not become actively involved in the internal affairs of the college."

As for the educational mission of the institution, the Board noted that:

> The major aim of Barber-Scotia College is to provide a secular education. The college does not stress religion or Presbyterian principles in its curriculum. Students are required to take one of the two religiously oriented courses that are offered, but both of these are surveys of various religions and are not limited to the teaching of Presbyterian principles. The record does

not indicate that religious doctrine affects the teaching of courses offered by the College for credit towards a degree. The College occasionally conducts religious observances, but student attendance is not mandatory. Decisions concerning the curriculum and course content are made by the College without the Church's involvement.

We therefore find that Barber-Scotia College is not a 'church-operated school.' Rather, it is a college of the kind found by the Supreme Court to be primarily concerned with providing a secular education, rather than with inculcating particular religious doctrines.

The NLRB held in Barber-Scotia that the college more closely resembles the Tilton institutions than the Lemon and Catholic Bishop institutions. Accordingly, the Board rejected the college's argument that the Board's assertion of jurisdiction would constitute an impermissible entanglement between government and religion.

College of Notre Dame, CA (1979)

In 245 NLRB No. 44, College of Notre Dame (1979), the NLRB issued a similar ruling with respect to the College of Notre Dame, a Catholic institution in Belmont, California. The college was originally established in 1851 by the Order of the Sisters of Notre Dame de Namur (an international religious teaching congregation), but was operated in 1979 by an independent board of trustees. There is no formal requirement that any particular number of the trustees must be members of the Order, but at the time of the NLRB ruling 9 of the 15 trustees were sisters of Notre Dame. The President of the college, who is ex officio a member of the board, is required by charter to be a member of the Order. The Roman Catholic Diocese of San Francisco, in which the college is located, does not exercise administrative control over the college, although the religious members of the Order are subject to the authority of the Archbishop of San Francisco in matters of church doctrine. The property and assets of the college are independently owned, although the articles of incorporation provide that, should the college be dissolved, the assets would be distributed to the Order of Sisters of Notre Dame de Namur.

The Board contended that "the purpose of the college as set forth in the articles of incorporation is entirely secular; namely, to provide a liberal arts education to qualified students regardless of religious orientation, as would any other public or private nonsectarian college." The decision quoted a statement in the student handbook, that the aim of the college is "to assist the student to acquire a deeper understanding of Christianity in its Catholic interpretation, to live and experience it relevantly; and to provide knowledge of other Christian and non-Christian religions." But the Board saw nothing "sectarian" in such a purpose. Rather, the Board declared, "It is clear . . . that the religiously oriented aspects of campus life are strictly optional." The Board found the curriculum of the college to be "nonsectarian." And it noted that, although one-third of the faculty are members of Catholic Orders, "decisions concerning hiring of both teaching and nonteaching personnel, as well as admission of students, are made without regard to religious preference."

The NLRB holding in this case declared that, despite the vestiges of a prior religious orientation and control, "the College of Notre Dame is not church-operated as contemplated by Catholic Bishop, and that the Board clearly has statutory jurisdiction over the Employer." Accordingly, the Board concluded that there was no First Amendment bar to its exercise of jurisdiction in the petition of the International Union of Operating Engineers, AFL-CIO, to be certified as the representative of service and maintenance employees of the college. The Board found the college fundamentally dissimilar to the "church-operated schools" of the Catholic Bishop decision and essentially similar to the nonsectarian, though religiously affiliated schools of Tilton.

We thus conclude that, unlike parochial elementary and high schools, the operation of the Employer does not involve 'substantial religious activity and purpose.'

It is certainly clear that its reason for being is not the 'propagation of religious faith.' Accordingly, we shall assert jurisdiction over the College of Notre Dame.

N.L.R.B. v. Saint Francis College (1977)

In N.L.R.B. v. Saint Francis College, F.2d 246 (1977), a case decided prior to the Supreme Court's decision in Catholic Bishop, the U.S. Court of Appeals for the Third Circuit supported the refusal of a Catholic college to bargain with a faculty union on grounds that the union unreasonably and arbitrarily excluded faculty who were members of the Franciscan Order. In 1974 the St. Francis College Education Association filed a representation petition with the National Labor Relations Board and subsequently won the representation election. At the representation hearing before the NLRB, St. Francis College objected, unsuccessfully, to the exclusion of Franciscans from the Association, asserting that the exclusion of this group of faculty violated their religious rights and vitiated the appropriateness of the bargaining unit. Following the election the college refused to bargain, and the NLRB then sought the assistance of the Court of Appeals in enforcing its "cease and desist" order, requiring the college to bargain.[1] The court denied the NLRB's petition, finding that the exclusion of Franciscan faculty from the union was an unreasonable and arbitrary action on the part of the NLRB.

St. Francis College, located in Loretto, Pennsylvania, was founded in 1847 by the Third Order Regular of St. Francis. In 1966 lay members were elected to the board of trustees and the college was separated from the Order. In 1973 the Order released the college from indebtedness resulting from the Order's original investments, in exchange for a tract of land. Also during that year Franciscan faculty members were placed under contracts with the college which were "largely identical" to those of lay faculty, and from that time forward Franciscan faculty no longer volunteered their time for college work but were compensated in full for the work for which they contracted.

The Franciscans continue to make annual donations to the college, typically amounting to about 50% of the salary amounts received by members of the Order. The Franciscan faculty have taken a vow of poverty.

The NLRB's exclusion of the Franciscan faculty from the faculty union was based on a previous decision of the Board in Seton Hill College, 201 NLRB No. 155, 82 LRRM 1434 (1973). In that instance the faculty was composed of 34 lay teachers and 58 Sisters of Charity of Seton Hill. The Sisters were excluded from the faculty bargaining unit on the grounds that they lacked a "community of interest" with the lay faculty members and "were in a sense part of the employer," since the Order owned and operated the college. St. Francis College objected to use of the Seton Hill precedent on two grounds: (1) First, the facts in the Seton Hill College and St. Francis College cases are different in important respects; and (2) Second, the reasoning in the Seton Hill decision has been seriously undermined by later Board decisions in D'Youville College (1976) and Niagara University (1976), in which religious faculty were included in the bargaining unit. Indeed, the Court of Appeals itself volunteered the additional information that religious faculty had been included in a bargaining unit by a decision of the Board prior to the Seton Hill decision (in Fordham University 1971).

The NLRB relied on two arguments: First, that the "special and complex relationship" between the Franciscan faculty and the administration of the college would present a conflict of loyalties for Franciscans if they were members of the union. Second, substantial differences in salary and benefits mean that the Franciscans' economic interests differ substantially from those of lay faculty. The Court of Appeals was not persuaded by either of these arguments and found that the NLRB had abused its discretionary authority in excluding the Franciscan faculty from the union.

The college argued, with the support, as amici, of the Pennsylvania Association of Colleges and Universities and the National Catholic Educational Association, College and

University Department, that exclusion of the Franciscans from the union violated the religious rights of the Franciscans. The court did not reach any of these arguments, however, since it was able to deny the NLRB petition on grounds of "non-religious neutral principles for appropriate unit determinations."

In a concurring opinion Circuit Judge Rosenn emphasized that, in his view, the decision of the court did not imply that religious faculty members could never be excluded from a faculty bargaining unit. In the St. Francis College instance, said Judge Rosenn, the alleged lack of a "community of interest" between lay and religious faculty and the "conflict of loyalty" arising from the "special and complex relationship" between the religious faculty and the college's Franciscan administrators were not documented in the record considered by the Board. A future case might present a different basis for exclusion, supported by evidence of record, and such a case, he contended, would have to be decided on its own merits.

We cite the St. Francis College case to emphasize that a number of colleges would choose to work with the NLRB in establishing a collective bargaining process, and would not wish to follow the Catholic Bishop/Barber-Scotia/Notre Dame strategy of challenging the jurisdiction of the NLRB in collective bargianing cases on grounds of a religious status which shields the institution from the provisions of the National Labor Relations Act. Indeed, we believe that the Catholic Bishop strategy would be successful only in institutions in which the religious and secular functions are so closely integrated that any government involvement in employment issues would violate the Religion Clauses. Many religiously affiliated colleges and universities would not succeed in that strategy.

Universidad Central de Bayamon v. N.L.R.B. (1985)

In Universidad Central de Bayamon v. National Labor Relations Board, 793 F.2d 383 (1st Cir. 1985), the U.S. Court of Appeals for the First Circuit split evenly on the question whether the NLRB had jurisdiction to require a Catholic university to enter into collective bargaining with a faculty union. A panel of three judges of the Court of Appeals, by a vote of 2-1, first granted enforcement of the NLRB's order requiring the University to bargain. But the full court subsequently vacated the panel's decision and reheard the case en banc. The full court was evenly divided as to the proper outcome and published two conflicting opiniions on June 13, 1986.

The Universidad Central de Bayamon was founded in Bayamon, Puerto Rico in 1961 by the Dominican Order and was separately incorporated in 1964 by the Regional Vicar of the Dominican Order and two other Dominican priests. The university is governed by a board of trustees, the majority of whom must be and are members of the Dominican Order. (In 1985 there were ten members of the board, six of whom were members of the Dominican Order and all of whom were Catholics.) Since 1970 the University has been financially self-sufficient.

The President of the University, who has broad powers and authority, must be a Dominican. The Regional Vicar of the Dominican Order has been President of the University and Secretary of the Board of Trustees since 1970. The University is part of a system of Dominican schools, including two elementary and secondary schools which are administered under the Board of Trustees of the University. The principals of these schools report directly to the Vice President of the University. In 1980 the University began operating a seminary, called the Center for Dominican Studies in the Caribbean (CEDOC), which offers a master's degree in theology. On review the NLRB exempted the CEDOC from its bargaining order, "because of the pervasively religious character of the program."

The University describes itself as being "a Catholic-oriented civil institution," whose mission is to provide "a humanistic education at an academic level." In 1970 a dispute arose between the Dominican Order and the local church hierarchy over control of the University. Because of

179

the dispute the University terminated its original organizational relationship as a branch of the Catholic University of Puerto Rico, the main campus of which is in Ponce. An agreement was reached between the Dominican Order and the Archbishop of San Juan, which reserved to the Order control over all matters relating to the religious orientation, educational philosophy, and internal discipline of the University, but recognized a "pastoral connection" between the University and the Archdiocese of San Juan. The agreement binds the University

> to keep the faith of the Roman, [Apostolic], and
> Catholic Church and a Catholic education[al] philosophy,
> in light of the Christian Revelation and guided by the
> teachings of the Doctors of the Church, foremostly,
> Saint Thomas Aquinas, and with the impulse of the
> theological and spiritual patrimony of the Order of Saint
> Domingo of Guzman, which has originated the
> University.

The full-time faculty include 49 lay faculty and 4 or 5 priests. There is no religious requirement for appointment to the lay faculty, although most are Catholic. The bylaws of the University require that faculty "possess the appropriate academic degrees, be of sound moral character, and show traits of pedagogical qualities." The University guarantees full academic freedom to its lay faculty. Nevertheless, all faculty are apprised of their responsibility to adhere to the Catholic philosophy of the University. The faculty contract requires faculty members "to know, respect, and uphold the University's philosophy," and the Faculty Regulations state that the faculty "shall at all times put into practice [the University's] philosophy of being a Catholic-oriented institution."

In its student admission policy the University "welcomes students of all denominations and faiths." Students are required to take one course in theology and three in philosophy. The theology course is usually taught by a Dominican, using a Dominican text; the philosophy courses, although more general in content, are taught with a

Catholic orientation. Regular masses are offered in the Dominican church adjoining the campus, but attendance, though encouraged, is not compulsory.

In 1979 a faculty union filed a petition with the NLRB, seeking recognition as the bargaining unit for all full-time teaching personnel of the University. The University opposed the petition, in part on the Catholic Bishop grounds that the Board's assertion of jurisdiction would violate the Establishment Clause. The NLRB's regional director denied the University's claim, finding that its educational aim was "entirely secular." The faculty then voted 41 to 9 to be represented by the union, which was certified by the NLRB in February, 1980.

The University refused to bargain with the union, maintaining its view that the NLRB lacked jurisdiction. Furthermore, in May and July of 1980 the University unilaterally promulgated a series of new requirements for faculty appointments, and discharged eight teachers who failed to meet the requirements. The union struck the University in September, 1980, but returned to work in November. The University refused to reinstate fifteen of the striking employees.

The union then brought unfair labor practices proceedings against the University. In March, 1982 and March, 1983 hearings were held before an administrative law judge, who found that the jurisdiction of the NLRB over the University was proper, because the University's "academic mission is secular." The administrative law judge relied on the Board's precedents (in Barber-Scotia and College of Notre Dame), which, as we have just noted, had refused to apply the Catholic Bishop precedent to colleges.

The Board ordered the University to bargain collectively with the certified union, to rescind the unilateral changes in requirements for faculty appointments on request of the union, and to offer discharged employees reinstatement in their former positions. The University appealed the NLRB

181

decision to the First Circuit, and the NLRB cross-petitioned for enforcement of its order.

Three members of the Court of Appeals found that the NLRB had properly asserted jurisdiction over the University and that such jurisdiction involved no violation of the First Amendment. Three other judges held that, since the University was controlled by the Dominican Order, the NLRB lacked jurisdiction. Because the court was evenly divided, both the petition of the University challenging the jurisdiction of the NLRB and the petition of the NLRB for enforcement of its order were denied.

The central issue in this case concerned the applicability of the Supreme Court's decision in Catholic Bishop to a religiously affiliated college or university. The two sides adopted conflicting interpretations of the reasoning of Catholic Bishop and came to irreconcilable conclusions.

One side, joining in Circuit Judge Coffin's opinion upholding NLRB jurisdiction, thought that the basic rationale of Catholic Bishop rested on "the unique church-teacher relationship existing in parochial secondary schools" and the role of such teachers in carrying out the educational mission of the church, as contrasted to the role of university-level teachers, who "are not expected to provide the intense inculcative religious experience for their students that is the norm in a religious elementary or secondary school." Coffin's opinion dwelt on the consistent tendency of the Supreme Court to treat church-operated colleges and universities as significantly different from church-operated elementary or secondary schools.

The other side, joining in Circuit Judge Breyer's opinion denying NLRB jurisdiction, contended that the NLRB's "finding that the Catholic Church does not control the University is legally unsupportable; it lacks 'substantial evidence' in the record." Breyer found evidence of a sectarian purpose and control in the documents propounding the University's mission, in the form of organizational and management control, in the qualifications and procedures followed in faculty appointments, and in the curriculum. Breyer saw no difference between the <u>Catholic Bishop</u> and <u>Bayamon</u> circumstances as far as the risk of state/religion entanglement is concerned. Furthermore, he argued, to refuse to apply <u>Catholic Bishop</u> in this case would be to undermine the entire rationale and purpose of that opinion, which sought to foreclose the kinds of governmental or regulatory intrusion into the activities of religious and religiously affiliated institutions which would be required to establish whether a given institution was "completely religious" or "merely religiously associated." Both "the language, reasoning, and purposes" of <u>Catholic Bishop,</u> said Judge Breyer, "make it applicable here."

Judge Coffin, on the other hand, declared, "We believe the language, reasoning, and purposes of <u>Catholic Bishop</u> guide us towards allowing NLRB jurisdiction over an institution (as described in the language of <u>Tilton</u>) 'with admittedly religious functions but whose predominant higher education mission is to provide . . . students with a secular education.'" Noting the NLRB's current disposition to retain jurisdiction over church-operated colleges and universities, Judge Breyer declared, "Whether this kind of institution of higher education falls within the strictures of <u>Catholic Bishop</u> is, in our view, an important, likely recurring, question, that calls for Supreme Court guidance."

The division of the court in <u>Bayamon</u> is, in our opinion, a clear indication of the uncertainty of the law affecting the employment rights of religiously affiliated institutions of higher education. The court was unable to reach agreement concerning either the degree of religiousness present in an institution with a strong religious affiliation and purpose, or the applicability to such an institution of statutory or constitutional exemptions based on religion.

RACE OR SEX DISCRIMINATION

2. Discrimination on the Basis of Race or Sex in Religiously Affiliated Schools

A number of recent judicial decisions have addressed the exercise of discrimination based on race or sex by religious organizations or religiously affiliated educational institutions. The right to exercise such discrimination, ostensibly from religious motivations, has been claimed as protected by the Religion Clauses of the First Amendment. A brief consideration of the reasoning followed in the disposition of these cases will contribute to our understanding of the legal principles affecting the exercise of religious preference in employment decisions in religious and religiously affiliated organizations.

McClure v. Salvation Army (1972)

In McClure v. Salvation Army, 460 F.2d 553 (5th Cir.), cert. denied, 409 U.S. 896 (1972), the Fifth Circuit Court of Appeals sustained the dismissal of a female minister's civil action against her employer, the Salvation Army, alleging that her employer had engaged in discriminatory practices against her in violation of Title VII of the Civil Rights Act. The court held that "Congress did not intend, through the nonspecific wording of the applicable provisions of Title VII, to regulate the relationship between church and minister." The court was guided by the principle that a secular court should not attempt to resolve civil disputes which would engage it "in the forbidden process of interpreting and weighing church doctrine."

The plaintiff alleged that she had received less salary and fewer benefits than those accorded similarly situated male officers, and that she had been discharged in retaliation for her complaints to her superiors and to the Equal Employment Opportunity Commission with regard to these practices. She and the Equal Employment Opportunity Commission, which joined in the appeal as amicus, contended that the exemption provided in Title VII permits a religious organization to discriminate only on the basis of religion, not on the basis of sex. The Fifth Circuit agreed with that

184

statutory interpretation, admitting that "the language and legislative history of Section 702 compel the conclusion that Congress did not intend that a religious organization be exempted from liability for discriminating against its employees on the basis of race, color, sex, or national origin with respect to their compensation, terms, conditions or privileges of employment."

This interpretation of the statute required the Court to address the question pressed by the Salvation Army in its defense, viz. that application of the provisions of Title VII to the relationship between it and its officers (a church and its ministers) is violative of the Religion Clauses of the First Amendment. The opinion of the court rehearsed a series of Supreme Court decisions confirming the autonomy of religious organizations in matters of church administration.[2] The court determined that applying the provisions of Title VII to the employment relationship between a church and its ministers would involve a form of state intrusion in matters which the Supreme Court has consistently declared to be "matters of singular ecclesiastical concern."[3]

The court found, therefore, that such application "would result in an encroachment by the State into an area of religious freedom which it is forbidden to enter by the principles of the free exercise clause of the First Amendment." Out of deference to the possibility that there might be some doubt concerning that constitutional judgment, however, the court found it possible (without citing supporting documentation from the legislative history) to read the intention of Congress in such a way as to avoid the constitutional question. The Supreme Court was apparently willing to acquiesce in this strategy, refusing to grant certiorari on appeal.

E.E.O.C. v. Mississippi College, (1980)

In E.E.O.C. v. Mississippi College, 626 F.2d. 477 (1980), the Fifth Circuit Court of Appeals refused to extend McClure's definition of the protected relation between a church and its ministers to cover the relation between a religiously affiliated college and its faculty. The court declared that "the employment relationship between Mississippi College and its faculty and staff is one intended by Congress to be regulated by Title VII," and it rejected the college's claim that application of Title VII to the college violates either the Establishment or the Free Exercise Clause. However, the court interpreted the language of Section 702 as excluding from the application of the Civil Rights Act "any employment practices of a religious educational institution that discriminates on the basis of religion, regardless of whether the religious discrimination is a pretext for some other type of discrimination."

The Mississippi College case rose from the refusal of the college to respond to an EEOC subpoena for voluminous statistical and documentary information which it claimed was needed in its investigation of a charge of discrimination on the basis of sex, filed against the college by a female faculty member. The EEOC sought enforcement of its subpoena through the U.S. District Court, which denied the petition, declaring that "the potential for involvement by the EEOC . . . into the internal affairs of Mississippi College clearly constitutes excessive entanglement, interference with the religious practice of the College and the Mississippi Baptist Convention, and an inhibition and chilling of the religious convictions held by the College and the Mississippi Baptist Convention." On appeal the Court of Appeals for the Fifth Circuit vacated and remanded the District Court judgment, declaring that the EEOC had a limited jurisdiction over the college and leaving for resolution by the District Court the question of what portions of the EEOC's subpoena should be enforced.

The appellate decision denied Mississippi College's contention, relying on McClure, that the EEOC had no jurisdiction to investigate employment relationships between a religious educational institution and its faculty. The court declared that such jurisdiction of the EEOC is limited, however, to other forms of alleged discrimination than

186

religious discrimination. Hence the information which the EEOC might appropriately obtain from college files would be limited to that required to determine whether the college is following discriminatory employment practices other than religious discrimination.

In McClure the Fifth Circuit determined that questions touching the relationship between a church and its ministers are matters of purely "ecclesiastical cognizance," and that ecclesiastical employment discrimination of any form lies beyond governmental examination. But in Mississippi College the court declared that the McClure precedent does not bar the EEOC from investigating allegations that a religiously affiliated college engages in discrimination based on sex or race. "The College is not a church," said the court. "The College's faculty and staff do not function as ministers." Hence the terms and conditions of faculty and staff employment in a college like Mississippi College do not lie beyond the range of Title VII regulation.

The court held that the College was fully protected under Title VII in the exercise of religious discrimination in employment decisions, and that an EEOC investigation concerning alleged discrimination on the basis of sex or race would at most impose only minimal burdens on the College's religious practices. The court reasoned, "The fact that those of the College's employment practices subject to Title VII do not embody religious beliefs or practices [with the possible exception of the appointment of women to teach religion courses] protects the College from any real threat of undermining its religious purpose of fulfilling the evangelical role of the Mississippi Baptist Convention, and allows us to conclude that the impact of Title VII on the free exercise of religious beliefs is minimal."

The court added that the United States has a "compelling interest" in eradicating discrimination in all its forms. It saw the proscription of race discrimination as particularly compelling, being mandated not only by congressional enactments but also by the Thirteenth Amendment. "We conclude that the government's compelling interest in eradicating discrimination is sufficient to justify the minimal burden imposed upon the College's free exercise of religious beliefs that results from the application of Title VII."

E.E.O.C. v. Southwestern Baptist Theological Seminary (1981)

In E.E.O.C. v. Southwestern Baptist Theological Seminary, 485 F.Supp. 255 (N.D.Tex.), revised in part, 651 F.2d. 277 (5th Cir. 1981), cert. denied, 456 U.S. 905 (1982), the Fifth Circuit extended the range of application of McClure's protected employment relationship between a church and its minister relation to cover the employment policies of a theological seminary with respect to its theological faculty and faculty supervisors, but not with respect to its support staff. The case arose from the refusal of the seminary to file a routine report required by the EEOC in pursuit of its statutory responsibility to obtain such reports as are reasonably necessary for determination of whether or not unlawful employment practices have been or are being committed by employers. When the EEOC brought suit to compel compliance, the District Court refused, finding that the application of Title VII to any aspect of the employment relationship between the seminary and its employees would violate both the Establishment and the Free Exercise Clauses. The Court of Appeals affirmed in part, and reversed and remanded in part, holding that judicial precedent excludes from governmental investigation the employment relationship of the seminary to its ministerial employees, but not the relationship to its non-ministerial employees.

The court applied both the McClure and the Mississippi College precedents in reaching its determination. The court saw the crux of this case as the question whether or not the seminary should be characterized as a church (analogously to McClure), or as a religiously affiliated educational institution (analogously to Mississippi College). The seminary claimed that it was a wholly religious institution, and that all its employees serve a ministerial function. The court accepted the determinations of fact below, and treated the faculty and administration, but not the support staff as "ministerial" for the purpose of applying McClure.

The Court of Appeals then responded to the District Court's finding that application of the reporting requirements of Title VII to the seminary would impair the seminary's free exercise rights and would foster an excessive governmental entanglement with religion. The Court essentially followed its reasoning in Mississippi College. The court saw any burden imposed on the seminary through EEOC reporting requirements limited to support staff as far less onerous than those involved in Mississippi College, as largely hypothetical, and as involving a minimal relationship between the seminary and the government. The nexus of the EEOC's investigatory jurisdiction, said the court, is strictly limited and "does not directly burden the exercise of any sincerely held religious belief." On the other hand, the weight on the side of the government's compelling interest in eradicating all forms of discrimination is also lighter in this case than in the Mississippi College case.

Ritter v. Mount St. Mary's College (1980)

In Ritter v. Mount St. Mary's College, 495 F.Supp. 724 (1980), a Maryland district court considered a sex and age discrimination suit, brought against a Catholic college under Title VII, the Equal Pay Act, and the Age Discrimination in Employment Act by a lay faculty member who had been denied tenure. The College moved to dismiss, contending that the court lacked jurisdiction under the federal statutes on grounds that the statutes were not intended by Congress to apply to church-operated schools. The College also alleged that application of these statutes to the College would violate the College's First Amendment rights. The District Court agreed with the College's contentions to the extent of finding insufficient evidence of a clear, affirmative Congressional intention that church-affiliated schools were to be included within the jurisdiction of the

RACE OR SEX DISCRIMINATION

Equal Pay Act and the Age Discrimination in Employment Act. But it did not agree with the College's claim with respect to Title VII, which it saw as clearly intended to reach religiously affiliated educational institutions, and it saw no violation of the Religion Clauses in applying the statute in this case. The College's motion (which the court construed as a motion for summary judgment) was therefore denied.

Mount St. Mary's College is located in Emmitsburg, Maryland, where it was established late in the 18th Century by a priest who had fled from the French Revolution. The College dates its founding from 1808, although the first state charter was not received until 1830. The College was very small throughout the 19th Century and well into the 20th, but grew rapidly after World War II. The first lay president was appointed in 1971. The College became coeducational in 1972 when its sister institution, St. Joseph College, was forced to close. In 1980 enrollment stood at about 1400 students.

The court noted that the College's objectives are "to provide a liberal arts education and a Catholic experience for its students." Fifteen semester hours in philosophy, ethics, and theology are required for graduation. Students are encouraged to attend regular worship services. Approximately 90% of the students and 80% of the faculty are Catholic. In 1978 out of a full-time faculty of 76, twenty-one were priests and one was a nun. Since its founding the College has viewed the appointment of qualified priests to the faculty as essential not only to teach theology courses, but also to "provide a spiritual dimension to the College consistent with its history, tradition and mission."

In Ritter the plaintiff, a fifty-seven year old Catholic and a former lay member of the faculty in the Department of Education, brought suit against the College, alleging sex and age discrimination in the College's denial of tenure and the subsequent non-renewal of her contract. In 1978 the plaintiff was considered for tenure along with four other faculty members, one of whom was a priest. Only the priest, who held appointment in theology and was subsequently appointed Vice President of the College, was granted tenure at the time. In December 1978 the plaintiff was notified by the President of the College that her tenure had been denied, and in March, 1979 she accepted a one-year terminal contract. Her suit, filed in March, 1980, alleged that in denying her tenure the College had discriminated against her on the basis of sex, as proscribed in Title VII of the Civil Rights Act and the Equal Pay Act, and on the basis of age, as proscribed in the Age Discrimination in Employment Act.

The College responded by contending that the District Court lacked jurisdiction in the case, on the grounds that Title VII, the Equal Pay Act, and the Age Discrimination Act "do not express a clear, affirmative intention to include within their scope religious, non-profit educational institutions such as the College." Furthermore, the College argued, even assuming arguendo that the statutes express such an intention, the application of the statutes to the College would involve an infringement of the College's rights under the First Amendment so as to prohibit the Court from considering the plaintiff's claims.

The point of departure for the court's determination of its jurisdiction was the methodology followed by the Supreme Court in Catholic Bishop, which had held that church-operated schools were not subject to the National Labor Relations Act. The court sought to employ the same methodology in determining whether or not Congress had demonstrated a clear and affirmative intent to include church-operated schools within the jurisdiction of the statutes under which the plaintiff's action was presented. The court found what it called irrefutable evidence of such an intent in the case of Title VII, but inadequate evidence in the case of the Equal Pay Act and the Age Discrimination Act.

The court followed common judicial precedent in holding that "Congress has shown a clear affirmative intention to include religiously affiliated schools within the scope of Title VII." Having determined the applicability of the statute, the court turned (in accordance with the Catholic Bishop methodology) to the question whether application of the statute in this case would violate the guarantees of the Religion Clauses.

The College saw the civil action as potentially infringing its right to give preference to priests in its faculty personnel policies. The College contended that its rights of religious free exercise would be unconstitutionally burdened by the court's review of its decison to grant tenure to a priest instead of to the lay plaintiff. The College viewed the suit as endangering "the tenure policies of the College as they may be influenced by consideration of clergymen eligible for tenure" and its policies on faculty salaries which were affected by its giving preference to clergy in faculty appointments.

The court viewed the issue more narrowly, however. The court thought that there might be some merit in the College's contention if the case involved a decision to grant tenure to a priest instead of a lay person. In that case, said the court, questioning the institutional policy or decision in a court of law might result in excessive entanglement, because it might (in the language of Catholic Bishop) "necessarily involve inquiry into the good faith of the position asserted by the clergy-administrators and its relationship to the school's religious mission." However, the court found nothing in the record to indicate that such was the case in this instance. The plaintiff strenuously argued that she was not challenging the College's decision to grant tenure to a priest instead of to her. She was not competing with a priest for the same position, she contended, nor was there any announced limitation on the number of tenured faculty position at the time.

The court declared, "Were this a case where a priest was granted tenure instead of a lay person because of the College's religious policy of promoting priests, such a decision could well be shielded from judicial scrutiny by the

192

First Amendment." But the court found nothing in the record to support the contention that there was any limitation on the number of faculty who could be granted tenure, so as to place a lay candidate in education in competition with a clergy candidate in theology for a tenured position.

The court also noted the Findings of Fact in <u>Roemer v. Board of Public Works of Maryland</u> (in which Mount St. Mary's College had been declared eligible for non-categorical state aid), which had indicated that "apart from the Theology Department, religion plays no part in tenure decisions" at the college. But if this is true, said the court, we fail "to see how the application of Title VII to this case would violate the first amendment."

The court's ruling denied that part of the plaintiff's action which was based on the Equal Pay and Age Discrimination Acts. The issue then depended on a determination (through a judicial hearing, rather than in a jury trial) of actual sex discrimination in the decision of the College to deny tenure to the plaintiff. The plaintiff's only ground of action then became a showing of actual sex discrimination. The court held that the religious character and purposes of the College did not shield it from an inquiry as to whether or not such discrimination had in fact occurred.

Russell v. Belmont College (1982)

A closely related case is <u>Russell v. Belmont College</u>, 554 F.Supp. 667 (1982), in which a district court in Nashville addressed the question of the applicability of the Fair Labor Standards Act and its amendment, the Equal Pay Act, to a church-controlled educational institution. Plaintiff, an assistant professor, brought action under Title VII and the Equal Pay Act, alleging discriminatory discharge and discriminatory treatment on the basis of sex in the compensation, terms, conditions and privileges of her employment. Belmont College moved for summary judgment, on the grounds that Congress did not intend the Equal Pay

Act to be applied to church-related educational institutions, and that application of the provisions of the Act would infringe the Free Exercise rights of the college. The District Court denied the motion, finding that Congress clearly intended the statute to apply to religiously affiliated schools, and seeing no merit in the college's claim that such application would violate the Religion Clauses.

The Tennessee court took note of the opinion of the Maryland court in Mount St. Mary that Congress had not demonstrated a clear, affirmative intention to include religiously affiliated schools within the scope of the Equal Pay Act. But it disagreed with the analysis presented in the Maryland opinion, acknowledging that only the Supreme Court could arbitrate the difference between the two courts.

The Belmont court was governed, it said, "by decades of judicial precedents interpreting the Fair Labor Standards Act of 1938" (the original statute governing the Equal Pay Act) as applying to religious and educational employers as well as to enterprises engaged in commerce. The court noted that the minimum wage requirements of the FLSA, for example, apply to all employers, and exemptions are only narrowly construed. The Equal Pay Act merely places new civil rights requirements on employers who were already subject to the minimum wage law. The court emphasized the declaration of the U.S. Supreme Court in Tennessee Coal Co. v. Muscoda Local, 321 U.S. 590 (1944), that the FLSA is "remedial and humanitarian in purpose" and that such a statute "must not be interpreted in a narrow, grudging manner."

Furthermore, the court contended, the interpretation under which it construed the statute as applicable to Belmont College involves no violation of the U.S. Constitution. The only constitutional question possibly posed by the application of the Equal Pay Act to Belmont College is the extremely narrow one "whether the First Amendment permits a church-controlled institution, . . . having employed a lay female teacher, to discriminatorily compensate its employees on the basis of sex." In order to justify its claim to such a constitutional guarantee, the college would need to show that "it is a sincerely held belief of the Baptist faith to discriminate on the basis of sex in the compensation of its employees." The College, the court said, has presented no such evidence.

The court tended to view the college's claim concerning a Free Exercise violation as too vague to be taken seriously. The college, said the court, failed to support its claim to a blanket Free Exercise exemption by specifying a reason for such exemption which was "related to the Baptist faith." The court could not "divine any reason that exercise of Belmont's religious belief will be threatened or hampered if required to pay its employees doing equal work equal pay regardless of sex."

In any case, said the court, the government has a compelling interest which would justify burdening the college's Free Exercise right to the extent required by the Equal Pay Act. The Equal Pay Act, it said, establishes a national policy of equal compensation for equal work, regardless of sex. There is, therefore, a compelling governmental interest which would "justify a burden, in this case minimum at best, to impose on Belmont College's exercise of religious beliefs the demands of the Equal Pay Act."

E.E.O.C. v Pacific Press Pub. Ass'n (1982)

A similar decision was reached by the Ninth Circuit in the case of a religiously affiliated publishing house in E.E.O.C. v Pacific Press Pub. Ass'n, 676 F.2d 1272 (9th Cir. 1982). The EEOC brought an employment suit against Pacific Press Publishing Association on behalf of a female employee, an editorial secretary. Upon determining that the employee was involved in bringing such suit, the General Conference of Seventh-Day Adventists, with which the Press was affiliated, passed a resolution recommending termination of the employee, on the grounds of her failure to adhere to Biblical teaching prohibiting lawsuits against the church and her unresponsiveness to spiritual counsel. Pursuant to this recommendation, the Press dismissed her.

The District Court found that the Press had violated Title VII in that it had exercised sex discrimination in denying the female employee monetary allowances paid to similarly situated male employees, and had terminated her employment in retaliation for participating in proceedings under the Civil Rights Act. The lower court decision was upheld by the Ninth Circuit Court of Appeals, which asserted that Congress clearly intended to protect employees of religious institutions under Title VII, and that enforcement of Title VII does not infringe religious freedom under the facts of this case.

In its opinion the court declared that, "Every court that has considered Title VII's applicability to religious employers has concluded that Congress intended to prohibit religious organizations from discriminating among their employees on the basis of race, color, sex, or national origin." Pacific Press argued, relying on McClure and Catholic Bishop, that the employment of the plaintiff was outside the application of Title VII, but the Court took the view that reliance on these precedents was misplaced. The employee in question is by no stretch of language a minister as in McClure, said the court, and the examination of the alleged discrimination involves no ongoing entanglement such as was involved in Catholic Bishop. The court rejected Pacific Press's "sweeping position that all employees at a sectarian publishing house are immune from EEOC scrutiny."

Nor did the court agree that requiring the press to refrain from discriminating against this employee infringes on its Free Exercise rights. The court observed that the Seventh-Day Adventist Church proclaims that it does not believe in discriminating against women and minority groups; hence enforcement of Title VII's equal pay provision cannot conflict with sincerely held religious beliefs of a Seventh-Day Adventist agency. The court took essentially the same view of the potential violation of the Establishment and Free Exercise Clauses that had been taken by the Fifth

Circuit in Mississippi College. Any governmental intrusion in ecclesiastical decisions which attended either circumstance was viewed by the respective courts as "acceptably limited both in scope and effect."

Bob Jones University v. United States, (1983)

In Bob Jones University v. United States, 461 U.S. 367 (1983), the U.S. Supreme Court upheld an Internal Revenue Service ruling, which denied tax-exempt status to a pervasively religious university on grounds of racially discriminatory policies and practices of the university. The Court determined that whatever Free Exercise right the university had with respect to its religious reasons for its policies prohibiting interracial dating or marriage were limited by a "compelling governmental interest" in protecting individuals from all forms of racial discrimination, even those forms which might arise from sincerely held religious beliefs. The Court's opinion declared that,

> The Government's fundamental, overriding interest in eradicating racial discrimination in education substantially outweighs whatever burden denial of tax benefits places on [the university's] exercise of their religious beliefs. Petitioners' asserted interests cannot be accomodated with that compelling governmental interest, and no less restrictive means are available to achieve the governmental interest.

In 1970 the Internal Revenue Service revised its interpretation of Section 501(c)(3) of the Internal Revenue Code concerning the granting of tax-exempt status to corporations organized for religious, charitable, or educational purposes. Prior to that time the IRS had granted tax exempt status to independent schools independent of racial admissions policies. In 1971 the IRS, responding to an injunction against it issued by a Mississippi court, promulgated Revenue Ruling 71-447, which stated:

RACE OR SEX DISCRIMINATION

Both the courts and the Internal Revenue Service have long recognized that the statutory requirement of being 'organized and operated exclusively for religious, charitable, . . . or educational purposes' was intended to express the basic common law concept [of 'charity] . . . All charitable trusts, educational or otherwise, are subject to the requirement that the purpose of the trust may not be illegal or contrary to public policy.

Based on "the national policy to discourage racial discrimination," the IRS then ruled that "a [private] school not having a racially nondiscriminatory policy as to students is not 'charitable' within the common law concepts reflected in" the Internal Revenue Code. In July 1970 the IRS announced that it could "no longer legally justify allowing tax-exempt status to private schools which practice racial discrimination" and that it could not "treat gifts to such schools as charitable contributions for income tax purposes." The term "racially nondiscriminating policy as to students" was defined to mean that "the school admits the students of any race to all the rights, privileges, programs, and activities generally accorded or made available to students at that school and that the school does not discriminate on the basis of race in administration of its educational policies, admission policies, scholarship and loan programs, and athletic and other school-administered programs." The IRS notified all private schools of its new standard by letter dated November 30, 1970, and announced its intention to deny tax-exempt status to private schools practicing racial discrimination.

Bob Jones University, located in Greenville, South Carolina, is a nonprofit corporation whose purpose is "to conduct an institution of learning . . . giving special emphasis to the Christian religion and the ethics revealed in the Holy Scriptures." The corporation conducts educational programs from kindergarten through graduate school, enrolling some 4,000 students at the post-secondary level. The institution has no formal affiliation with any religious denomination, but it is pervasively religious. The Supreme Court opinion described it as "both a religious and

198

educational institution." Its teachers are required to be "devout Christians," and entering students are "screened as to their religious beliefs." Student conduct is closely regulated by standards promulgated by University authorities.

The sponsors of the University, the Court noted, "genuinely believe that the Bible forbids interracial dating and marriage." Prior to 1971 Negroes were not admitted as students, but in the 1970's provision was made for admitting Negroes under certain conditions. At the time of the Supreme Court decision the University continued to deny admission to applicants engaged in an interracial marriage or known to advocate interracial marriage or dating. A student disciplinary rule expicitly prohibited interracial dating.

From 1971 until 1978 the University was involved in extended litigation with the IRS concerning its tax-exempt status. In 1978 the U.S. District Court for the District of South Carolina held that revocation of the University's tax-exempt status exceeded the delegated powers of the IRS, was improper under the IRS rulings and procedures, and violated the University's rights under the Religion Clauses of the First Amendment. In 1980 the Court of Appeals for the Fourth District reversed, upholding the IRS's interpretation of charitable trust law.

The Supreme Court decision in the case was combined with its review of Goldsboro Christian Schools v. United States, which raised essentially the same issues.[4] The Supreme Court, with only Justice Rehnquist dissenting, affirmed both of the appellate decisions below, declaring that "neither petitioner qualifies as a tax-exempt organization under Sect. 501(c)(3)."

The opinion of the Court, which was delivered by Chief Justice Burger, declared,

It would be wholly incompatible with the concepts underlying tax exemption to grant tax-exempt status to

199

racially discriminatory private educational entities.
Whatever may be the rationale for such private schools'
policies, racial discrimination in education is contrary to
public policy. Racially discriminatory educational
institutions cannot be viewed as conferring a public
benefit within the . . . 'charitable' concept or within
the congressional intent underlying Sect. 501(c)(3).

The University contended that, even if the IRS policy is
valid as to nonreligious independent schools, it cannot
constitutionally be applied to schools that engage in racial
discrimination on the basis of sincerely held religious
beliefs. This contention, said the Court, presented claims
concerning the Free Exercise Clause "not heretofore
considered by this Court in precisely this context." The
Court had no difficulty in treating the claims, however.

The Court quickly reaffirmed its long-standing principle
that the Free Exercise Clause constitutes an "absolute
prohibition" against any governmental regulation of religious
beliefs. The Court made no attempt to judge the beliefs of
appellants respecting the religious basis of their racial
policies, and thought any governmental regulation of such
belief would be entirely improper. Moreover, the Court
stated, the Free Exercise Clause provides substantial
protection for lawful conduct grounded in religious belief,
but it does not protect unlawful conduct.

The Supreme Court has never interpreted the Free
Exercise Clause to mean that all burdens on religion are
unconstitutional. In Bob Jones the Court cited its 1982
pronouncement in United States v. Lee, 455 U.S. 252, 257-
258 (1982): "Not all burdens on religion are unconstitutional
. . . The state may justify a limitation on religious liberty
by showing that it is essential to accomplish an overriding
governmental interest." Such an interest may induce the
Court "to allow even regulations prohibiting religiously based
conduct." There is no simple judicial formula for
determination of the circumstances under which a
"compelling governmental interest" will override a Free
Exercise right, but the Bob Jones decision can leave no

doubt that a religiously affiliated college or university may not carry on any form of discrimination based on race without sacrificing its eligibility for federal tax exemption of for other forms of federal financial assistance.

In weighing the burden on Free Exercise against some public benefit or governmental interest, the Court has been generally unwilling to require action which would directly burden the religious practice when the state's interest might be achieved by accomodating religion.[5] In the <u>Bob Jones</u> case, however, the Court saw no possibility of accomodating the religious beliefs and practices of petitioners within the scope of the compelling governmental interest, nor did it find any "less restrictive means" for achieving the governmental interest.

The Court held that the governmental interest in eradicating racial discrimination in education is compelling and easily "outweighs any burden denial of tax benefits might place on petitioners' exercise of their religious beliefs."[6] The entire Court was in agreement that there is a compelling national interest in eradicating racial disrimination and that this interest might at times override Free Exercise rights.

Justice Rehnquist, dissenting, and Justice Powell, concurring, both argued that it is Congress, however, not the IRS or the Court, that is the properly constituted authority for specifying what is the compelling governmental interest with respect to racial discrimination, and voiced deep misgivings about the tendency of the Court's decision to assume functions reserved by the Constitution to Congress. As Rehnquist put it:

> I have no disagreement with the Court's finding that there is a strong national policy in this country opposed to racial discrimination. I agree with the Court that Congress has the power to further this policy by denying Sect. 501(c)(3) status to organizations that practice racial discrimination. (Footnote: I agree with the Court that such a requirement would not infringe on

petitioners' First Amendment rights.) But as of yet Congress has failed to do so. Whatever the reasons for the failure, this Court should not legislate for Congress."

Gay Rights Coalition of Georgetown Law Center v. Georgetown University (1987)

In Gay Rights Coalition of Georgetown Law Center v. Georgetown University, 536 A.2D 1 (D.C. App. 1987), the Court of Appeals of the District of Columbia required a Catholic university to grant two student homosexual groups equal access to certain university facilities and services, without regard for the sexual orientation of such groups, even though the university, as a Catholic institution, is religiously and morally opposed to homosexual practices and life-styles. The court refused to accept the University's claim that its Free Exercise right exempted it from compliance with a District of Columbia statute proscribing discrimination on the basis of sexual orientation.

The suit of the Gay Rights Coalition was brought against the University on the basis of the District of Columbia Human Rights Act, which provides that,

> It is an unlawful discriminatory practice ... for an educational institution: (1) To deny, restrict, or to abridge or condition the use of, or access to, any of its facilities and services to any person otherwise qualified, wholly or partially, for a discriminatory reason, based upon the race, color, religion, national origin, sex, age, marital status, personal appearance, sexual orientation, family responsibilities, political affiliation, source of income, or physical handicap of any individual.

The statute defines "sexual orientation" as meaning "male or female homosexuality, heterosexuality and bisexuality, by preference or practice." The prohibition of discrimination on the basis of sexual orientation in the District of Columbia was originally enacted as a regulation in 1973, and was elevated to a statutory footing in 1977, when the District was granted Home Rule. The Court of Appeals accepted the view of the District of Columbia Council that eradicating discrimination on the basis of sexual orientation, "along with all other forms of discrimination unrelated to individual merit," was essential to eliminating "recurrent political injustice and build[ing] a society which encourages and expects the full contribution of every member of the community in all their diversity and potential."

In 1977 a group of homosexual students of Georgetown University formed a group called Gay People of Georgetown University (GPGU), whose purposes included the following:

1. To provide an atmosphere in which gay people can develop a sense of pride, self-worth, awareness, and community.
2. To provide information and encourage understanding and dialogue between gay and non-gay people.
3. To provide a forum for the development of responsible sexual ethics consonant with one's personal beliefs.
4. To establish a program of activities which reflect the above purposes.

In the academic year 1978-79 GPGU obtained a Student Government Charter from the Student Activities Commission (SAC), with ratification by the Student Senate. Under Georgetown University policy, such recognition represented "the interest of the Student Government and the entire student body." It allowed the group to use University facilities for its activities, to apply for lecture fund privileges, to receive financial counsel from the SAC comptroller, to use campus advertising, and to petition to receive assistance from Student Government.

The group was unsuccessful, however, in its repeated attempts to obtain recognition at the second and third tiers of support available to Georgetown University student groups. At the second tier, called "University Recognition," certain additional privileges are granted, viz.: use of a mailbox in the SAC office, use of the Computer Label Service and mailing services available to student groups, and the opportunity to apply for institutional funding. The third tier of support, called "University Funding," may be sought only by groups which have already obtained "University Recognition," although there is no guarantee that direct financial support will be granted to those groups which apply.

In granting the initial charter to GPGU, the Student Activities Commission emphasized that its purpose was to "provide a forum where all students of Georgetown may come to understand the concerns of gay students." In a public statement the SAC declared, however, "The recommendation for a charter does not mean that SAC is making any statement on the rightness or wrongness of homosexuality or is implying that the University is making such a statement."

University officials in the Student Affairs area sought to assure the gay students access to University facilities and services without endorsing the GPGU as an "official activity of its Student Affairs programs." In early 1979 an Associate Dean of Student Affairs informed the Student Government that the University would welcome, but not endorse the GPGU as an "official activity," and that the University would not contribute to the support of the organization by granting University funds, by providing subsidized office space, telephone services, office supplies, and equipment, or by granting authorized use of the name "Georgetown University." The ruling was appealed through several levels of the administration, finally reaching President Timothy J. Healy, S.J., and was upheld at all levels.

A similar chain of events occurred in the Georgetown University Law Center, where the Gay Rights Coalition had been formed in 1978-79. The group's application for University Recognition was denied on the basis of the University's action respecting the Gay People of Georgetown University. In a letter to the Dean of the Law Center in

RACE OR SEX DISCRIMINATION

May, 1980, President Healy explained, "The University's decision is not a reflection on or a judgment of the personal choices of its individual members, but rather reflects a judgment of what is appropriate for Georgetown as an institution."

The two gay groups brought suit against the University, alleging that the denial of "University Recognition," together with the increased access to facilities and services which that status entails, violated the Human Rights Act of the District of Columbia. Georgetown presented two defenses: First, that the denial of "University Recognition" was not an act of discrimination on the basis of sexual orientation; Second, that even if its actions had been taken on the basis of sexual orientation, they were protected by the Free Exercise Clause of the First Amendment.

The Superior Court ruled that the University's actions were, in fact, discriminatory on the basis of sexual orientation, but that they were protected by the Free Exercise Clause of the First Amendment. On appeal the Court of Appeals upheld the finding that discrimination had occurred, but reversed the trial court's holding that the D.C. statute violated the University's Free Exercise rights.

Georgetown University's status as a Roman Catholic university was fully acknowledged by the court. Its Catholic philosophy and Jesuit relationship were viewed by the court as entirely compatible with its professed intention of providing "a secular education, albeit one that is informed by Christian values." The openness of the University and its acceptance of a secular educational role were seen as fully possible without abandoning the religious heritage and present relationship of the institution. The court rejected the student groups' contention that the University's acceptance of certain federal funding on condition that it not be used "for religious worship or a sectarian activity," operates as a waiver of its right to raise a Free Exercise defense. The court had no doubt that the status of the university as a religiously affiliated institution allowed it to rely on a Free Exercise right against any action of government forcing it to "embrace a repugnant philosophy."

The court found, however, that the University could be expected to comply with the D.C. statute without "endorsing" homosexuality, contrary to its conscience. The burden of the court's opinion was to construe the statute in a manner which would permit its constitutionality to be upheld. "Interpreting the Human Rights Act so as to require Georgetown to 'endorse' the student groups," the court held, "would be to thrust the statute across the constitutional boundaries set by the Free Speech Clause and also, where sincere religious objections are raised, the free Exercise Clause." But such an interpretation, said the court, is not required.

The court distinguished between a statutory requirement of equality of treatment with respect to facilities and services without regard to sexual orientation, on the one hand, and "university recognition" in the sense of "endorsement" of the values and beliefs of the student groups, on the other. It is only the former, said the court, and not the latter that is required by the D.C. statute. The court construed the statute as "requir[ing] Georgetown to equally distribute, without regard to sexual orientation, the tangible benefits" involved in "University Recognition." It did not understand the statute to require the University to "endorse" a practice or life-style which it finds morally offensive.

Both University policy and the petition of the gay rights groups had combined the "endorsement" and the "tangible benefits" aspects of "University recognition." The University saw no conflict with its own principles in the granting of "student body endorsement" status to the gay rights groups. Under University policy, however, the "University Recognition" status sought by the groups was construed to involve a determination by the University that the student organization so recognized was "successful in aiding the University's educational mission in the tradition established by its founders." The University took the view that it was prevented by its Catholic philosophy and relationship from allowing gay rights groups to apply for University funding or subsidies and to use the name "Georgetown University."

The court's opinion, however, called for severing this "artificial connection" between what it regarded as two distinct issues, the issue of "endorsement," which it agreed could not be compelled by government, and the issue of "equal treatment," which it thought was the only concern of the Human Rights Act. The statute, the court determined, did not require the University to endorse homosexual orientation, but only to allow homosexual students access to certain University facilities and services and to other "tangible benefits of recognition." The court argued that since no "endorsement" of homosexual orientation was implied by the "recognition" required by the statute, the statute did not infringe the university's Free Exercise right.

Although the court did not agree with the University's claim that "recognition" was tantamount to "endorsement," it was prepared to grant that "the enforcement of the Human Rights Act with regard to the tangible benefits imposes a burden on Georgetown's religious practice sufficient for it to invoke the Free Exercise Clause." The court then turned to determining whether or not there was an "overriding governmental interest in the eradication of sexual orientation discrimination," which would outweigh the burden on the University's Free Exercise right.

The court concluded that "the Council of the District of Columbia acted on the most pressing of human needs when incorporating into the Human Rights Act its view that discrimination based on sexual orientation is a grave evil that damages society as well as its immediate victims." The court agreed that "the eradication of sexual orientation discrimination is a compelling governmental interest," which outweighs the small burden which enforcement of the Act might impose on the University's free exercise of religion. Hence the University's status as a religiously affiliated university does not exempt it from compliance with the statute. The court held:

> On statutory rather than on constitutional grounds, we affirm the trial court's conclusion that Georgetown need not grant 'University Recognition' to - - and thereby endorse - - the student groups. The Human Rights Act does, however, mandate that the student groups be given equal access to any additional 'facilities and services' triggered by that status. Georgetown's asserted free exercise defense does not overcome the Human Right's verdict that the tangible benefits be distributed without regard to sexual orientation.

On statutory rather than constitutional grounds, the Court of Appeals affirmed the trial court's holding that Georgetown University may not be required by law to grant the student groups "University Recognition," as that status is defined in the University's policies and criteria. But it reversed the trial court's ruling that the University's Free Exercise right relieves it of its obligation under the law to provide the tangible benefits associated with "University Recognition" without regard to sexual orientation.

Two judges dissented from this holding and would affirm the trial court's finding for Georgetown on constitutional grounds. Judge Nebeker, retired, expressed his opinion in the strongest terms:

> Today the court uses the state's power to force a religious body, contrary to its basic tenets, to provide services and facilities to those who advocate and proselytize abnormal and criminal sexual practices. . . . The homosexual orientation as defined by one's sexual practice at issue here has a stark inconsistency with established criminal law. . . . I find no factor favoring a state interest under the Act which can be balanced against Georgetown's rights. Indeed, there is reason to hold absolute Georgetown's first amendment rights. . .
> Surely this court's holding against Georgetown University raises first amendment issues warranting

closest review by the ultimate adjudicators of the meaning of these important provisions.

The basis of the Georgetown opinion is a District of Columbia statute, and the decision does not apply outside that jurisdiction. However, the court saw the D.C. legislation as "pioneering" in the area of discrimination on the basis of sexual orientation, and it compared "the mounting response to the problems gay people face" to "the local antidiscrimination measures, which paved the way for the Federal Civil Rights Act of 1964." A similar statute has been enacted by the State of Wisconsin, and many other states have executive orders prohibiting discrimination on the basis of sexual orientation in public employment.

The Georgetown case was concerned, of course, with student rights rather than employment discrimination. Presumably, however, the court's reasoning would be similar if it were presented with a case where Georgetown University (or some other religiously affiliated college) refused for religious reasons to hire a homosexual employee.

3. Summary

The process of judicial decision is typically one of balancing conflicting interests. The liability of independent and religiously affiliated colleges and universities in such an area as employment practice is not defined by a few abstract concepts or doctrinal generalizations, but through determination of the precise limits which should be placed on the action of one party by virtue of a legally specifiable duty owed to another party. Such determination must take into consideration the changing requirements of individual and social well being as these may be reflected in the developing law. The law seeks to combine consideration of the rights of independent and religiously affiliated institutions with consideration of their duties and responsibilities as agencies of educational, social, economic, and cultural benefit. The analysis of preferential hiring in religiously affiliated institutions of higher education, in other words, seeks to recognize both the autonomy and the accountability of such institutions.

In actions alleging employment discrimination on the basis of race, the courts have been strongly influenced by regard for what they have seen as a national interest in eradicating all forms of employment discrimination on the basis of race. The courts have also been guided by acceptance of a compelling state interest in removing all employment discrimination on the basis of sex. When these state interests come into conflict with religious tenets, the courts have generally judged that any burden placed on institutional Free Exercise rights by enforcement of civil rights or labor law is justified by the weight of the public interest.

The courts have been unwilling, on First Amendment grounds, to pass judgment on the legality of employment decisions of churches and religious organizations with respect to their clergy. Furthermore, courts have been willing to extend the protection of the church-clergy relationship to cover the relationship of seminaries and schools of divinity to their faculties and administrative officers, although not to other staff. However, the courts have explicitly refused to allow extension of the same protection to the relationship of religiously affiliated colleges and universities to their faculties.

Except for the instance of employment of clergy and clergy-like personnel, the reliance of religiously affiliated institutions of higher education in race or sex discrimination cases on a general exemption based of an institutional Free Exercise right under the First Amendment has not been successful. The U.S. Supreme Court's Free Exercise jurisprudence has developed mainly in cases involving the rights of individuals. The Court recognizes a right of Free Exercise for institutions, but it tends to favor individual rights to protection from employment discrimination on the basis of race or sex ahead of an institutional right of Free Exercise. The courts have refused to become engaged in substantive questions of the sincerity or philosophical-ethical justifiability of religiously based institutional policies on racial or sexual relationships, and they continue to regard the constitutional protection of beliefs, whatever their nature, as absolute and unconditional. But the courts have consistently been willing to burden the Free Exercise rights of institutions when the compelling state interest in eradicating racial or sex discrimination is in question.

The Supreme Court decision in <u>Catholic Bishop</u> is a somewhat different case, since it was based on statutory rather than constitutional interpretation. But the institutional exemption from government regulation of employment relationships allowed in that case was limited to the National Labor Relations Act and to parochial elementary and secondary school systems. Lower courts and regulatory agencies have not permitted extension of the same exemption to institutions of higher education, although the precedents in this area are not well established. And lower courts have generally read the legislative history of the Fair Labor Standards and Equal Pay Acts as requiring the application of these acts to religiously affiliated educational institutions as employers.

Courts generally respect the integrity of internal procedures by which colleges and universities reach faculty personnel decisions of various kinds. However, courts are prepared to become involved in the protection of individual rights where there is prima facie evidence that internal procedures fail to protect individuals in their civil rights. Judicial procedures respecting the burdens of proof carried by the individual and the institution, respectively, in such cases are well established.

NOTES TO CHAPTER SIX

1. Refusal to bargain is often the only way an employer can obtain judicial review of a bargaining unit determination by the NLRB. The Board has wide discretion in determining a bargaining unit; the Board need not select the most appropriate unit; any unit that is an appropriate one will do,

even if there are several possible units. Courts are generally reluctant to disturb NLRB determinations, following the admonishing of the Supreme Court in Packard Motor Car Co., 330 U.S. 485, 491 (1947): The determination of an appropriate unit "involves of necessity a large measure of informed discretion, and the decision of the Board, if not final, is rarely to be disturbed."

2. Watson v. Jones, 13 Wall. 679, 80 U.S. 679 (1871); Gonzalez v. Roman Catholic Archbishop, 280 U.S. 1 (1929); Kedroff v St. Nicholas Cathedral, 344 U.S. 94 (1952); Presbyterian Church in United States v. Mary Elizabeth Blue Hull Memorial Presbyterian Church, 393 U.S. 440 (1969).

3. Cf. Rayburn v. General Conference of Seventh-Day Adventists, 772 F. 2d 1164, Fourth Circuit (1985).

4. Goldsboro Christian Schools offers programs from kindergarten through the twelfth grade. The Schools are closely related to the Second Baptist Church of Goldsboro, North Carolina, although separately incorporated.

5. Cf. Sherbert v. Verner, 374 U.S. 398 (1963).

6. In a footnote the Court emphasized: "We deal here only with religious schools - - not with churches or other purely religious organizations; here the governmental interest is in denying public support to racial discrimination in education" (emphasis in original). The remark suggests the Court's concept of a hierarchy of religious and religiously affiliated institutions, of which some are "purely religious" and others are religious in part, such that their varying degrees of religiousness would require or permit varying forms of regulation and/or exemption. Presumably, religiously affiliated colleges and universities are farther down in the hierarchy than parochical elementary and secondary schools or theological schools, and are thus less likely to be exempted from the general nondiscrimination requirements of public law.

CHAPTER SEVEN

INSTITUTIONAL AUTONOMY AND
THE EXERCISE OF RELIGIOUS PREFERENCE

The theory under which American law recognizes the autonomy of religiously affiliated colleges and universities in the area of employment decisions is not fully systematic. The case law is relatively undeveloped, since the number of civil actions specifically addressed to the question remains small, despite an increase of such actions in the last fifteen years. On the other hand, the actions of legislatures are affected by the compromises inherent in the political process and by the limitations of legislative resources for close legal analysis. The law continues to exhibit a tendency to define the scope of the regulatory authority of government over religious and religiously affiliated organizations on an ad hoc and pragmatic basis, without the benefit of a coherent theory of the autonomy of such institutions.

Nevertheless, some trends can be identified. In two recent cases a virtually unanimous Court took action which significantly narrowed the autonomy of independent colleges and universities (in <u>Grove City v. Bell</u>, 1984) and significantly broadened the autonomy of churches (in <u>Corp. of Presiding Bishop v. Amos</u>, 1987). In a series of lower court cases the judicial system has exhibited a definite preference for reaching decisions on religious discrimination in higher education employment, not by applying broad exemptions based on institutional autonomy or religious affiliation, but by applying precedents which treat colleges and universities equally with other employers.

1.   The Scope of Federal Regulation

<u>Grove City College v. Bell</u> (1984)

In <u>Grove City College v. Bell</u>, 465 U.S. 555 (1984), the U.S. Supreme Court ruled that an independent college was subject, as a recipient of federal financial assistance, to the provisions of Title IX prohibiting sex discrimination, even

213

though the institution did not receive any direct federal financial assistance. The fact that some of the college's students received federal aid was deemed sufficient for a determination that the college was a recipient of federal financial assistance under the meaning of federal law. The Court declared, however, that the aid received by Grove City College did not trigger institution-wide coverage of federal statutes and regulation, but that such coverage was limited to the institutional program actually receiving aid (in this case the student financial aid program).

In 1976 the Department of Education (then organized as the Office of Education under the Department of Health, Education, and Welfare) sought to obtain from Grove City College (as well as from all other American colleges and universities) the Assurance of Compliance which the Department requires in order to document that recipients of federal financial assistance are satisfying the nondiscrimination requirements of federal law. The Assurance required the college to agree to

> comply, to the extent applicable to it, with Title IX . .
> . and all applicable requirements imposed by or pursuant
> to the Department's regulation . . . to the end that . .
> . no person in the United States shall be . . . subjected
> to discrimination under any education program or
> activity for which [it] receives or benefits from federal
> financial assistance from the Department.

The Department's requirement of an Assurance of Compliance from Grove City College was based on the fact that a number of the college's students had received federal financial assistance under the Basic Educational Opportunity Grants (BEOG) Program and the Guaranteed Student Loans (GSL) Program. The college refused to comply, contending that students' receipt of financial aid under these programs did not make the college a recipient of federal financial assistance and thereby cause it to be subject to the regulations of Title IX. The college also objected to the requirement that it assure its compliance not only with existing law and regulations, but also with future amendments and interpretations thereof.

Following the college's refusal to submit the required Assurance of Compliance, the Department of Education initiated administrative proceedings, which resulted in an order terminating all financial assistance until the college executed the Assurance and satisfied the Department that it was in compliance with the regulations. Suit was brought against the Department by the college and four students whose financial aid had been cut off. The issue was pursued in Federal District Court and in the Court of Appeals for the Third District, and eventually reached the U.S. Supreme Court.

In refusing to execute the Assurance the college did not wish to take issue with the nondiscrimination purposes of federal law, nor to protect itself in any discriminatory practices. There were no findings of fact at any point in these judicial proceedings which in any way suggested that the college was engaged, or wished to engage, in any form of discrimination on the basis of sex. On the contrary, the college has a long and enviable record of respect for individual freedom and civil rights. In defending its refusal to execute the Assurance of Compliance the college sought to focus on the jurisdictional question of whether, given its institutional policy of accepting no public funds, it was subject to any form of governmental regulation.

Grove City College is an independent college of liberal arts, located in western Pennsylvania, just north of Pittsburgh. The college is related to the United Presbyterian Church. The college describes itself as a private institution, "guided by deeply held moral, religious, and political beliefs, which endeavors to maintain both a Christian world-view and a freedom philosophy." In the initial judicial proceeding at the U.S. District Court for the Western District of Pennsylvania, Pres. Charles S. Mackenzie stated that those who guide the affairs of Grove City College believe that freedom and Christian faith are interelated and interdependent. He continued, quoting from an official institutional document:

> Grove City College exhibits its own independence and freedom by rejecting funding from any goverment agency. Though charges to its 2200 students are among the lowest of any quality college in America, for many years the college has operated 'in the black' and has no indebtedness. Efficiency and productivity are carefully balanced with a high academic program. Grove City's total charges are about $2,000 lower than average charges of other private four-year colleges. This is accomplished without government funding, which is avoided to preserve the college's independence and freedom.

The college has a long history of independence, which is carried out in financial affairs as well as in educational programs. All buildings and major capital improvements have been funded from private monies, and operating income is drawn substantially from gifts, endowment, and student fees. The college has historically maintained a very low level of indebtedness, even on income-generating facilities like dormitories and the student union, with the result that it has been able to partially subsidize the cost of educational programs from non-tuition revenues.

Only a relatively small proportion of Grove City students have been recipients of federal student aid. Of some 2,200 students, approximately 140 (approximately 6%) were eligible in 1979 for Basic Educational Opportunity Grants, and 342 students (about 15%) had secured loans from private lending institutions under the Guaranteed Student Loan program. The college has declined to participate in the so-called "campus-based programs" of student financial aid, such as the Supplemental Educational Opportunity Grants Program (SEOG), the College Work-Study Program, or the National Direct Student Loan Program, participation in which would have involved the college in direct administration of the aid. Under each of these programs federal funds are paid directly to the institution for dispersal to students judged to be eligible.

The college assists students to apply for any federal financial assistance for which they might qualify. This assistance, as President Mackenzie testified, is limited to providing information to students and, "upon the request of the student and at the student's sole discretion," providing certain financial information and/or a certification of the student's enrollment "to any organization, private or governmental, which requires information about students who request the financial assistance necessary to complete their educations." Although some Grove City College students received federal aid under the BEOG and SDL programs, they received these funds directly from the federal government, and the college's involvement was entirely limited to providing information to the federal agency concerning the student's enrollment status. These facts concerning the college's involvement in the BEOG program were not disputed in the record.

The U.S. District Court in Pittsburgh held:

1) That the Basic Educational Opportunity Grant (BEOG) program in which Grove City College students participate is Federal assistance to the college and brings it within the provisions of Title IX.

2) That the Guaranteed Student Loan (GSL) program is exempted specifically by the statutory language from coverage under Title IX and is hence not considered by this court to be Federal financial assistance to the college.

3) That HEW may not lawfully demand that the college execute the Assurance of Compliance, because said form presently improperly requires the college to abide by implementing regulations of the Department which exceed the authority granted to it by Congress. (The court did not hold, however, that the college is totally exempted from executing a proper Assurance under all circumstances.)

4)   That HEW, under no circumstances, can use the sanction of terminating a student's Federal financial assistance (BEOG, for example) because of failure of the college to comply with Title IX or its implementing regulations unless and until there is a showing of actual sex discrimination involving student programs at the college.

On appeal the Third Circuit Court of Appeals in Philadelphia reversed the District Court decision. Grove City then appealed the appellate decision to the U.S. Supreme Court. The issues presented to the U.S. Supreme Court in this case were the following: (1) Whether Title IX applies at all to Grove City College, which accepts no federal grants but enrolls students who receive federal grants that must be used for educational purposes; (2) If Title IX applies, whether its coverage is institution-wide or is limited to the specific program receiving aid; (3) Whether federal assistance to eligible students may be terminated solely because the college violates Department regulations by refusing to execute an Assurance of Compliance with Title IX; (4) Whether application of Title IX to Grove City College infringes the First Amendment rights of the college or of its students.

The Supreme Court's opinion was delivered by Justice Byron White. The Court was unanimous in holding that Grove City is a "recipient of federal financial assistance" under the language of Title IX and that it is required to issue a Certificate of Compliance. The Court was also unanimous in finding that application of Title IX to the college involves no infringement of its First Amendment rights. The Court was divided, however, on the question whether the coverage of Title IX is institution-wide or program-specific and on whether it is either appropriate or necessary for the Court to express an opinion on this matter in reaching its decision in this case.

The Court rejected the college's contention that Title IX coverage is foreclosed because federal funds are granted to the college's students rather than directly to one of the college's educational programs. It based this holding on "clear statutory language, powerful evidence of Congress' intent, and a longstanding and coherent administrative construction of the phrase 'receiving Federal financial assistance.'"

However, the Court took the view that the "education program or activity" of the college that is properly characterized as "receiving federal financial assistance" is not the entire college, but only the student financial aid program, to which federal funds are allocated. The opinion of the Court declared that receipt of BEOG's by some of Grove City's students does not trigger institution-wide coverage under Title IX, even if the federal funds eventually reach the general operating budget of the college. In purpose and effect, BEOG's represent federal financial assistance only to the financial aid program, said the Court, and it is that program that is subject to regulation under the nondiscrimination provisions of Title IX.

Justice John Paul Stevens contended, in his opinion concurring in the result, that a holding that the college is a recipient and is accordingly required to issue a Certificate of Compliance would have been sufficient to affirm the judgment under review. In adding a judgment on the scope of program coverage the Court, he said, is deciding an issue which is not in dispute. Furthermore, he contended, such a judgment would require evidence concerning which of the college's program in fact receive or benefit from federal financial assistance. Until the Court has information concerning how the benefits are allocated, he maintained, "it is inappropriate to give advice about an issue which is not before us."

In an opinion, dissenting in part, Justice Brennan presented an extended analysis of the statutory history to show that Congress intended the statute to be applied to the entire institution receiving federal assistance. Allowing Title IX coverage for the financial aid program but rejecting institution-wide coverage, he declared "may be superficially pleasing to those who are uncomfortable with federal

219

intrusion into private educational institutions, but it has no relationship to the statutory scheme enacted by Congress." He was joined in his opinion by Justice Marshall.

The Court viewed the Assurance of Compliance required by the Department as having a limited function. It is intended, on its face, to require recipients to provide assurance that "each education program or activity operated by . . . [them] which receives or benefits from Federal financial assistance" will be operated in compliance with the nondiscrimination requirements of the Title. Accordingly, the Court thought that an institution's refusal to execute the Assurance of Compliance would be sufficient ground for terminating federal assistance to the specific program for which such assurances were not given. The Court determined that under the language of the statute it could not sustain the college's contention that program termination required a finding of actual discrimination.

The Court gave only the briefest consideration to the college's contention that the First Amendment rights of the college and of its students were infringed by a law which makes the receipt of federal assistance conditional on the institution's compliance with nondiscrimination on the basis of sex. The Court disagreed with this contention:

> Congress is free to attach reasonable and unambiguous conditions to federal financial assistance that educational institutions are not obligated to accept. Grove City may terminate its participation in the BEOG program and thus avoid the requirements of [nondiscrimination]. Students affected by the Department's action may either take their BEOG's elsewhere or attend Grove City without federal financial assistance. Requiring Grove City to comply with Title XI's prohibition of discrimination as a condition for its continued eligibility to participate in the BEOG program infringes no First Amendment rights of the College or its students.

RELIGIOUS PREFERENCE

Following the Supreme Court decision Grove City College took further steps to protect its institutional autonomy from governmental regulation. The college obtained private funds to replace the BEOG (Pell Grants) program which had made it subject to the coverage of federal law, and discontinued its participation in that federal program. The cost of such replacement has been about $400,000 per year. The college has continued its participation in the GSL program, however, basing that participation on the District Court's finding (which was never overturned) that the GSL program did not provide a basis for federal claims of jurisdiction and accountability. In addition the college has incurred legal fees of another $400,000 in the course of this litigation.

Justice Powell wrote a reluctantly concurring opinion, in which Chief Justice Burger and Justice O'Connor joined, in which he recorded his view that the Grove City "case is an unedifying example of overzealousness on the part of the Federal Government." The Department of Education, he observed, has prevailed after taking "this small independent college, which it acknowledges has engaged in no discrimination whatever," through six years of litigation to establish the very narrow principle that receipt of BEOG's brings the college's financial aid office within the coverage of Title IX. "I cannot believe," he concluded, "that the Department will rejoice in its victory."

In a conference presentation sponsored in 1988 by the Center for Constitutional Studies, President Mackenzie viewed the Grove City decision in terms of the dialectics of autonomy and accountability in American higher education. He remarked,

> When I first went into education years ago, it seemed that universities, like churches, transcended, evaluated, judged public policy. But today universities more and more are becoming subservient and compliant to the compelling interest of public policy as defined by a coalition of special interest groups linked up to the bureaucracy. However, if universities become

221

instruments of state policy, they will do little for society in the years that lie ahead. They will lose what little objectivity they have left. They will find that the creativity and the vision needed to inspire and invigorate a society are stifled. Then the ideals of society, and eventually the noblest and most humane goals of government itself, will be frustrated. Only as universities are autonomous and free to fulfill their true character will government itself fulfill its most humane purposes.

The Supreme Court, however, saw no threat to the autonomy of an independent college in the action of the Department in requiring "reasonable" assurances that any program receiving federal financial assistance was in compliance with the nondiscrimination provisions of the law. If Grove City College, in its concern to preserve its autonomy in some more comprehensive meaning of the term, is unable to provide such assurances, then, said the Court, its choice of independence simply means that it cannot participate in any way in federal programs of student aid. Of course, the college has every right to make that choice. But in the Court's view, its choice in no way creates an abridgement of its rights under the First Amendment.

Subsequent to the Grove City decision, Congress enacted the Civil Rights Restoration Act of 1987, which changed the definition of "program" under Title IX (and three other statutes) and extended the coverage of civil rights legislation to include an entire college or university, "any part of which is extended Federal financial assistance." Under this extended definition a college's receipt of indirect federal assistance through a student financial aid program brings the entire college, in all its operations, within the scope of the Title IX prohibition against discrimination on the basis of sex, as well as of all other applicable federal regulations. Whether the Court would continue to see no abridgement of the college's First Amendment rights in that circumstance is an issue which would have to be tested in a new case.

2. Religious Preference in Church and College

King's Garden, Inc. v. FCC (1974)

In an early precedent the Court of Appeals of the D.C. Circuit refused to allow the exercise of religious preference in the employment of all personnel in a radio station owned and operated by a religious organization. In King's Garden, Inc. v. FCC, 498 F.2d 51 (D.C. Cir.), cert. denied, 419 U.S. 996 (1974), the court upheld a ruling by the Federal Communications Commission, which declared that under the Civil Rights Act religious tests were appropriate in the appointment of employees of religiously oriented radio station only in the case of "persons hired to espouse a particular religious philosophy over the air." The court concluded that a religious corporation holding a broadcasting license was not exempt from the general ban against employment discrimination on the basis of religion, noting that Congress had given "absolutely no indication that it wished to impose the [Title VII] exemption upon the FCC."

King's Garden is a non-profit, religious, inter-denominational organization engaged in a number of ministries, including operation of Radio Stations KBIQ-FM and KGDN in Edmonds, Washington. The stations are licensed by the Federal Communications Commission. In 1971 the FCC received a complaint alleging discriminatory hiring practices in the stations and requesting enforcement of the FCC rules prohibiting employment practices that discriminate on the basis of race, color, religion, national origin, or sex.

The complainant stated that in seeking employment at the stations as an announcer or newsman he was asked: "Are you a Christian?", "How do you know you are a Christian?", "Is your spouse a Christian?", and "Give a testimony." The complainant contended that such questions "obviously have no bearing on a person's ability to handle a job in broadcasting, and could only be used to discriminate against potential employees, because of their religious beliefs."

In response to the received complaint the FCC found that the hiring policy of King's Garden "discriminates on the basis of religion as to all station personnel, and is not, therefore, in compliance with Sections 73.125 and 73.301 of the Commission's rules."[1]   The FCC acknowledged that King's Garden was eligible under the Civil Rights Act for an exemption allowing the exercise of religious discrimination in employment "in those certain circumstances where religion . . . is a bona fide occupational qualification reasonably necessary to the normal operation of that particular business or enterprise," but held that it was not eligible for the general exemption of Section 702.   The ruling of the FCC emphasized the responsibility of King's Garden "to operate in the public interest, as defined by the Commission's rules and policies."   The FCC ruling states:

> The Commission does not believe that religion is a qualification that is 'reasonably necessary' to all aspects of the stations' normal operations.   In keeping with the exemptions you cite from the Civil Rights Act of 1964, the Commission believes that those persons hired to espouse a particular religious philosophy over the air should be exempt from the nondiscrimination rules.   But also in keeping with the very limited nature of the exemptions afforded by the 1964 Act, the Commission does not see any reason for a broad interpretation that would permit discrimination in the employment of persons whose work is not connected with the espousal of the licensee's views.[2]

When the National Religious Broadcasters requested a clarification of the applicability of the FCC ruling in the King's Garden decision to various employee categories, the FCC identified a number of positions where it thought a religious qualification would be clearly appropriate.   The Commission cited as examples writers and research assistants hired to prepare programs espousing the licensee's religious views, or persons hired to answer religious questions on a call-in program.   On the other hand, the FCC declared that religious qualifications would clearly not be appropriate for announcers. In other job categories the Commission was unwilling to issue a general declaratory ruling, preferring to have "specific factual settings" in hand before making any determinations. "We can say generally," said the FCC, "that our present rules proscribe religious discrimination in employment practices and that the exemption from those rules set out in the King's Garden decision is limited to those who, as to content or on-the-air presentation, are connected with espousal of the licensee's religious views."[3]

King's Garden appealed the FCC decision to the D.C. Court of Appeals, claiming the statutory and constitutional right to discriminate on religious grounds with respect to all positions of employment in its radio stations. King's Garden relied on the exemption provided in the Civil Rights Act, Title VII, Section 702, which provides: "This subchapter shall not apply . . . to a religious corporation, association, educational institution or society with respect to the employment of individuals of a particular religion to perform work connected with the carrying on by such corporation, association, educational institution, or society of its activities." The radio station argued that the FCC Rules cannot be exercised contrary to the religious exemption provided in federal law. King's Garden further contended that the anti-discrimination rules of the FCC abridged their First Amendment rights.

King's Garden's appeal was denied by the Court of Appeals, which took the view that the 1972 Title VII exemption, allowing the exercise of religious preference in employment for all activities of religious corporations, "is of very doubtful constitutionality" on both First Amendment and Fifth Amendment grounds.[4] The Court declared that it could conceive of no valid secular purpose being served by the "unbounded exemption" of the 1972 amendment, which requires no showing that the job in question involves a religious activity of the religious corporation. The court further declared that it found no indication that Congress intended to impose the broad exemption on the FCC. It affirmed the FCC's rulings, declaring that the Commission operates under a mandate given by the Communications Act, that it is not required to define its concept of the "public interest" in terms of the broad exemption of the Civil Rights Act, and that the limited exemption which the FCC currently recognizes to its own anti-bias rules adequately protects a sectarian licensee's rights under the Communications Act and the First Amendment.

The court saw the broad 1972 Civil Rights exemption as potentially immunizing "virtually every endeavor undertaken by a religious organization" from the requirement of nondiscrimination on the basis of religion. The exemption seemed to the court to shelter all kinds of activities which have not the slightest claim to protection under the First Amendment. The list of exempt activities, said the court (in flippant earnestness), might include "a trucking firm, a chain of motels, a race track, a telephone company, a railroad, a fried chicken franchise, or a professional football team." In creating such a broad exemption, declared the court, "Congress placed itself on collision course with the Establishment Clause." Prior to 1972 Congress had been reasonably successful in walking the "tightrope" between the two religion guarantees of the First Amendment. Now, said the court, "we must see to it that Congress does not slip off."

Such constitutional dicta were not required, however, for the court's decision, which was based finally on statutory interpretation. The court found that the FCC's own rules, promulgated under the Communications Act, made ample provision for exempting employment "connected with the espousal of the licensee's religious views." Application of these rules to the employment policies and practices of licensed broadcasters would involve no abridgement of their Free Exercise rights, said the court, because those rules have no substantial connection with religious program content, but deal only with positions connected with programs having no religious dimension. "A religious group," the court concluded, "like any other, may buy and operate a licensed radio or television station. . . . But, like any other group, a religious sect takes its franchise 'burdened by enforceable public obligations.'"

226

The court recognized that, in upholding the FCC's regulatory scheme, it was inviting "continuing judicial scrutiny" of the determinations made by the Commission as to what activities and positions of broadcasters are religious and thus exempt from the nondiscrimination rules. However, the court limited its judgment in this case to whether or not the religious exemption provided by FCC rules was "facially adequate." The FCC, noted the court, "has set itself the difficult task of drawing lines between the secular and religious aspects of the broadcasting operations of its sectarian licensees. Though this is a delicate undertaking, it is one which the First Amendment thrusts upon every public body which has dealings with religious organizations." The court admitted that there might well prove to be problems of application, "but they will be questions for another day."

The process of judicial determination contemplated by the D.C. Court of Appeals, however, is one which the legislative history of the 1972 Civil Rights amendments shows the Congress clearly wished to avoid.[5] In broadening the scope of the religious exemption to cover all activities of religious organizations, Congress chose not to assert any compelling public interest which justified infringing on the Free Exercise rights of such organizations. The Congress was also guided by the apprehensions of a number of its own members, as well as the experience of the judicial system, that questions of church operations and administration cannot be resolved by government without excessive entanglement in matters of singular ecclesiastical concern. We share the view expressed by a Michigan Law Review commentator who said that the court's dictum in King's Garden "underestimates the extent to which government proscription of religious discrimination interferes with the free exercise of religion and overestimates the extent to which the 1972 exemption establishes religion."[6] As we shall see, the D.C. Court's view of the constitutionality of the broad religious exemption of Title VII was later explicitly rejected by the U.S. Supreme Court.

RELIGIOUS PREFERENCE

Corporation of the Presiding Bishop v. Amos (1987)

In Corporation of the Presiding Bishop of the Church of Jesus Christ of Latter Day Saints v. Amos, 107 S.Ct. 2862 (1987), several individuals, employed by corporations owned by the Mormon Church, were fired because of their inability or refusal to satisfy certain religious tests for employment. The employees brought suit against the church in the District Court of Utah, claiming violation of federal and state employment discrimination laws. The church operations in question were a clothing mill known as Beehive Clothing Mills and a public gymnasium known as the Deseret Gymnasium. The employees were a secretary in the personnel department of the clothing mill, three seamstresses, and a building superintendent at the gymnasium. All five were fired from their jobs solely because they were unable or refused to satisfy the Mormon church's "worthiness" requirement for "temple recommends." To obtain the required standing an individual must satisfy church authorities that he observes such standards as regular church attendance, tithing, and abstinence from coffee, tea, alcohol, and tobacco.

The Church moved to dismiss on grounds of Title VII of the Civil Rights Act of 1964, which exempts churches and religious organizations, including religious corporations, associations, societies, and educational institutions, from discrimination claims with regard to religion and allows them to engage in religious discrimination in all their activities. The District Court found for the plaintiffs, declaring that the religious exemption relied on by the Church had been rendered unconstitutional by the amendment of 1972, when Congress removed the "religious activities" limitation in the original exemption clause. The court ruled that the exemption as amended, when applied to secular, nonreligious activities, violates the Establishment Clause of the First Amendment.[7] The decision was upheld by the Court of Appeals of the State of Utah.

The U.S. Supreme Court agreed to review the District Court judgment and to decide whether Congress acted unconstitutionally when it amended Title VII, Civil Rights Act of 1964 . . . to permit religious employers to hire only members of their own faith, regardless of the nature of the employment activity, thus making it unnecessary for federal courts to decide whether particular activities of religions are in fact religious.

Attorneys on the Church's side argued that the decision of the lower court would create "a new test that requires broad scrutiny of the tenets, ritual, and administrative practice of religions for the purpose of determining what is and what is not 'religious.'" The U.S. Solicitor General agreed, declaring in a brief supporting the church's appeal that the decision of the lower court had invalidated what he called a sensible congressional effort to avoid constitutional problems, to avoid excessive government entanglement in religion, and to uphold First Amendment values.

On the other side, lawyers for the employees argued that the case was a clear instance of a religious employer's using the exemption clause "to coerce religious loyalty through the economic power that an employer enjoys over employees." They contended that the Church's employing the religious requirement that its employees must tithe should be viewed as a strategy for gaining unfair economic advantage over its private-sector competitors. The Utah chapter of the American Civil Liberties Union assisted in legal representation of the workers.

Among the issues at stake in this case was whether or not religious and religiously affiliated institutions shall have the right to determine in which of their activities and for which of their personnel a religious qualification for appointment is essential to the purposes and mission of the enterprise. The District Court opinion would assign to the courts the authority to determine the conditions under which the exemption for religious discrimination is permissible for such institutions.

229

RELIGIOUS PREFERENCE

The <u>Amos</u> case was decided by the U.S. Supreme Court on June 24, 1987. By a unanimous decision the Court supported the Church's appeal and reversed the judgment of the District Court, declaring that application of the Section 702 exemption to the secular nonprofit activities of religious organizations is permissible under the U.S. Constitution and does not violate the Establishment Clause of the First Amendment. The decision, which was delivered by Justice Byron White, strongly affirms the right of religious organizations to engage in religiously preferential hiring in all their activities, as long as these activities remain within the nonprofit sector.

The Court cited its long-standing recognition of the right of government to accomodate religious practices without violating the Establishment Clause. It recognized that "at some point" such accomodation might devolve into an unlawful fostering of religion, but it did not agree that this point had been reached in the circumstances of <u>Amos</u>. The decision reaffirmed the principles for judging the constitutionality of religious exemption statutes which were promulgated in <u>Lemon v. Kurtzman.</u> The <u>Lemon</u> decision, said the Court, "aims at preventing the relevant governmental decisionmaker - - in this case Congress -- from abandoning neutrality and acting with the intent of promoting a particular point of view in religious matters." The <u>Amos</u> Court upheld the statute in question on the grounds that its clear purpose was to minimize governmental interference with the decision making process in religions.

The Court held that governmental accomodation of religion is not the same as an establishment of religion. "A law is not unconstitutional simply because it <u>allows</u> churches to advance religion, which is their very purpose." For a law to be judged unconstitutional under the Establishment Clause it would have to be shown that the "<u>government itself</u> has advanced religion through its own activities and influence." The line between accomodation and establishment, the Court noted, "is hardly a bright one," and fear of potential liability which might arise from decisions of a court which did not understand the religious tenets

230

involved might well have a chilling effect on the way in which a religious organization seeks to carry out its religious mission.

The Court found no evidence that either the intention or the effect of the 702 exemption as amended was to single out a religious entity for special benefits. The Court held, "It cannot be seriously contended that Section 702 impermissibly entangles church and state; the statute effectuates a more complete separation of the two and avoids the kind of intrusive inquiry into religious belief that the District Court engaged in in this case." The statute, said the Court, is merely a proper act of government in lifting a regulation which would burden the exercise of religion. The statute is "neutral on its face and motivated by a permissible purpose of limiting governmental interference with the ability of religious organizations to define and carry out their religious missions." It would be a significant burden on a religious organization, the Court argued, "to require it, on pain of substantial liability, to predict which of its activities a secular court will consider religious."

Justice William Brennan, in his concurring opinion (in which Justice Marshall joined), saw the case as presenting a confrontation between the rights of religious organizations and those of individuals. An exemption from Title VII's proscription against religious discrimination, he said, favors institutional rights but restricts individual rights. The protection of institutional rights, he said, is in fact essential to the protection of individual rights, because "for many individuals, religious activity derives meaning in large measure from participation in a larger religious community." Hence it is entirely proper for Congress to protect institutions in their rights of self-determination and preferential selection of employees, since "the autonomy of religious organizations often furthers individual religious freedom as well."

This rationale, Brennan admits, would seem to imply that religious organizations should be permitted to discriminate on the basis of religion (and so infringe on the religious liberty of individuals) only with respect to their religious activities, so that a determination would have to be made on a case-by-case basis whether an institutiional program or activity is religious or secular. However, this theoretical distinction between religious and secular is not self-evident in practice. To determine whether a particular activity or program is religious and therefore exempt from the proscription against religious discrimination would, said Brennan, involve the government in an entangling intrusion which would both offend the Establishment Clause and chill the organization in its Free Exercise.

Brennan stressed, however, that it is in the non-profit activities of religious organizations that the exemption is most likely to be appropriate. When the activities of a church have the color of a for-profit function, the claim that they are infused with a religious purpose loses its plausibility. On the other hand, the non-profit activities of a church are likely to present cases in which classification of the activities as religious or secular will be "a close question." Brennan would therefore provide a categorical exemption from nonprofit activities of religious organizations, as demarcating "a sphere of deference with respect to those activities most likely to be religious." He would permit infringing on an individual employee's Free Exercise rights in those instances in which the institutional exercise of religious discrimination would be most likely to authentically reflect the community's self-definition. "While every nonprofit activity may not be operated for religious purposes, the likelihood that many are makes a categorical rule a suitable means to avoid chilling the exercise of religion."

Justice Sandra O'Connor took a similar view in her concurring opinion. Given the likelihood that a nonprofit activity will be, in fact, involved in the organization's religious mission, she said, "the objective observer should perceive the government action as an accomodation of the exercise of religion rather than as a government endorsement of religion." When the activities in question are organized for profit, however, the significance of the exemption is less clear. "I emphasize that under the holding of the Court, and under my view of the appropriate Establishment Clause analysis, the question of the constitutionality of the Section 702 exemption as applied to for-profit activities of religious organizations remains open."

The unanimity of the Amos Court is startling in several respects. The decision affirmed the autonomy of an institution in a manner which appears to many commentators to be clearly at the expense of the rights of individuals. Furthermore, a number of the findings of fact, as established in the trial court, are disturbing to anyone concerned for proper personnel procedures. All of the employees in question had worked at their jobs for a number of years before being confronted quite suddenly with the requirement of satisfying the religious worthiness standards of the Mormon Church as a condition of continued employment. Personnel policies and procedures adopted by the Mormon Church in 1969, requiring that "continued employment in the Church is dependent on the employees living their lives so as to be worthy of temple recommends," had not been enforced prior to 1980.

The employees in question were engaged in clerical, maintenance, transportation, or manufacturing work, which could easily be classified as secular and non-religious in function.[8] The factual background for the lower court decision stipulates that "at no time did any of the plaintiffs' positions require any of them to describe, explain, or proselytize the doctrine and beliefs of the Mormon Church. At no time did any of the plaintiffs' positions require any of them to engage in worship, ritual, or ministerial duties of the Mormon Church nor in matters of Mormon Church administration."

In addition, there are ample lower court precedents for the opposite finding than the one reached by the Amos court. The opinion of the District Court had reviewed these precedents at considerable length and had reached essentially the same conclusion as had been reached in

King's Garden concerning the constitutionality of the Section 702 exemption. Many observers expected the Supreme Court to be at least divided on the constitutional question.

The Amos decision rejects the argument that the exemption for religious discrimination in employment should be limited (in the language of Title VII) to "those certain instances where religion . . . is a bona fide occupational qualification reasonably necessary to the normal operation of that business or enterprise." If there had previously been any doubt about the authority for a broader exemption for religious organizations, any such doubt was effectively removed by the Amos Court. The Court issued an unambiguous rebuttal to those sectors of the judiciary and the government bureaucracy who had thought of the amended Section 702 exemption as "on collision course with the Establishment Clause."

The constitutionality of the religious exemption in Section 702 has thus been explicitly confirmed by the Supreme Court. The basis of the Court's decision, however, was not the Free Exercise Clause, but the "benevolent neutrality" of the Establishment Clause, which "will permit religious exercise to exist without sponsorship and without interference." The opinion leaves open the question of a Free Exercise right which exempts religious organizations from the proscription of religious discrimination in employment in all their activities.

The implications of the decision for religiously affiliated colleges and universities remain unclear. The vagueness of the legal definition of the term "religious organization" persists. Nor is the law clear as to how "religious" an institution of higher education must be in order to qualify for the broad exemption of Section 702. It is quite possible, furthermore, that the courts will restrict the religious exemption to the "religious," as distinguished from the "secular" programs of religiously affiliated colleges and universities. In that case the basis for permitting religious discrimination in employment would come down to the bona fide occupational qualification test, which is available, of course, to all employers.

Seattle Pacific University v. Orin C. Church (1986)

In August, 1983 Orin C. Church, a Catholic, appeared at the personnel office of Seattle Pacific University, which is related to the Free Methodist Church, to apply for a job as a warehouseman. When he was not permitted to apply on the grounds that he would not be able to satisfy the University's requirement that its employees must be professing evangelical Christians and members of a local church, he filed a discrimination complaint with the Washington State Human Rights Commission and the Equal Employment Opportunity Commission. The EEOC promptly served notice to the University of an employment discrimination charge by Mr. Church under Title VII of the Civil Rights Act of 1964.

In October, 1984 the EEOC staff issued a finding of reasonable cause that the University had unlawfully discriminated against Mr. Church and asserted the Commission's jurisdiction over the case. The University and its sponsoring religious organization, the Free Methodist Church, then filed suit in U.S. District Court, moving to dismiss Church's complaint on the grounds that the EEOC did not have jurisdiction because of the University's exempt status, and declaring that action against the University by the Commission would violate the University's federally protected statutory and constitutional rights. The University's complaint for declaratory and injunctive relief was filed in District Court in December of 1984.

The University based its complaint on grounds of both the federal Constitution and federal civil rights statutes. It sought injunctive relief and a judgment declaring:

(a) That plaintiff is a religious institution or association vested with rights under the First Amendment of the U.S. Constitution;

(b) That plaintiff's exercise of religious preference in hiring for an employment position at the University comprises an expression of a sincerely held religious conviction which is protected under the First Amendment of the U.S. Constitution;

(c) That, by virtue of the religious nature of the plaintiff institutions and the religious underpinnings of their hiring policy, plaintiffs are exempt from any complaint, investigation, proceeding, or action alleging employment discrimination on the basis of religion or creed . . . filed with any court of law or equity, or with any administrative agency, and brought under [state or federal law];

(d) That said exemption constitutes a reasonable governmental accomodation of sincerely held religious beliefs and practices.

In answering the University's complaint to the District Court and its request for injunctive relief, the EEOC admitted that the University was a private, religiously affiliated institution of higher education, but denied that it qualified for the exemption contained in Section 702 of Title VII "with respect to the employment of warehousemen." (The EEOC attorneys were basing their interpretation of Title VII in part on the Utah District Court decision in Amos v. Presiding Bishop, which had just been reached on January 11, 1984, 594 F.Supp. 791.)

The Commission also disputed the University's claim that it was a religious institution within the meaning of the Washington Anti-Discrimination Law. In its October "finding" the Washington State Human Rights Commission explicitly declared its understanding that "religious non-profit organizations are 'employers' within the meaning of (state law) RCW 49.60 when the employment transaction in question involves a job which is non-religious in nature." The University replied that all its employees were involved in the religious aspects of its educational mission and that even a warehouseman could be a role model for a religious community.

RELIGIOUS PREFERENCE

The EEOC took the view that Seattle Pacific University was not a religious institution under state law, that the university was not exempt from any complaint, investigation, proceeding, or action alleging employment discrimination on the basis of religion or creed, that the University's policy of exercising religious preference in the hiring of a warehouse worker was not entitled to protection under state or federal law or under the First Amendment of the U.S. Constitution, and that the University's First Amendment rights had not been violated by any action of the Commission.

The EEOC and the U.S. Attorney contended that the District Court lacked jurisdiction in the Seattle Pacific complaint because no prima facie case for the infringement of the University's constitutional rights had been made. The EEOC further contended that its acceptance of a charge of discrimination against the University in no way violated the University's First Amendment rights, and that the Commission needed to have an opportunity to conduct its fact-finding investigation before the University's complaint would be "ripe" for judicial review. Extensive legal maneuvering occurred, focusing on the question whether the EEOC had the right to proceed with its investigation and whether the university had exhausted its available administrative appeals and should be allowed to bring suit in the federal courts.

After nearly two years of motions and counter-motions, EEOC officials finally withdrew their claim to jurisdiction on the basis of their discovery of "new" information concerning the appropriateness of religious qualifications for non-academic positions at Seattle Pacific University. Mary Tennyson, an Assistant Attorney General representing the EEOC, explained to the press that an investigator for the Commission had learned that many University employees, including someone like a warehouse worker, "have contacts with students in a supervisory role. That was something we didn't know." The new information led the state to conclude that the University was, in fact, a religious organization under Washington law and that it was therefore exempt from the state's anti-discrimination statute. With the agreement of the University, in March, 1986 Judge Kaufmann of the District Court dismissed the University's complaint, and no formal judicial determination of its merit was required.

Seattle Pacific University was well prepared, because of its clearly stated employment policies and practices and carefully documented relationships with its sponsoring religious body, to defend its claim that religious preference was appropriate in hiring for all its positions. The institution functions within a long-standing tradition according to which all people within the church, whatever their specific vocations, have a decisive role in the evangelical task. The institution was able to cite instance after instance in which religious conversion or development had been decisively affected by the quality of routine contacts with a cook or a janitor. However, the basis of its successful defense against a challenge to its right to exercise religious preference in employment for all positions, nonacademic as well as academic, was essentially (at least as far as the governmental agencies viewed it) a factual confirmation that religion was a bona fide occupational qualification for all employment positions at Seattle Pacific University.

The preliminary finding of the State Human Rights Commission that Church had reasonable cause for a discrimination suit against the University seems not to have been well researched. The judicial process was prolonged by a certain amount of posturing by both parties with respect to procedural and jurisdictional questions. The University was put to considerable expense in defending itself against an attempt at regulation which was probably ill advised.

The case illustrates precisely the kind of burden on institutional Free Exercise which both the Congress and the Supreme Court have sought to relieve. It is not yet clear whether regulatory agencies and courts will continue to be engaged in secular determination of the appropriateness of religious qualifications for various kinds of positions in religiously affiliated colleges and universities.

Pime v. Loyola University of Chicago (1986)

Several recent judicial decisions reveal a continuing reluctance on the part of courts to allow religiously affiliated institutions of higher education to depend on the general exemption for religious organizations and religiously affiliated educational institutions, and an inclination to require them, instead, to demonstrate that the exercise of a religious test in academic employment is a case of use of a bona fide occupational qualification.

In Pime v. Loyola University of Chicago, 803 F.2d 351 (7th Cir. 1986), the United States Court of Appeals for the Seventh Circuit upheld a decision of a United States District Court affirming the right of Loyola University of Chicago under the Civil Rights Act of 1964 to reserve a number of tenure track teaching positions in the Department of Philosophy for Jesuits. Jerrold S. Pime had brought suit against Loyola, claiming employment discrimination against him on the basis of his having been told that a faculty vacancy for which he wished to apply was being reserved for Jesuit applicants.

In the fall of 1978 there were 31 tenure track positions in the Loyola Department of Philosophy, seven of which were held by Jesuits. One of the Jesuit incumbents had resigned and two others were about to retire. The Department of Philosophy, concerned about retaining a Jesuit presence among the faculty, passed a resolution, upon the chairman's recommendation, "that for each of the three vacant positions we seek to hire a professionally competent Jesuit philosopher."

Pime, a Jew, had taught in the Department on a part-time basis since 1976, apparently receiving indications that his work was approved. He expected to receive his doctorate in June, 1979. Knowing of the upcoming vacancies in the department and of the resolution passed by the

239

faculty in the fall of 1978, Pime asked the department chairman whether there would be a full-time tenure track position for him at Loyola. The chairman replied that he saw no prospect of a position for Pime in the next three or four years. Disappointed, Pime left Loyola after the spring semester. He then filed a timely charge of employment discrimination with the Equal Employment Opportunity Commission and, upon receiving notice of his right-to-sue, initiated his action against the University.

Loyola affirmed two defenses: (1) The University has the right, as a Catholic and Jesuit university, to require its employees to be Jesuits under Section 703(e)(2) of the Civil Rights Act, which permits an educational institution to employ persons of a particular religion if the institution is "in whole or substantial part, owned, supported, controlled, or managed . . . by a particular religion or by a particular religious corporation, association, or society;" and (2) The University has the right under Section 703(e)(1) to employ an individual "on the basis of his religion, sex, or national origin in those certain instances where religion, sex, or national origin is a bona fide occupational qualification reasonably necessary to the normal operation of that particular business or enterprise."

In 1984 the District Court gave judgment in favor of Loyola upon finding that, for the vacancy for which Pime wished to apply in the Department of Philosophy, being a Jesuit was a bona fide occupational qualification.[9] Pime appealed, challenging the finding of a BFOQ. Loyola also appealed, challenging the District Court's judgment that the University could not rely on subsection 703(e)(2). The U.S. Court of Appeals for the Seventh Circuit found no error in the decision of the District Judge and affirmed the judgment of a BFOQ. However, the court did not support the University's claim to a defense on the basis of its being a religious employer.

The appellate court's decision in Pime was based on the finding that in this case the requirement that a candidate for the philosophy vacancy in question must be a member of the Society of Jesus constituted a bona fide occupational qualification (BFOQ) under the terms of the Civil Rights Act. The University was thus permitted to rely on Subsection 703(e)(1) of the Act. The District Court found that the Department of Philosophy had made a bona fide determination of qualification for the three existing vacancies in reserving them for Jesuit candidates; and the Court of Appeals agreed that "having a Jesuit presence on the Philosophy faculty is 'reasonably necessary to the normal operation' of the enterprise, and that fixing the number at seven out of thirty-one is a reasonable determination." However, the court did not sustain the University's contention that it could also rely on subsection 703(e)(2).[10]

Loyola was founded by the Jesuit order in 1870, but it is now incorporated not as a religious corporation, but as "an ordinary nonprofit corporation." Financial contributions from the Jesuit order make up only one-third of one percent of the university's annual income. The University's bylaws require that a third of the trustees must be Jesuits, and although that is a minority, it is enough to block amendments to the bylaws. The president of the University is required to be a Jesuit.

In his concurring opinion, Court of Appeals Judge Posner declared that, while agreeing with the decision of the Court, he would have preferred that it had been based not on either subsection of the exemption clause, but on the finding of fact that there was no prima facie violation of Title VII, given the lack of evidence of discriminatory intention or effect. However, unlike Judge Fairchild, the Senior Circuit Judge who wrote the Pime opinion, Judge Posner was willing to address, "for the sake of completeness," the claim of Loyola University to a broad exemption under Section 702(e)(2), as a university that "is, in whole or in substantial part, owned, supported, controlled, or managed by a particular religion or by a particular religious corporation, association, or society."

RELIGIOUS PREFERENCE

That description of Loyola, said Judge Posner, would have been apt at its founding in 1870. But the ownership and control of the university by Jesuits is now much less obvious. It is no longer a religious or sectarian school in the narrow sense. Judge Posner asked, "Is the combination of a Jesuit president and nine Jesuit directors out of twenty-two enough to constitute substantial control or management by the Jesuit order?"

There is no case law pertinent to this question, Judge Posner answered. Nor does the statute provide the answer. Corporate-control and state-action analogies are too remote to be illuminating. And the legislative history, though tantalizing, is inconclusive. Congress, said Judge Posner, seems to have been cognizant of the variations in degrees and forms of religious involvement among religiously affililiated institutions of higher education, but "neither the statute nor the legislative history indicates where in the continuum Congress wanted to make the cut."

Judge Posner ventured some speculations about what might happen if the court had to really decide whether Loyola qualified for the broad exemption:

> If the governance arrangements of Loyola are
> typical of those of Catholic universities, then I would
> have little doubt that Loyola was within the protection
> of the religious-employer exemption. . . . They may not
> be typical. . . If Loyola, perhaps in order to attract
> financial or other support from non-Catholic sources . .
> . has attenuated its relationship to the Jesuit order far
> beyond that of other Catholic universities, there would
> be a serious problem in holding that it could
> nevertheless discriminate freely in favor of Catholics.

Such speculations in a legal opinion raise serious questions and apprehensions about the predictability of judicial interpretation of the Title VII exemptions. Judge Posner interposes them in his opinion mainly to show that there are pitfalls in applying the facts of the Pime case to determine precedent for either of the exemptions claimed by the University, and to argue for his preference for a decision based not on an exemption clause, but on the failure of plaintiff to show that there was any violation of Title VII, given the lack of evidence of either discriminatory intent or discriminatory effect. His hypothetical speculations, however, indicate that at least one very gifted and influential federal judge is quite uncertain of how the broad exemption of Section 702(e)(2) would be applied by the courts to religiously affiliated colleges and universities. Our guess is that, under his understandings, a very large majority of religiously affiliated colleges and universities would not qualify for the broad exemption.

The decision reached in this case was quite satisfactory to independent and religiously affiliated higher education in its outcome, but troubling in many of its implications. The judicial finding vindicated Loyola University's faculty employment policy. But a number of issues affecting the interpretation and application of the exemptions under the Civil Rights Act remain unresolved.

The District Court found that Jesuit-ness was indeed, for the philosophy vacancy in question, a bona fide occupational qualification, and the Seventh Circuit Court of Appeals agreed. The court found that there was something common-sensically right about a priest's teaching philosophy in a Catholic school. Clearly, it has been the intention of Congress that the system of American justice should continue to permit religiously affiliated colleges and universities to have independent discretion in such a matter as this. But when this principle was presented by the Loyola University to a court of law, the court preferred to limit its application to cases where a religious qualification could be shown to be a bona fide occupational qualification. The court refused to allow a general religious exemption for a religiously affiliated university.

On balance the Pime case should have been an easy case. It was relatively easy to explain why a Jesuit university ought to be able to reserve some positions in its philosophy faculty for Jesuits. It was an easy case, and yet the courts struggled with it, reaching essentially a split decision after twenty months of deliberation.

Maguire v. Marquette University (1987)

In Maguire v. Marquette University, 814 F. 2d 1213 (7th Cir. 1987), the Seventh Circuit Court of Appeals had a further opportunity to decide a Title VII claim against a religiously affiliated university. The case is not a clear one, due to changes in the grounds of action presented by the plaintiff. The Court of Appeals eventually disposed of the case by determining that the plaintiff had failed to establish a prima facie case of discrimination.

Between 1976 and 1984 Marjorie Maguire, who holds a Ph.D. degree in Religious Studies from The Catholic University of America, applied repeatedly for a faculty position in theology at Marquette University, a Jesuit institution, and was each time denied an appointment. In 1984 she brought suit under Title VII, alleging that Marquette had refused to hire her because she was a woman. In addition to alleging general sex discrimination, the plaintiff challenged the validity of the University's use of "Jesuit preference" in respect to its hiring in the theology department.

The University replied by filing a motion for summary judgment on the grounds that its policy of giving preference to Jesuits did not constitute sex discrimination, and that being a Jesuit was a bona fide occupational qualification for the position of a theology professor at a Jesuit university. While this motion was pending the plaintiff requested permission to supplement her original complaint on the basis of information which, she claimed, had come to light in the course of discovery, viz. that the University's grounds for not hiring her had actually been "perceptions and/or misperceptions of (its) agents concerning the plaintiff's views respecting the moral theology of abortion and/or the public policy of abortion in a pluralistic society and the relationship between the two." She therefore added a pendant claim that her rights had been violated under the terms of the Wisconsin law of academic freedom.

The pendant claim changed the entire nature of the civil action. Indeed, Dr. Maguire's previous claim that her denial of employment had been based on her sex was effectively removed by her own shift to a different basis of the suit. The question became whether the University had the right to exercise religious preference in appointments in theology and whether it was under any legal obligation to appoint to its theology faculty persons who explicitly disagreed with Catholic doctrine.

The University contended that sex discrimination had nothing whatever to do with its decision not to hire Dr, Maguire, that her credentials had been judged by a properly conducted academic review to be not competitive with those of other applicants, and that, even if they had been competitive, she would not have been hired because of "her perceived hostility to the institutional church and its teachings, and to the goals and mission of Marquette." The University maintained that it was permitted to exercise religious preference in this case by the exemption provided in Title VII. The institutional decision was upheld by the court, although no determination had to be made concerning the merits of the University's argument.

The District Court granted the University's motion for summary judgment, declaring that a federal court is not

> the appropriate forum in which to decide who should teach in the theology department of a Catholic university. . . . Such an inquiry would require the Court to immerse itself not only in the procedures and hiring practices of (the department) but, further, into questions of what it is to be a Catholic. That question is one the First Amendment leaves to theology departments and church officials, not federal judges.[11]

Dr. Maguire appealed to the U.S. Court of Appeals for the Seventh Circuit, the same court that had delivered the

245

Pime decision. There in March, 1987 the decision of the District Court in dismissing the plaintiff's Title VII claim was affirmed. The Court of Appeals again thought it unnecessary to decide on the university's claim as a religious employer under the Title VII exemption, because it found that no valid claim of discrimination had been made by the plaintiff.

The plaintiff's original complaint of sex discrimination had been undercut by her own amended complaint, which alleged that the University's grounds for refusing to hire her was not sex bias, but the University's "perceived or misperceived consideration of plaintiff's views" on abortion. Her amended claim of discrimination on grounds of her views on abortion and violation of her academic freedom had been dismissed by the District Court, which held that the plaintiff had failed to show that the Wisconsin law of academic freedom was intended to govern the hiring decisions of a private university. In its own judgment the Court of Appeals expressed its opinion that Wisconsin law "in no way limits the right of a private university to reject otherwise qualified applicants for positions as professors because of their opinions or beliefs;" but it thought that the District Court was procedurally in error in reaching the merits of plaintiff's claim in this matter. Accordingly, the decision of the circuit court in dismissing the state law claim on academic freedom was vacated.

The basis of the appellate decision was, therefore, not a determination of Marquette's eligibility for the religious-employer exemption or even a determination of whether Jesuit-ness was a bona fide occupational qualification for a position in theology. The Court found it possible to resolve the case on a much narrower ground: the plaintiff had simply failed to make out a valid claim to sex discrimination under Title VII. Having determined that the plaintiff's claim of discrimination under Title VII fails as a matter of law, the court found it unnecessary to decide what were the University's rights as a religious employer, or what were the conditions under which a religious qualification might be a bona fide occupational requirement for a theology position, or what were the plaintiff's rights to academic freedom.

Marquette University was eager to present its claims as a religious employer for adjudication by the court and to obtain confirmation of the legitimacy of religious criteria of employment in religiously oriented institutions. The District Court had agreed with the University's claim that it was entitled to the statutory exemption as a religious employer and that its practice of giving preference to Jesuits in theology appointments and requiring theology faculty to be in agreement with Catholic teaching was protected by this exemption. But the Court of Appeals did not reach this question.

3. Summary

The judicial decisions surveyed in this chapter have resolved a number of questions affecting the exercise of religious preference in employment decisions at religiously affiliated institutions of higher education, but they have left a number of important questions unresolved. The clarifications are welcome, even though they have not always been of the sort that the independent sector would have liked. The remaining uncertainties are, perhaps, not life-threatening for religiously affiliated higher education, but they are still troubling.

The Supreme Court has removed any lingering uncertainty as to whether indirect aid reaching a religiously affiliated educational institution causes the institution to become a "recipient" of federal aid and thus to fall within the jurisdiction of the federal proscriptions against discrimination in programs receiving federal assistance. Federal law and regulations continue to allow that organizations which are "ultimate" beneficiaries of federal aid programs are not "recipients" and are thus not subject to federal regulation. But indirect aid, even tax exemption, triggers the jurisdiction of civil rights law. As Grove City shows, an independent educational institution cannot avoid government regulation simply by refusing direct federal aid.

The subsequent enactment of the Civil Rights Restoration Act of 1987 further clarifies the scope of federal regulation that is triggered by a determination that an institution is a recipient of federal assistance. Under present law an institution that is a recipient of either direct or indirect federal assistance is subject to the requirement of institution-wide compliance with federal nondiscrimination regulations.

The Supreme Court has also resoundingly confirmed the constitutionality of the Title VII exemption for religious organizations and religiously affiliated educational institutions, even as broadened by the 1972 amendment. The right of churches and religious organizations to exercise religious preference in employment decisions affecting all their activities has been upheld. This clarification brings with it a major strengthening of the capacity of such organizations to provide for the religious identity and integrity of their programs and ministries. The confirmation is limited, however, to the non-profit activities and programs of religious organizations, and the ground of the confirmation of these institutional rights is the Establishment Clause, rather than the Free Exercise Clause. The Free Exercise claims of religious organizations remain limited by potentially conflicting individual rights and compelling state interests.

Still unresolved are questions affecting the eligibility of religiously affiliated institutions of higher education for the exemptions which are assured to religious organizations themselves. On the continuum of religiousness, colleges and universities as a class continue to be regarded by courts and regulatory agencies as essentially different from parochial elementary and secondary schools as a class. Many religiously affiliated colleges and universities may expect to be treated more like religious broadcasters than like parochial schools, subject to regulation in "the public interest." Within the group of religiously affiliated colleges and universities, it is not clear at what point on the continuum of religious affiliation or orientation an institution begins to be defined as a "religious" organization. The resulting uncertainty about the applicability of statutory exemptions from general anti-discrimination requirements seems likely to continue indefinitely.

The following appear to be the major options available to religiously affiliated institutions of higher education in establishing a claim to an exemption from the general statutory prohibition against religious discrimination in employment:

1. An institution that is pervasively religious might qualify for exemption as a religious organization. It should be remembered, however, that colleges and universities are very unlikely to be considered churches. The broad right to exercise religious and religiously based discrimination in churches is probably available to seminaries, schools of divinity, rabbinical schools, and most Bible schools and Bible colleges.

2. If an institution cannot qualify for the general exemption of Title VII as a religious organization, it may still discriminate religiously in all its positions if it is "in whole or in substantial part owned, supported, controlled, or managed by a particular religious [organization]" or if its curriculum "is directed toward the propagation of a particular religion." For all but the most sectarian institutions of higher learning, that test comes down, largely, to the issue of the nature of the organizational relationship with a sponsoring religious body.

3. If an institution cannot qualify for either of the previous exemptions, it is required to justify any exercise of religious discrimination in employment by a showing that religion is, in the specific job, "a bona fide occupational qualification reasonably necessary" to carrying out the institution's educational mission. The institution must then be prepared to give evidence of a nexus between particular positions for which religious preference is

exercised and the religious character of the institutional mission.

There is no assurance that religiously affiliated colleges and universities have a First Amendment right to discriminate in all their employment decisions on the basis of religion. Even if there were an institutional Free Exercise right, an institution might find its right restricted by conflicting individual rights or by a compelling state interest. Religiously affiliated colleges and universities will probably continue to face challenges from individuals and regulatory agencies concerning the practice of religious discrimination in academic and support staff positions perceived as being remote from the religious mission of the enterprise.

NOTES TO CHAPTER SEVEN

1. Section 73 of the FCC's Rules promulgates the following General Policy: "Equal opportunity in employment shall be afforded by all licensees or permittees of commercially or noncommercially operated standard, FM, television or international broadcast stations . . . to all qualified persons, and no person shall be discriminated against in employment because of race, color, religion, national origin, or sex." 47 C.F.R. 73.125(a), 73.301(a), 73.599(a), 73.680(a), 73.793(a). The Commission traces its authority for issuing such a regulation to the Communications Act of 1934, which mandates the Commission to regulate broadcast licensees "as public convenience, interest, or necessity requires." In memoranda issued in 1968 and 1969 the FCC explained its Rule on equal opportunity in employment as based on the clear "National policy against discrimination in hiring" and the nature of broadcasting as a mass media form, requiring "a Federal license under a public interest standard."

2. 34 FCC 2d 937, 24 RR 2d 281 (1972); affirmed on reconsideration 38 FCC 2d 339, 25 RR 2d 1030 (1972). The decision was affirmed after enactment of the 1972 amendment to the Civil Rights Act, which broadened the

exemption in Section 702.

3. In Re Request of National Religious Broadcasters, Inc., 43 FCC 2d 451 (1973).

4. That view was specifically rejected by the U.S. Supreme Court in its Amos decision in 1987.

5. Cf. E.E.O.C. v. Pacific Press Pub. Ass'n, 676 F. 2d 1272 (1982); see above pp. 195-197.

6. Notes: "The Constitutionality of the 1972 Amendment to Title VII's Exemption for Religious Organizations," Michigan Law Review, Vol. 73, January, 1975, pp. 538-560.

7. 594 F. Supp. 791 (D.C. Utah).

8. The District Court developed and applied a three-part test to determine whether an activity is religious. The test involves a progressive series of determinations as to: 1) the financial and managerial tie between the religious organization and the activity at issue; 2) the nexus between the primary function of the activity and the religious rituals or tenets of the religious organization; and 3) the nature of the relationship between the job and the religious rituals and tenets of the religious organization and matters of church administration. 594 F. Supp. 791,799 (Utah 1984). The Supreme Court found this proposed test not particularly helpful.

9. 585 F. Supp. 435.

10. The court did not directly deny the university's claim to a broad exemption under Section 702(e)(2). Finding it possible to decide the case on the basis of the Section 702(e)(1) BFOQ exemption, the court thought it unnecessary to reach the university's claim of a broad exemption.

11. 627 F. Supp. 1499.

CHAPTER EIGHT

RELIGIOUS PREFERENCE AND ACADEMIC FREEDOM

The chief virtue in any community of learning is its autonomy, which is the root of its integrity. Freedom is the essential environment of all education. Freedom to inquire is the foundation of scholarship; freedom to explore creates the dialectics of all teaching and learning.

Legal scholars are divided on the question whether the American Constitution protects the community of learning in its academic freedom. There is general agreement, however, that the chief defense of the freedom of the academy must come from within the academy itself - - from the vitality of its traditions and the effectiveness of its own procedures for protecting the life of the mind. Defenses against improper pressures from without are needed at times, and the law may be an important instrument in establishing necessary safeguards. But the freedom of a community of learning comes from within itself.

We contend that religiously affiliated higher education in its fullest expression is dominated by a broader concept of freedom than is possible in any other system of education. The life of learning in the religiously affiliated college or university holds the promise of a comprehensive, coherent, and integrated educational experience, including examination of the religious and values-related issues which lie at the foundation of human autonomy in its fullest expression. Religiously affiliated higher education needs to be at least as assiduous in its defense and pursuit of freedom as any other sector of education. It is not enough for religiously affiliated higher education to secure the right to exemptions from the general requirements of freedom that are in force in other sectors of the academy. A religiously affiliated college or university must establish itself as a place where freedom can be as complete as it can possibly be in the House of Intellect.

Yet a religiously oriented program of education is widely viewed as inherently involving a compromise of the freedom to inquire and to learn. And any exercise of religious preference in employment decisions in a religiously affiliated college or university is widely assumed to involve a compromise of the academic ideal. Furthermore, the model of teaching most commonly identified in the law with religiously oriented educational institutions is indoctrination in the "tenets" of the sponsoring religious organization, the "inculcation" of values through systems of conditioning and control - - procedures which have no place in the higher learning. The law often fails to do justice to the traditions of freedom and critical thought in the religiously oriented college or university. There is a great deal of confusion, too, among the faculty of many religiously affiliated institutions as to the meaning of freedom in the area of religious and value-related inquiry. A new initiative is required at the moment to reassert the tradition of freedom in the life of the religiously affiliated college or university.

1. The Virtues of the Academy

No institution of learning can be value-neutral. The pulse of its life is evaluation. It evaluates judgments, it evaluates the achievement of students, it evaluates the performance of teachers and of administrative staff. And it establishes educational goals and policies which express its underlying values. It is the concept of excellence (virtue) which brings all the activities and processes of the higher learning to perfection and fulfillment.

The central concern of the university is cultivation of academic virtue. Education is not merely the formation of competence, or preparation for skillful performance, or the acquisition of the data of learning. Education is the cultivation of respect for excellence, which is the supreme value of the university.

An academy of learning presupposes certain qualities which are necessary for its own functioning. Every institution of higher learning must make provision for the protection and nurture of those qualities, for without them it cannot do its work. What, then, are the values which belong essentially to the life of learning?

Obviously, an academy of learning values truth, and it values critical and rigorous inquiry as the indispensable means to the pursuit of truth. Accordingly, an essential academic virtue would be the capacity to distinguish reliably between critically supportable judgments and those which will not stand up under critical scrutiny, the ability to recognize the difference between valid and invalid inferences, the skill of identifying fallacies in argumentation and non-rational appeals in persuasive discourse.

With respect to the observation of phenomena and the collection of data, the virtue of the scholar is precision in measurement and accuracy in reporting. With respect to the scope of investigation, the excellence of scholarship is comprehensiveness and inclusiveness, which may be understood in either historical or logical terms. With respect to the promulgation of results, excellence in the scholar means articulateness, aptness/elegance of expression, and order. If, as Alfred North Whitehead suggested, education is "the imaginative consideration of learning," then the power of imagination is what gives higher education its special excellence.

Above all, perhaps, an academy of learning values freedom - - the freedom to inquire, the freedom to teach, and the freedom to learn. Academic freedom is the most cherished tradition of education, and provision for the continued protection and nurture of that tradition is one of the deepest administrative concerns of every academy of learning. The academy is based also on respect for personality and on the teacher's virtue in serving the development of another person. The act of education is an inherently self-giving act. Its aim is the realization of the highest human potential in every individual. Closely related to this value is the academy's historic commitment to the idea of justice, to fairness in judgment based on available information, and to the restraint of prejudice and bias in both belief and inter-personal relationships. The academy is a community, and it makes a virtue of collegiality as a means of bringing the best minds and competence to bear on the treatment of both scholarly and policy questions on the merits.

Excellence is essential to freedom. That is true both for individuals and for society. Indeed, one of the important lessons of history is that individual and social excellence are interdependent. Personal freedom - - the freedom to do, to think, to reason - - is conditioned by competence; and the viability of free institutions depends on the virtue of the people who make those institutions work. A democracy built on mediocrity will never achieve the highest ideal of human freedom. The great test confronting our society from the beginning has been on the question whether we shall be able to combine excellence with equality, whether we shall succeed in honoring excellence in its highest forms while giving opportunity and respect to every human being regardless of background, station, or calling.

Every academy of learning is called to the contemplation and advocacy of excellence, of virtue. The university is called to the nurture of its own virtue. It cannot depend on others to develop and protect the excellence on which its life and work depend. It must act so that it can safely assume the values which are essential to academic pursuits. And it must protect the integrity of the community of learning.

2. Education and Indoctrination

The means by which the academy nurtures the values on which its life depends cannot be inconsistent with its own methodologies. The methods of scholarship are those of critical inquiry, and the methods of education are those of rational analysis. The freedom of the higher learning cannot be advanced by authoritative systems or control mechanisms which restrict inquiry. In pursuing its ideals the university must remain true to its selfhood.

ACADEMIC FREEDOM

Robert M. MacIver says that, amid all the divisions and fragmentations of the American university, there is unanimity on one issue: American scholars all affirm "the intrinsic worthwhileness of the knowledge of things, the moral and spiritual value of the integrity of mind that steadfastly seeks the truth, refusing to yield to biases within and pressures without, determined, so far as may be, 'to strive, to seek, to find, and not to yield.'" The university, he says, is true to itself and makes its best contribution to society when it "makes the inculcation of this virtue its special concern."[1]

His choice of the term "inculcation" is unfortunate, if revealing. For it expresses the common, often unwitting, assumption of the academy that it can deal with virtue only through strategies of "inculcating," "producing," or "creating" the perspectives, dispositions, and habits which are desired. Academic freedom requires something more. It requires the preservation of a non-indoctrinative educational method even when the university is concerned with the formation of virtues about which it cannot help but care.

One of the central issues of educational theory concerns the distinction between education and indoctrination. Indoctrination is a process of leading an individual or group to adopt a belief or standard of conduct without adequate consideration of the grounds of that belief or standard -- i.e. without taking into account the freedom of the learner to make his own independent assessment of the justifiability of the belief or standard through applying a rule of warranted inference. Education, on the other hand, is a process of human development through reasoned investigation as conducted within the scholarly disciplines as currently constituted. The freedom which is essential to education depends on a cooperative search for truth through open and rational inquiry.

Indoctrination is the imposition of particular beliefs, doctrines, or standards of worth on persons without respecting their capacity for free inquiry and critical judgment. It is the conditioning of individuals to accept certain standards for belief and conduct without the guidance of self-conscious and critical assessment of the basis of such standards. Indoctrination conditions rather than educates. Education, on the other hand, is always dialectical, being based on a method of criticism. Instruction depends on the learner's freedom; indoctrination treats the learner as an object to be controlled or manipulated.

Indoctrination is commonly associated with any form of moral or religious education. It is widely assumed, even by the courts, that an indoctrinative method is characteristic of a religiously affiliated school, at least when it begins to treat theological or religious topics. But moral education, properly understood, is the process of showing the student how to do moral thinking. It is a matter not of transmitting values, but of teaching what counts as an adequate basis for accepting a value. It is only when moral education is pursued in a manner which emphasizes the methodology of moral decision that it will be taken seriously within the higher learning. Whenever the academy treats values-related issues it must do so in the spirit of respect for freedom and for truth.

Values education is a process of enabling students to strengthen their capacities for thinking about moral and religious issues and for forming justifiable and reliable value judgments. Values education is not merely a process of causation leading predictably to specified patterns of behavior or belief. It is a process of enabling each student to independently confirm the warrantability and reliability of value judgments through the application of critical thought and informed scholarship. Values education, in other words, helps every individual to judge for himself.

The process of education is concerned at every stage with nurturing the autonomy of learners. Hence an authoritative or indoctrinative approach to teaching, if ever appropriate in education, must always be viewed as provisional at best and as requiring specific justification of its utility in realizing the long-term goal of nurturing every individual's autonomy.

The act of education is based on respect for personality. Indoctrination, on the other hand, seeks to anticipate choice. An education which seeks to fix beliefs in a learner without examination of their justifying grounds only enslaves him to his teachers. No teaching, as William Kilpatrick says, can be ethically defensible which knowingly and deliberately hides from any person any matter within his grasp which would help him to think more adequately.

Freedom is founded on seriousness of inquiry; and inquiry in a university classroom is founded on a dialectical method of instruction. A college in which there is nothing but authoritative advocacy may succeed in indoctrinating, but it cannot educate. A true religious faith will always allow for flexibility in theological articulation and for progress in theological science so as to guarantee freedom in the scholarly examination of its meaning and implications. In theological education, too, "fundamental doubt is the father of knowledge."

3. The Denominational University

Religiously affiliated colleges and universities have historically accepted the particular mission of showing how religious values may be integrated with scholarship and with all of life. A whole system of education has been founded on a theological understanding which seeks the synthesis of faith and learning, on an educational model which contemplates the permeation of the teaching/learning process by religious values and purposes, and on a social ideal which contemplates the penetration of the common life of the campus by the discipline and sensitivities of a community of faith.

Such a collegiate model, of course, is no longer widely endorsed, either in circles of American higher education generally or within church-related higher education in particular. It is well known that George Bernard Shaw viewed the very idea of a Catholic university as an illusion - - indeed, as a contradiction in terms. The idea of the university as a place of untrammeled inquiry cannot be reconciled, Shaw contended, with the imposition of creedal limitations on the results of inquiry by the sponsoring religious community. A college is a college, said Shaw, just as a hospital is a hospital, regardless of whether or not it is run by a church. What is, perhaps, less known is that Shaw's opinion is widely shared in circles of American higher education today.

John Cogley, writing from a Catholic perspective, once predicted that the day would come when historians would find the idea of a Catholic college or university as incredible as the idea of the papal states appears today. While steadfastly confessing his own Catholicism, Cogley maintains that a college with a creedal base is a contradiction in terms. He is appalled by the idea that a university should be in a position of advocacy with respect to ideology or any proposition currently debated by responsible scholars, or that it should play favorites among the giants of intellect. The university, says Cogley, bears witness not to ideology, but only to the integrity of its own processes of scholarly investigation. And it exists not to strengthen students' earlier commitments, but to enable them to make meaningful, informed adult choices. In so doing it doesn't play with loaded dice.

Cogley is not advocating that Marquette or Notre Dame should be dismantled, or even that religion should no longer be allowed to be of central interest in such universities. He thinks that there is good reason for the church to operate universities, just as there is good reason for it to operate hospitals. But "they should be universities, period," he says. "God knows we need universities that are truly universities. Any group that adds to their number will have the nation in its debt." But the universities of the church, he maintains, need to be "pluralized, ecumenized, and universalized in order to be transformed into genuine universities in a pluralistic, ecumenical, and philosophically many-mansioned world."[2]

259

A Protestant version of Cogley's point of view appears in Harvey Cox's The Secular City. The university, says Cox, has always been a problem for the church. But the alienation between the two is now wider than ever. The growing separation of college and church is, he thinks, an inevitable - - and quite proper - - expression of the end of the church's dominance in Western culture. The secularization of the church is bound to lead to the secularization of the university. He writes,

> The whole idea of a 'Christian' college or university after the breaking apart of the medieval synthesis has little meaning. The term Christian is not one that can be used to refer to universities any more than to observatories or laboratories. . . . The idea of developing 'Christian universities' in America was bankrupt before it began.[3]

In 1945 the celebrated Harvard report on "General Education in a Free Society" took the view that formation of a program of general education on the basis of a supposed religious or theological integration would never work under modern conditions - - except, possibly, for a few isolated institutions. Religion, said the committee, "is not now for most colleges a practicable source of intellectual unity."[4] The committee based its conclusion ostensibly on its assessment of the tension between sectarianism and democracy in the pluralistic American society, but the judgment also had a deeper intellectual root. The problem stems in part from fundamental doubts, entertained in many sectors of the academy, about the logical basis of theological method.

The fact is that the classic model of a Christian college has become more and more rare in the real world of American higher education today. In its survey of church-sponsored higher education in the mid-sixties the Danforth Commission on Church Colleges and Universities assessed the extent to which such institutions were effectively helping their students to develop a vital religious perspective from which to view life and learning and concluded:

A few church colleges are engaged in significant demonstrations, but, on the whole, church-related education is not doing much better in helping students face fundamental questions than are other institutions. Much of the confusion and uncertainty regarding this responsibility which one finds in public and independent colleges and universities, and indeed in the world at large, is also present in church-related institutions of higher learning.[5]

Researchers would doubtless reach similar conclusions twenty years later. The Danforth project identified two more or less typical patterns. On the one hand, there were church-related colleges whose curricula and personnel were virtually indistinguishable from those of so-called "secular" institutions. On the other hand, there were more theologically determinate colleges which were dogmatically restricting freedom of inquiry and of learning within authoritative creedal constraints. Rarely did the investigators find a sense of the essential unity of faith and learning, derived from clear theological understanding integrated with rigorous and free inquiry.

Theodore M. Hesburgh, as is well known, has made a special effort at Notre Dame (and throughout American Catholic higher education, where he has had such a powerful influence) to prove Bernard Shaw wrong. One of the many tributes which were paid to Father Hesburgh in his remarkable career was his being given the Alexander Meiklejohn Award for Academic Freedom by the American Association of University Professors in 1970. It was the first time anyone from a Catholic university had been so honored. In accepting the award Hesburgh reaffirmed the ideal concept of a Catholic university, as developed by a group of North American Catholic educators in the so-called Land O'Lakes Statement in 1967:

ACADEMIC FREEDOM

The Catholic university today must be a university in the full modern sense of the word, with a strong commitment to and concern for <u>academic excellence</u>. To perform its teaching and research functions effectively, the Catholic university must have a true autonomy and academic freedom in the face of authority of whatever kind, lay or clerical, external to the academic community itself. To say this is simply to assert that institutional autonomy and academic freedom are essential conditions of life and growth and indeed of survival for Catholic universities as for all universities.[6]

In the Catholic university, said Hesburgh, there can be "no theological or philosophical imperialism," no intellectual boundaries and no barriers, no outlawed books or subjects. Scholarship in the Catholic university is no different from what it is in any other place. The Catholic university honors and respects all scientific and disciplinary methodologies; it draws knowledge from all the traditions of mankind; it explores the insights of every age and seeks to extend the frontiers of advancing knowledge in every possible way.

Hesburgh's essential answer to Shaw is that the Catholic university does not cease to be free just because it is Catholic. The university is not the church; it is not even the church teaching. It is "a place - - the only place -- in which Catholics and others, on the highest level of intellectual inquiry, seek out the relevance of the Christian message to all of the problems and opportunities that face modern man and his complex world."[7]

The church, says Hesburgh, has nothing to fear from creative criticism springing from the community of scholars who, while loving the church and desiring to participate in its continual reformation, remain steadfast in their autonomy and "creative disaffiliation." In a word, says Hesburgh, "if the prophetic, creatively critical mission of the church-related institution of higher learning is not vital and courageous," then its role in mediating between the sacred and the secular, between the believing and the unbelieving,

262

between church and society will become suspect; and there would then be "no easier option for the generality of mankind but to write off the Christian college and university as Cox has done."[8]

William J. Byron, S.J., President of The Catholic University of America, takes the same view. Every collegiate community, whether Catholic or not, says Byron, is committed to the search for truth. Hence open inquiry in a Catholic college or university is neither unusual nor threatening. Byron writes:

> Truth is both the norm and goal of the continuing quest which is the Catholic college. There is no truth which can be labelled inappropriate or inadmissible in a Catholic college, where the search for truth is conducted within the context of disciplines and forms of creativity which belong in any authentic academic setting. . . . The university is the best place the Church has to meet its young in a spirit of open inquiry on solid intellectual grounds bordered only by a full range of academic disciplines to guide the development of human understanding. In such a setting faith has nothing to fear.[9]

In any academy of learning there are limits on academic freedom. Byron notes several which are common to all academic settings: the limits of truth, of scholarly discipline, of responsible inquiry and responsible communication of the results of inquiry. Every teacher's academic freedom is restricted by the freedom (as well as by the limitations) of the students he is trying to teach. Academic freedom is limited in its expression not only by truth, but also by human prudence, which refrains from communication of truths which cannot be assimilated and interpreted on their merits. There are also limits which inhere in the social context and constituency within which the academy functions. In public institutions such limitations may arise out of the circumstances of public policy and public opinion. Similarly, says Byron, in the religiously affiliated college or university there are ecclesial limits on academic freedom.

Such limits are not necessarily inconsistent with the ideal of respect for truth and human rights which is the foundation of academic integrity. Faith-related limits, says Byron, need not violate the essential meaning of academic freedom when they are authentically shared by the religious tradition or community with which the institution has chosen to be associated. Nor are theological limits in any way inappropriate as long as they are drawn by truth and prudence. Furthermore, says Byron, the theological tradition of the church-related college is not a static creed, but "a living and growing reality." A theologically conditioned education is not a process of authoritative advocacy of revealed truth, but a "communion with the community of faith" which any particular theology is intended to serve.

Religiously affiliated higher education always functions in continuity with a particular religious tradition. Reflection on past understandings is the point of departure for its inquiry, but its special responsibility is to discover new and deeper understandings of its tradition and to construe it in new relationships and applications. In this process of adaptation tensions with conventional understandings are sure to arise. A "new and deeper understanding" of the historic faith might be viewed in some quarters not as continuity but as discontinuity with the religious tradition.

The religiously affiliated college or university, says Byron, needs a procedure for deciding whether a given theological innovation represents a continuous advance of the tradition or a discontinuous break with it. He advocates a process for shared examination of such questions by university and church, by theologians and bishops; but he thinks that, in the last analysis, the formal determination is the province of the church. The church is the guardian of its own traditions. Catholic theology must proceed, therefore, with due respect for the teaching authority of bishops.

ACADEMIC FREEDOM

Byron thinks the church has much at stake, however, in rightly deciding this close question. If the church's decisions have the effect of infringing the competence and freedom of theological inquiry, the church itself will suffer. It will not grow in its understanding of the full implications of its faith and will lose its vitality and effectiveness in a rapidly changing world.

The church and the university are united in their need for freedom. Unresolved tensions between church authorities and university scholars concerning the advance of religious understanding may at times appear as violations of academic freedom. But for Byron a larger freedom is at stake: the freedom of church and university to advance the essential purposes and mission of the tradition they share.

Not all religiously affiliated colleges and universities see themselves in such terms. Some would impose creedal constraints on academic inquiry, on the selection of teaching/learning materials, and on the selection of personnel. Some would disavow our theory of instruction, as distinguished from indoctrination, and would view their mission in terms of "inculcating values" and creating beliefs. And some would say that what is most urgently needed in religiously affiliated higher education today is not greater emphasis on the traditions of academic freedom, but restoration of the authority of traditional values and beliefs in the disciplines of teaching and learning.

Yet even the more strongly creedal colleges and universities need to provide for the development of new perspectives on authoritative formulations, in order that cherished ideals may be adapted to changing circumstances. In all communions religiously affiliated educational institutions function out on the edge of this continuing adaptation, working to construe historic confessions in new applications.

As Nels Ferre says, the church-related college serves a flexible faith, an ecumenical and inclusivist point of view, and if it restricts the scope of scholarly exploration by sectarian pronouncements, it will only destroy itself. He writes:

> At whatever point the mind is forbidden to probe any subject, precisely there it loses its confidence in its own usefulness or in its being needed, and develops fears and frustrations in relation to the fenced-off area. ... Intellectual no-trespassing signs frustrate and give us basic insecurities. When men are not allowed to interpret revelation for themselves on account of its absolute authority, but must accept it as it is, the mind, by thus being fenced off and deprived of its rightful function, feels frustrated.[10]

The common understanding of academic freedom views it in terms of the right to pursue truth without constraints imposed by doctrines, individuals, or agencies which are external to scholarship itself. Such an understanding emphasizes freedom of investigation, of advocacy, of educational exposition. The Hesburgh concept of academic freedom involves also the "freedom to be." It values not only freedom to pursue the truth, but freedom in the truth. And it declares that a program of education can be an instrument of freedom in the fullest sense only if it is comprehensive in its engagement with all the questions of human thought and experience, including questions of faith and value.

The task of administrative leadership in religiously affiliated higher education centers on the formation of a community of learning in which freedom in this larger sense is possible. Part of that task is to recruit, appoint, and support individuals who possess qualities which contribute to the formation of the environment in which the freedom to think and to be can be nurtured. This means that the employment practices of an institution dedicated to the pursuit of this more comprehensive idea of freedom will be significantly different from those of an institution in which a more limited idea of freedom functions. Mere conformity to a doctrinal or behavioral standard is not enough. An informed sensitivity to the heritage of faith and value, a caring commitment to the continuing adaptation and reformation of structures and ministries, and the capacity for creative criticism are among the academic qualities which a religiously affiliated college or university needs to do its work.

The legal and social foundations of such an understanding of the task of religiously affiliated higher education are in need of confirmation and clarification. The precedents of academic appointment policy have been dominated for several generations by a concept of academic freedom which does not serve the purpose. And the law of higher education almost completely misunderstands the operations and requirements of religiously affiliated educational institutions functioning with this broader concept of freedom. A new tradition of freedom needs to be articulated and implemented, both within the academy and in the larger social and legal framework, if the distinctive promise of religiously affiliated higher education is to be realized in this country.

4. The Freedom of the Scholar

Academic freedom is the most deeply cherished tradition of the modern university. It has several dimensions. In its individual dimension it concerns the rights of scholars to pursue truth wherever it leads. In its institutional dimension it is the corresponding responsibility of scholarly and educational institutions to protect scholars from any hazards or threats which might prevent them from carrying out their obligations in the pursuit of truth.

As defined in the classic formulation of Arnold O. Lovejoy, academic freedom

> is the freedom of the teacher or research worker in higher institutions of learning to investigate and discuss the problems of his science and to express his conclusions, whether through publication or in the instruction of students, without interference from political or ecclesiastical authority, or from the

administrative officials of the institution in which he is employed, unless his methods are found by qualified bodies of his own profession to be clearly incompetent or contrary to professional ethics.[11]

Several aspects of Lovejoy's definition are noteworthy. First, it focuses on professorial autonomy vis a vis administrative and hierarchical authorities, which are viewed as external to the scholarly discipline within which the professor works. Second, it assumes that the only restraints which may be placed on the activities of teaching or research are those which may be imposed by professional or scholarly peers. Third, it defines freedom mainly in terms of the individual's expression or publication of whatever conclusions his scholarship has reached. (In other words, academic freedom is a special instance of freedom of speech and expression.) Fourth, it limits the concept of academic freedom to learning at an advanced level, and fails (we assume deliberately, rather than inadvertently) to recognize any claim to academic freedom at the elementary or secondary education levels.

If now we ask whence the right to academic freedom arises, we may receive a variety of answers. As Lovejoy sees it, academic freedom is demanded by the social role of the scholar. His function as expert informant or adviser of the community requires that he be "set apart" to pursue his investigations free from bias or interference. The scholar's office, says Lovejoy, is analogous to that of a judge, and requires that he be both competent and disinterested.

But most important, the community of scholars constitute an outpost of the intellectual life of civilized society charged with widening the domain of the human mind. And the performance of this function is certain to mean, at times, that widely or generally held beliefs will be undermined. The scholar cannot perform this function, says Lovejoy, if he is "shackled by the requirement that his conclusions shall never seriously deviate either from generally accepted beliefs or from those accepted by the persons, private or official, through whom society provides the means for [his] maintenance." The principle of academic freedom is thus the paradoxical one that "those who buy a certain service may not . . . prescribe the nature of the service to be rendered."

Others have contended that academic freedom (in something like Lovejoy's concept) is guaranteed by the U.S. Constitution as a special instance of freedom of speech and expression. The protection of the rights of academicians has, indeed, been pursued at times in the courts, and with some success. But the legal vindication of the right of the scholar is by no means as facile as the academic rhetoric through which it is claimed.

William Van Alstyne complains that the meaning of the term, "academic freedom," has been debased by a "promiscuous usage" which has obscured the difference between academic freedom simpliciter and freedom of speech and expression as a universal civil right, regardless of one's vocation. Academics have sometimes claimed a special protection for freedom of political expression and participation which is due them because of their distinctive social function. Such an "errant claim" of academic freedom, Van Alstyne contends, only obscures the authentic issues and invites public indifference and cynicism toward the academy. And the impression has been created that academic freedom involves claims to a form of employment security available to no other profession. The resulting confusion, says Van Alstyne, has even made it "difficult for the courts of this country to recognize an authentic academic-freedom case when they have had one."[12]

Van Alstyne cites a number of dicta in Supreme Court decisions touching the subject of academic freedom, but finds no clear constitutional doctrine. The judicial system, he says, has not yet responded to those (including himself) who have been urging acknowledgement of "a separately-identifiable First Amendment right to academic freedom." The chances for development of a clear constitutional definition of academic freedom might have been improved, he suggests, if the academic community had limited its own

269

claims to the rights which belong more properly to the academic function.

In 1937 a survey by the Yale Law Journal of the topic, "What the law can do to protect academic freedom," came to the conclusion that, "It is extremely difficult to frame a legal action through which the courts can give relief against . . . unwarrantable limitations on academic freedom." Academic freedom, commented the Journal, is neither a property right nor a constitutional privilege, nor is the term so defined by the history of judicial usage that an action against an alleged interference with academic freedom might be presented in a justiciable form. Furthermore, there is the added barrier of judicial reluctance to intervene in the internal affairs of an educational institution, except in cases of an apparent breach of contract or a breakdown of established administrative procedures. Courts might be persuaded to address the question of the authority under which an academic employment action was taken, but not the propriety of the action. The commentator concluded, "It seems unduly optimistic to look to the courts for the development of effective legal protection for academic freedom, at least pending an improvement in the concrete provisions made for such rights in statutes and customary contracts."[13]

Of course, that summary was prepared before the 1940 Statement of Principles of Academic Freedom and Tenure, published jointly by the American Association of University Professors and the Association of American Colleges, and before the firming up of faculty contracts in many American colleges and universities. Yet the capacity of American law to address the issue of academic freedom remains limited. Almost twenty-five years later a Wisconsin professor found essentially the same condition as was noted by the Yale researcher, declaring that, "A reading of hundreds of cases has yielded very few opinions which pay any attention to the subject of academic freedom, and, much less, show any genuine appreciation of either its meaning or importance. . . . So far as academic freedom and tenure in colleges and universities are concerned, American decisional law may be described as formless and almost rudimentary."[14]

In a perceptive article contributed to a 1963 symposium, William P. Murphy reviewed a long series of recent cases which he saw as opening up the possibility of "a substantial degree of judicial protection of academic freedom as a right recognized and guaranteed by the United States Constitution." What he found, however, was a good deal of judicial rhetoric together with the potential for procedural, but not for substantive, safeguards. He reported that there was still no clear case in which the Supreme Court had unambiguously confirmed the constitutional basis for invalidating termination of a teacher because of a violation of academic freedom. What the law had provided was protection from summary dismissal without a hearing.[15] Thomas Emerson, writing at about that same time, reached a similar conclusion, declaring that, "The decisions of the Supreme Court until now have not utilized the First Amendment in any unique way in the academic freedom area."[16]

Murphy expressed the opinion that at best American law could never be more than "an occasional valuable ally in the struggle for academic freedom." The essential line of defense of academic freedom, he said, would continue to be "vigilant and determined self-help activity within the academic community itself." Indeed, the academy has understandable reasons for being reluctant to aggressively pursue legal remedies for violations of academic freedom. As an AAUP commentator put it on one occasion, "What the Court gives, it can also take away. Moreover, in the process it may unwittingly persuade many people that only those principles of academic freedom that are finally recognized by the courts as law need be observed, [with the result that] academic freedom may be left in a weaker position than it was before it became a concern of law."[17] Or as Thomas Emerson puts it, "The gap between the claims made on behalf of academic freedom and the claims the courts are presently likely to recognize is apparently a wide one."[18]

In a more recent survey of the constitutional basis of academic freedom, Robert M. O'Neil sees a somewhat greater potential for legal remedies to protect academic freedom. He, too, sees the potential as limited, however. He does not find that traditional issues of academic freedom are central to the judicial docket. He sees an emergence of non-constitutional, statutory safeguards, somewhat reducing the urgency of First and Fourteenth Amendment protections. He thinks that loyalty oaths, legislative investigations, and dismissals for political activity are largely threats of the past. And he notes a trend toward greater concern about conflicting claims to academic freedom among various constituencies within academic institutions, suggesting that these are dilemmas which colleges and universities might be well advised to keep out of the courts.

O'Neil identifies several judicial precedents which assure a core protection of classroom utterance, but he remarks that courts continue to show a certain deference to the uniqueness of the academic environment and procedures. He warns that "resort to the courts for vindication of academic claims is not always wise," and urges modest expectations of what judicial procedures might accomplish. He advises that "one should look to constitutional litigation only for those safeguards that are unavailable from any other source."[19]

Mark G. Yudof sees serious problems in the understanding of academic freedom in terms of the personal autonomy of the scholar-teacher (what he calls the first "face" of academic freedom).[20] Yudof's problems concern not only the grounds on which any claim to scholarly autonomy might be justified, but also the compatibility of such a concept with the social mission and function of education. Yudof thus sees a second "face" of academic freedom, which emphasizes the rights and responsibilities of governmental agencies in formulating educational programs in the public interest. The "government expression face" of academic freedom places an appropriate restriction on the autonomy of individual teachers, subject to the limitation that government action may not be calculated to stamp out unpopular or competing ways of thinking.

Yudof also distinguishes a third "face of academic freedom," namely, the autonomy which belongs to educational institutions, particularly to those functioning in the independent sector. Under this aspect academic freedom is the independence of academic organizations, under governmental charter, from the control of political and economic power. Institutional academic freedom protects an independent school from an overreaching governmental authority and restricts any tendency, under the "government expression" face of academic freedom, for government to exercise too strong an initiative in suppressing competing viewpoints and ideologies in the educational system. Each of these aspects of academic freedom - - the personal autonomy, the government expression, and the institutional autonomy faces - - is limited by the other aspects, says Yudof, and the interplay among these aspects must be recognized in any comprehensive analysis of the concept.

It is not enough to interpret academic freedom as the right of the scholar to pursue truth wherever it leads. In American higher education the function of the scholar is primarily that of a teacher, but his _Lehrfreiheit_ is inescapably limited by the _Lernfreiheit_ of his students and by the social accountability of every act of education. Nor may academic freedom be claimed merely as a device for protecting the interests of academicians as an elite group of citizens, for that would merely convert the concept to a partisan tactic. As Edmund Pincoffs says, the public long ago learned to recognize the ways in which academic special pleading and post hoc rationalization can be passed off as impartial analysis and reasoned defense.[21] Many people see the autonomy claimed by professors as nothing but a mythology which they use to defend their job security.

The constitutional freedom of the scholar, like that of the ordinary citizen, is unlimited and unconditional in so far as it concerns his beliefs. The right to believe what one chooses is generally available even in the most totalitarian of regimes. It is when the citizen begins to express or act on his beliefs that restrictions arise. So, too, for the academician. Freedom of expression is quite broad in this country, but there are points where such freedom runs into conflict with other freedoms, both individual and institutional, and where external restraints may be lawfully placed on both academic speech and action.

Sweezy v. New Hampshire (1957)

In the period of the loyalty oaths and investigations into subversive activities during the 1950's and 1960's, a number of challenges to the freedoms of scholars and teachers reached the courts.[22] Perhaps the most famous is Sweezy v. New Hampshire, by Wyman, Attorney General, 354 U.S. 234 (1957). The case concerned an investigation by the state attorney general, acting on behalf of the New Hampshire State Legislature, into possible violations of the Subversive Activities Act of 1951, to "determine whether subversive persons as defined in said act are presently located within this state." The term "subversive person" was construed to mean "any person who commits, attempts to commit, or aids in the commission of any act intended to overthrow or assist in the overthrow, destruction, or alteration of the constitutional form of government of the United States or of the State of New Hampshire."

Paul Sweezy, a visiting lecturer at the University of New Hampshire, was summoned to appear before the Attorney General and testified at length on two occasions concerning his past activities and associations. During the course of the inquiry, Sweezy declined to answer several questions concerning his knowledge of the Progressive Party or members of the Progressive Party, questions concerning a humanities lecture he had delivered in a course at the University of New Hampshire, and questions concerning his personal beliefs. He gave as the defense for his refusal not his privilege against self-incrimination under the Fifth Amendment, but his view that the questions were not pertinent to the state's inquiry and violated his rights under the First Amendment.

ACADEMIC FREEDOM

A state court found Prof. Sweezy guilty of contempt of court, and the State Supreme Court affirmed. The Court conceded that the right to lecture and the right to associate with others for a common purpose were constitutionally protected freedoms which had been abridged through this investigation. It declared that these rights were not absolute rights, however. The court admitted that the inquiries authorized by the State Legislature had interfered with the defendant's free exercise of those liberties, but contended that such interference was justified by "the need for the legislature to be informed on so elemental a subject as the self-preservation of government."

The scope of the investigation which the Attorney General was authorized by state law to undertake was extremely broad. The New Hampshire Supreme Court noted that the potential sweep of the definitions of "subversive person" and "subversive organization" extended to conduct "only remotely related to actual subversion and which is done completely free of any conscious intent to be a part of such activity." Nevertheless, the questions which Prof. Sweezy refused to answer concerning the subject matter of his university lectures were deemed by the state courts pertinent for the purpose of determining whether or not he was a "subversive person." Similarly, the inquiries concerning the plaintiff's knowledge of the Progressive Party were deemed to fall within the Attorney General's mandate to obtain information as to whether or not that party and its predecessor are or were subversive organizations.

The U.S. Supreme Court reversed by a 6-2 majority, with Justices Clark and Burton dissenting. The majority was divided on the grounds of the reversal, however, and Justice Clark declared in his dissenting opinion that only four justices joined in "the principal opinion." Justice Whitaker did not participate in the decision. The opinion of the Court was delivered by Chief Justice Earl Warren.

ACADEMIC FREEDOM

The U.S. Supreme Court reversed the judgment of New Hampshire, not by stating a broad interpretation of First Amendment rights, but merely by disagreeing with the factual determination as to whether infringment of individual rights was justified in this instance. The opinion of the Court included considerable rhetoric concerning the importance of free universities in a democratic society. The Court decided the question on a more narrow basis, however, holding that the scope of the investigating authority delegated by the legislature to the Attorney General was too broad to assure the Court that the information sought was really essential to the legislature's fundamental purpose.

There is no question, said the majority opinion, "that legislative investigations, whether on a federal or state level, are capable of encroaching upon the constitutional liberties of individuals." When the encroachment is in the area of the First Amendment rights of individuals, however, the power of compulsory inquiry must be carefully circumscribed, and particularly so in the academic community. When an investigation "is invested with a broad and ill-defined jurisdiction," said the Court, the necessary safeguards of individual liberty are not present, and the risk of unnecessary infringement on individual liberties is great. Under the circumstances of Sweezy the Supreme Court found that the infringement of plaintiff's constitutional rights was not justified.

Even Justice Felix Frankfurter's concurring opinion, much celebrated for its rhetorical defense of the tradition of academic freedom, does not articulate a precise constitutional interpretation of the rights of the teacher/scholar. As Frankfurter saw it, the decision of the Court involved "balancing two contending principles - - the right of a citizen to political privacy, as protected by the Fourteenth Amendment, and the right of the State to self-protection." He thought, however, that the plaintiff was fully justified in refusing to answer questions either about his university lecture or about his political activity in the Progressive Party. In both instances, said Justice

276

Frankfurter, the questions of the attorney general were an impermissible intrusion of government into protected areas of individual privacy, there being no evidence that those individual liberties were compellingly subordinate to an interest of the state.

The Sweezy opinion includes language indicating a recognition by the Court of a basic right of academic freedom. Chief Justice Warren wrote:

The essentiality of freedom in the community of American universities is almost self-evident. . . To impose any strait jacket upon the intellectual leaders in our colleges and universities would imperil the future of our country. . . . Scholarship cannot flourish in an atmosphere of suspicion and distrust. Teachers and students must always remain free to inquire, to study, and to evaluate, to gain new maturity and understanding; otherwise our civilization will stagnate and die.

And Justice Frankfurter added:

For society's good - - if understanding be an essential need of society - - inquiries into these problems, speculations about them, stimulation in others of reflection upon them, must be left as unfettered as possible. Political power must abstain from intrusion into this activity of freedom, pursued in the interest of wise government and the people's well-being, except for reasons that are exigent and obviously compelling.

Justice Frankfurter's opinion also included a formulation of an institutional right of academic freedom, often cited in recent commentaries as Frankfurter's "four freedoms" principle:

It is the business of a university to provide that atmosphere which is most conducive to speculation, experiment, and creation. It is an atmosphere in which there prevail 'the four essential freedoms' of a university - - to determine for itself on academic grounds who may teach, what may be taught, how it shall be taught, and who may be admitted to study.

Actually Frankfurter's words have no significance de jure. For one thing, they do not occur in the opinion of the Court. But neither are they Frankfurter's own formulation. They are quoted by him in a strongly rhetorical paragraph from a statement on The Open Universities of South Africa, prepared by a group of senior scholars at two universities, with the participation of their respective chancellors, both of whom Frankfurter particularly respected as former members of the South African judiciary. The rhetorical force of the "Four Academic Freedoms" formulation, and its use by a Supreme Court Justice of Frankfurter's standing, have earned it a very wide circulation in American discussions of the legal rights of universities. The fact remains, however, that the Sweezy decision is less explicit in clarifying a constitutional right of academic freedom than it is reputed to be.

Barenblatt v. United States (1959)

In Barenblatt v. United States, 360 U.S. 109 (1959), the U.S. Supreme Court upheld the conviction of Lloyd Barenblatt, a teacher at Vassar College, for contempt of Congress for refusing to answer questions put to him by the House Committee on Un-American Activities concerning his membership in the Communist Party during the period when he was a graduate student and teaching fellow at the University of Michigan. The decision again required the Court to weigh the conflicting constitutional claims of congressional authority and individual rights.

Barenblatt, who had refused to answer questions not on Fifth Amendment (self-incrimination) grounds, but on First and Fourteenth Amendment grounds, was convicted of contempt and was fined and imprisoned. The Supreme Court was divided 5-4 in upholding the judgment. Justice Black wrote a long dissenting opinion, in which Chief Justice Burger and Justice Douglas joined. Justice Brennan, after

278

agreeing with Black's analysis, added a brief dissenting word of his own.

The Court had no difficulty affirming a Congressional "power of inquiry," which it said was as broad as its potential power to enact and to appropriate as provided by the Constitution. The Court noted, however, that there were a number of limitations to the Congressional authority to inquire, including some imposed by the Bill of Rights. In this instance, however, Congressional investigation of "the extent of a nation-wide, indeed, world-wide problem," namely, the spread of Communist influence, appeared to the Court to have been justifiably exercised and properly limited to an area of Congressional authority under the Constitution.

The significance of <u>Barenblatt</u> is not in its judgment, but in its dicta. Justice John M. Harlan, writing for the majority, explained the limitations of the decision by citing the principle of academic freedom. "Broadly viewed, he wrote, "inquiries cannot be made into the teaching that is pursued in any of our educational institutions. When academic teaching-freedom and its corollary learning-freedom, so essential to the well-being of the Nation are claimed, this Court will always be on the alert against the intrusion by Congress into this constitutionally protected domain." Harlan distinguished, however, between an inquiry the purpose of which was to judge the content of teaching, which he judged to be impermissible, and an inquiry the purpose of which was to determine "the extent to which the Communist Party has succeeded in infiltrating into our universities," which he thought fell well within the authority of Congress.

The Court refused to treat the Communist Party as just another political association or to treat any educational institution as "a constitutional sanctuary from inquiry into matters that may otherwise be within the constitutional legislative domain." The Court thought that the exercise of congressional investigative rights in this case was justified by "the long and widely accepted view that the tenets of the Communist Party include the ultimate overthrow of the Government of the United States by force and violence," and noted that this view of Communism had been given formal expression by the Congress in the Subversive Activities Control Act of 1950 and the Internal Security Act of 1950. "We think," declared Justice Harlan, "that investigatory power in this domain is not to be denied Congress solely because the field is education."

Justice Hugo Black's long dissent makes no mention of a special right of academic freedom, but it presents one of the most eloquent of the Supreme Court's many defenses of First Amendment rights. Black disagreed with the suggestion that laws abridging freedom of expression or association might be justified by a congressional or judicial balancing of governmental interests against individual rights, or that such freedoms might be abridged when the "national security" is at stake, or that the ordinary requirements of the Bill of Rights do not apply when the Congressional investigating committee is merely after Communists, who "do not constitute a political party but only a criminal gang." Such redefinitions of the First Amendment seemed to Black highly arbitrary and dangerous. He declared:

> Today's holding, in my judgment, marks another
> major step in the progressively increasing retreat from
> the safeguards of the First Amendment. . . Ultimately
> all the questions in this case really boil down to one -
> - whether we as a people will try fearfully and futilely
> to preserve democracy by adopting totalitarian methods,
> or whether in accordance with our traditions and our
> Constitution we will have the confidence and courage to
> be free.

Keyishian v. Board of Regents (1967)

In Keyishian v. Board of Regents, 385 U.S. 589 (1967), the U.S. Supreme Court issued, perhaps, its most direct affirmation of the constitutional right of academic freedom. The case arose as a challenge to the constitutionality of Section 3021 of New York's Education Law and Section 105 of the Civil Service Law, which provided that "treasonable or seditious utterances or acts" were sufficient grounds for dismissal from service in the educational system of the state. Appellants were members of the faculty of the University of Buffalo, originally owned and operated by a private corporation but brought into the state system in 1962, at which time the faculty became state employees. Their employment had been terminated when each had refused to comply with a requirement of the university trustees, acting under the regulations of the State Board of Regents and the laws of the state, that they certify that they were not Communists. The U.S. Supreme Court held the New York loyalty oath law unconstitutional.

In an earlier case testing the New York loyalty oaths for educators, Adler v. Board of Education, 342 U.S. 485 (1952), the Court had upheld the dismissal of a number of public school teachers who had refused to declare that they were not members of any of the organizations listed by the Board of Regents as organizations which "advocate, advise, teach, or embrace the doctrine that the government should be overthrown by force or violence or any other unlawful means.". In that case the Court distinguished between the right of individuals "to assemble, speak, think, and believe as they will," which is, of course, protected under the Constitution, and their "right to work for the State in the school system on their own terms," which, the Court said, has neither a statutory nor a constitutional basis.

The state, said the Adler Court, has the authority to lay down reasonable terms of employment in the public school system, and the Court did not find the state's requirement for such employment unreasonable in this case. However, the Court specifically reserved judgment in Adler on the constitutionality of Section 3021, holding only that if, under the procedures set up in New York, "a person is found to be unfit and is disqualified from employment in the public school system because of membership in a listed organization, he is not thereby denied the right of free speech and assembly."

In Keyishian, however, the Court was presented with a direct challenge to the constitutionality of the New York requirement. Furthermore, it was presented with a case involving faculty appointments at the higher education level, to which the provisions of Section 3021 had been extended subsequent to Adler. By a 5-4 majority (with Justices Clark, Harlan, Stewart, and White dissenting) the Court held the New York laws "unconstitutionally vague, since no teacher can know . . . what constitutes the boundary between 'seditious' and nonseditious utterances and acts," and since some provisions of the laws "may well prohibit the employment of one who advocates doctrine abstractly without any attempt to indoctrinate others or to incite others to action, and may be construed to cover mere expression of belief."

Justice William Brennan's majority opinion recognized that the state has a legitimate interest in protecting its educational system from subversion, but it found that the intricacy and uncertainty of the administrative means by which the state was pursuing that interest constituted "a highly efficient in terrorem mechanism," which would inevitably stifle "that free play of the spirit which all teachers ought especially to cultivate and practice." Brennan wrote:

> Our Nation is deeply committed to safeguarding academic freedom, which is of transcendent value to all of us and not merely to the teachers concerned. That freedom is therefore a special concern of the First Amendment, which does not tolerate laws that cast a pall of orthodoxy over the classroom. . . The classroom is peculiarly the 'marketplace of ideas.' The Nation's future depends upon leaders trained through wide exposure to that robust exchange of ideas which discovers truth 'out of a multitude of tongues, [rather] than through any kind of authoritative selection.'

It should be emphasized that this unambiguous affirmation of the constitutional basis of academic freedom was issued in the setting of a public system of education and does not necessarily apply in the independent and religiously affilated sector. But the Court's intolerance of administrative mechanisms which would cast a "pall of orthodoxy" over a college or university is in the spirit of an academic tradition shared by both public and independent institutions.

5. Religious Orthodoxy and Academic Freedom

Robert MacIver speaks of three lines of attack on the tradition of academic freedom, the economic line, the religious line, and the line of social tradition (morals), and he requires the academy to vigorously defend itself from each. He sees the religious line of attack as involving the same kind of threat to the intellectual and moral integrity of the university as any other. Like Bernard Shaw, he has no doubt that the very concept of a denominational university involves a compromise of the academic ideal. He cheerfully recognizes the contributions made by religiously affiliated institutions both in the advancement of learning and in the struggle for academic freedom, but he thinks their denominational sponsorship and creedalism constitute a significant, although perhaps tolerable, restriction on the freedom of the academy.

The exercise of any type of religious test in a public or non-denominational university, says MacIver, would be completely unacceptable. The university may not be limited in its pursuit of truth by any a priori creed, whether political, economic, or religious. To limit the search for truth, he contends, is also to misdirect it. The university may never allow any area susceptible of scientific investigation to be fenced off as protected by some religious authority.

MacIver means neither to prohibit university study of religious and theological subjects by the ordinary methods of inquiry nor to contend that science holds the answers to any and all human questions. He contends only that the idea of the university makes no allowance for an authoritative ecclesiastical prescription of the content of

283

truth in advance of inquiry. A truth that is "given" need not be sought.

> Those who advocate that the university should take a definitely religious stand are in their proselyting zeal committing themselves to a total perversion of the function of the university. They would revert to the intellectual confusion of earlier times, when a superimposed prior 'truth' retarded the advance of knowledge and thus tended to imprison the inquiring mind. To make the university a center for the propagation of any creed, of any system of values that divides group from group, is to destroy the special quality and the unique mission of the university as a center for the free pursuit of knowledge wherever it may lead.[23]

The university is not the church, says MacIver, even though he recognizes the right of churches to conduct universities. A university may not be sectarian. Creedal indoctrination is beyond its province. The university serves all mankind and cannot be drawn into the religious divisions which create alienation in the human community. The methods of university scholarship and the processes of its reasoning are independent of any doctrinal assumptions, and the course of its investigations are not determined in advance.

In an appendix to his book MacIver offers a gesture to a special concept of academic freedom in the denominational university. Such a university, he grants, cannot be expected to make academic appointments purely on the basis of the professional competence and personal integrity of candidates, since the institution may need to have assurances that its teachers will be in harmony with the faith to which it adheres. MacIver notes that there is, of course, no single pattern of creedal "bindingness" which covers all the diversity that is found among religiously affiliated instituions. To this we readily agree. But we find his view of the freedom required by the concept of the religiously affiliated college or university fundamentally flawed and profoundly misleading. What is more painful is that his is a view which is widely accepted in both educational and legal circles.

MacIver sees the religiously affiliated university as having a double function. One function it shares with every institution of higher learning; the other it shares with its sponsoring church. The one function involves openness in the search for truth; the other involves a doctrinal commitment which sets limits on the range of inquiry. Any theological commitments which the denominational university as an institution postulates in carrying out its religious function seem to MacIver to create some kind of limitation on its academic freedom. "Any such institution," he maintains, "differs in certain relevant respects from the nondenominational kind."[24]

MacIver erroneously assumes that the values by which a religiously affiliated college or university lives have a fundamentally different character and foundation from those which underly the functioning of a nondenominational university. But the religiously affiliated university is no less committed to the openended pursuit of truth and is no less anxious to avoid static or preconceived doctrinal formulations. The aims of education at the religiously affiliated college concern neither orthodox opinion nor behavioral conformity, but maturity in well-formed belief and responsible action. Accordingly, an indoctrinative or authoritative approach to education is as counter-productive in the religious as in the secular college.

The religiously affiliated college or university values the pursuit of truth more than its possession. Its educational aims center on the process by which values are reflectively formed, rather than on the substantive or conventional norms by which belief and action are to be judged. The religiously affiliated college or university is no more "doctrinally" oriented than is any other university which views truth, beauty, and justice as excellences for human life. Its creeds, to the extent it employs them, are not tenets, but symbols; its confessions are not prescriptive, but heuristic; its aim is not doctrinal orthodoxy, but the freedom of a mind growing in its knowledge of the truth.

Like any other educational enterprise the religiously affiliated college or university must be able to recruit and retain teachers and other staff who possess the scholarly, professional, and personal qualities suited to guiding students in the direction of such freedom. A process of selection is involved in its personnel system, but it is a process which is entirely compatible with the concept of academic freedom. For the aim of this selection is not to facilitate "inculcation" of desired values or indoctrination in prescribed beliefs, but to assure the free interplay of minds in the shared search for greater maturity and understanding. The faith that is sought in educational leaders at the religiously affiliated college or university is defined not in terms of its doctrinal content or its apologetic persuasiveness, but in terms of a religion-based personal wholeness and vocation which can make the undergraduate experience uniquely fulfilling.

MacIver misunderstands the nature of the personnel requirements of a religiously affiliated college or university. He also fails to grasp the nature of the moral and religious values which lie at the base of our common life. He tends to think of religious and moral development as discontinuous with the life of learning and as gratuitously added to university education by conditioning or by choice.

MacIver's view of the denominational university is essentially that of the AAUP-AAC 1940 Statement of Principles on Academic Freedom and Tenure, which stated: "Limitations of academic freedom because of religious or other aims of the institution should be clearly stated in writing at the time of the appointment." This provision assumes several things: (1) It assumes that the exercise of religious preference in academic appointments constitutes a limitation of academic freedom; (2) It assumes that such limitations will be creedal and can be articulated in the form of tenets which scholarship and teaching may be expected to respect; (3) It assumes that any limitation of academic freedom by virtue of the religious affiliation or purpose of the institution should be mutually stipulated by contract at the time of initial appointment.

In the mid-sixties some members of the AAUP became increasingly troubled by what they called the "ambiguous status" to which the 1940 statement appeared to assign the faculties of church-related colleges and universities. A Special Committee on Academic Freedom in Church-related Colleges and Universities was formed, "to study and make more explicit the meaning" of the 1940 statement. After a number of meetings the Committee issued its report, including a working draft of a Statement on Academic Freedom in Church-related Colleges and Universities, which was published in the AAUP Bulletin in 1967.

The Committee's report reaffirmed the long-standing AAUP position on restrictions on academic freedom in church-related institutions: "In light of the historic commitment of the academic community to academic freedom, and the dangers inherent in restrictions on that freedom, even when these are believed to be essential to the accomplishment of basic institutional aims, the Committee urges that religious privilege not be employed to provide a sanctuary in which to avoid the full responsibilities of institutions of higher education." The Committee took the view that any imposition of limitations on academic freedom in church-related colleges and universities "raised grave problems of professional concern for the academic community." And it gratefully noted "the emerging tendency of church-related colleges and universities to waive, or drastically restrict, the use of the [AAUP] limitation clause." Included in the recommendations of the draft Statement were the following:

1. Any limitation on academic freedom should be essential to the religious aims of the institution, and should be imposed only after consultation among faculty, administration, and governing body. Student opinion on such limitation also would be helpful.

2. Such limitation with its supporting rationale and relevance to the institution's educational objectives should be clearly stated in writing with reasonable particularity and made a matter of public knowledge. A copy of this statement should be provided to prospective teachers at the beginning of negotiations for appointment.

3. The faculty member should respect the stated aims of the institution to which he accepts an appointment, but academic freedom protects his right to express, clarify, and interpret positions - - including those identified as his own - - which are divergent from those of the institution and of the church which supports it.

The Statement was never formally adopted by the Association, but in 1969 a joint committee of the AAUP and the Association of American Colleges (which had joined in the original 1940 Statement) met to reevaluate the Statement of Principles. In 1970 the AAUP (without the support of the AAC) adopted a series of "Interpretive Comments" on the 1940 Statement, which explicitly abandoned the earlier accomodation to church-related institutions with the comment: "Most church-related institutions no longer need or desire the departure from the principle of academic freedom implied in the 1940 Statement, and we do not now endorse such a departure."

A further clarification was issued by the AAUP in 1976 in a brief statement On Discrimination: "The Association is committed to use its procedures and to take measures, including censure, against colleges and universities practicing illegal or unconstitutional discrimination, or discrimination on a basis not demonstrably related to the job function involved, including but not limited to age, sex, physical handicap, race, religion, national origin, marital status, or sexual or affectional preference" (Our emphasis). Under this latest formulation the AAUP has declared its opposition to all employment discrimination on the basis of religion (including religiously based discrimination on the basis of sexual orientation), subject to an exemption for

288

positions where religion is a bona fide occupational qualification.

The pronouncements of the AAUP are accorded much less respect by higher education administrators these days than was the case thirty or forty years ago. Nevertheless, they represent a wide-spread consensus among academicians. The exercise of religious preference in academic employment at religiously affiliated institutions of higher education is tolerated, but not endorsed, in the American academy. And it is generally viewed as involving a compromise and limitation of academic freedom, which is thought to be more complete at institutions which exercise no such preference. The present challenge to religiously affiliated higher education is to demonstrate its commitment to the highest ideals of teaching and scholarship, and to propound a theory of academic freedom suited to its distinctive mission.

The functional definition of academic freedom is spelled out in institutional procedures governing academic appointments and termination. The rights of academic freedom and tenure are abstractions until due process is defined. In most institutions there is no concept of an academic-freedom right of initial appointment. (The same is true of a First-Amendment right to appointment, although there are statutory proscriptions against nondiscrimination in employment.) Furthermore, the procedures of most institutions provide for termination "without cause" during the period of probationary appointment, although academic freedom rights are guaranteed during the probationary period. However, due process for academic appointments typically provides at some point (for example, after the awarding of tenure) for termination only "for cause," with hearings at which parties may present and rebut statements explaining or justifying the challenged action.

Such procedures are no less important for religiously affiliated colleges and universities than for other types of institution. Indeed, the specification of administrative due process in academic and nonacademic employment decisions is critical to the effective exercise of religiously preferential hiring within the traditions of academic freedom. Most of the conflicts which arise in this area can be traced to poor documentation and implementation of these procedures.

Curran v. Catholic University of America (1989)

Perry A. Zirkel remarks that, "The umbrella provided by constitutional academic freedom is relatively small, thin, and tattered."[25] His understanding of the limitations of constitutionally protected academic freedom was illustrated recently in the case of Father Charles E. Curran, a tenured professor of theology at The Catholic University of America, who was suspended from his teaching position after the Vatican had determined that he held heterodox views on sexual ethics which made him unfit to teach theology in an ecclesiastical faculty. When Catholic University suspended him from his teaching position, Curran brought suit, claiming breach of contract, Curran v. Catholic University of America, Civil Action No. 1562-87, Sup.Ct. D.C. (Feb. 28, 1989). The suit was denied by the Superior Court of the District of Columbia, which tried the case in seven days of testimony without a jury. The court held that Catholic University had no contractual obligation to retain Curran as a teacher of Catholic theology after his ecclesiastical commission had been withdrawn.

The Catholic University of America has an unusual church relationship. It is the only American Catholic university which is chartered by the Vatican, but the University also has a civil charter as an independent institution governed by a self-perpetuating Board of Trustees. The Board has forty members, half clergy and half lay. In addition there are two ex officio members, the Chancellor of the University, who is the Archbishop of Washington, and the President of the University. The Holy See does not directly control the University, which is governed as an independent institution by the Board of Trustees, but it exercises a considerable influence over broad University policy.

ACADEMIC FREEDOM

The University awards ecclesiastical degrees in theology, philosophy, and canon law. In these departments faculty are required to hold an ecclesiastical commission, which authorizes them to teach in the name of the Church. Ecclesiastical commissions are found at Catholic University only in the faculties of theology, philosophy, and canon law. Other faculty of the University participate in some degree in the teaching mission of the church, but without any tie to an ecclesiastical faculty and thus without requiring a commission to teach officially in the name of the Church. Prof. Curran had taught theology at Catholic University with an ecclesiastical commission for a number of years and had earned tenure.

In April, 1979 Pope John Paul II issued an apostolic constitution, <u>Sapientia Christiana</u>, which contained new laws and regulations governing eccesiastical faculties. Under these regulations all those who teach disciplines connected with Catholic faith and morals are required to obtain a canonical mission from the Church, "for they do not teach on their own authority but by virtue of the mission they have received from the church."

In July, 1986 the Sacred Congregation for the Doctrine of Faith, with the approval of Pope John Paul II, notified the Chancellor of the University that Prof. Curran had been found to be not suitable or eligible to exercise the function of a professor of Catholic theology. The finding was the outcome of a seven-year investigation of Curran's writing, focused primarily on his dissent from official church doctrine in the area of sexual ethics and human life issues. In January, 1987, Prof. Curran was suspended from teaching in the Theology Department at Catholic University, and in March, 1987 he filed suit against Catholic University in Superior Court of the District of Columbia for breach of contract.

The decision to withdraw Curran's ecclesiastical commission was made by the Board of Trustees, on the basis of the declaratory judgment of the Sacred Congregation for the Doctrine of Faith (and the Pope) and the recommendation of the Chancellor (who was free to take what he considered to be "appropriate action" upon receipt of the declaratory judgment of the Vatican). The corporate decision of the University did not remove Prof. Curran's tenure. Furthermore, the decision was made in accordance with customary University procedures, which included evaluation by an ad hoc committee appointed by the Academic Senate. The faculty committee expressed its willingness to accept removal of Prof. Curran's canonical mission "if, but only if he were offered an alternative teaching assignment in his area of competence within the Department of Theology or elsewhere within the university."

The University construed Prof. Curran's area of competence broadly, as including moral theology and/or social ethics. Accordingly, when the Board of Trustees removed Curran's canonical mission on the basis of the Vatican finding, it instructed the administration to invite him to teach social ethics in the University's School of Arts and Sciences. Curran, however, was unwilling to accept such an appointment, contending that his competence was in the area of Catholic theology and that his accepting such a reassignment would amount to his accepting restrictions on his academic freedom as a scholar and teacher of theology.

One of the points at issue in Prof. Curran's suit concerned his contention that at the time of his tenure contract with the University in 1971, there was no requirement that he hold a canonical mission in order to teach theology at Catholic University. The University contended that the requirement of a canonical mission had been continuous since its inception in 1937, and had been confirmed by revised Canonical Statutes issued by the University in 1981, pursuant to Sapientia Christiana. Upon reviewing this disagreement the court determined that "as of 1981, if not before, Professor Curran had, and was required by his own contract to maintain, a canonical mission." The court reasoned that both parties were aware of the University's special church relationship and that neither could have reasonably expected the University to ignore an authoritative directive from the Vatican.

ACADEMIC FREEDOM

Curran viewed his conflict with the Vatican and Catholic University as part of his personal struggle to advance the integrity and autonomy of an academy of learning functioning within the context of the Roman Catholic church. He had previously articulated his own theory of the relationship between academic freedom, on the one hand, and the Catholic university and Catholic theology, on the other. Curran saw academic freedom, which he understood in essentially the MacIver-AAUP sense of the term, as essential for the very existence of a university and as indispensable in its pursuit of its mission in preserving, imparting, and discovering truth. Freedom, said Curran, is what distinguishes a university from a propaganda institution or a center of indoctrination.[26]

Curran noted that before Vatican II it was widely assumed that full academic freedom could not exist in a Catholic college or university. At that time, he said, academic freedom was generally viewed by Catholic educators as limited by doctrinal tests, imposed with the sanction of ecclesiastical authority, which could be evoked at any time, without appeal, to settle controversies concerning matters of faith. In the 1960's, however, Curran saw significant changes in American Catholic colleges and universities. The changes were reflected, for example, in a symposium held at The University of Notre Dame in 1966,[27] and in the 1967 Land O' Lakes Statement on "The Nature of the Contemporary Catholic University," cited above.[28] Curran welcomed the new view of academic freedom in the colleges and universities of the Church.

Curran saw the academic freedom of the Roman Catholic theologian not only as critical to the integrity of theology as a scholarly discipline, but also as indispensable, in the long run, to the health of the Church and of the teaching mission of the Church. Curran saw theology not as a "scientific discipline" seeking doctrinal certitude based on a deductive methodology, but as "interpretation of the sources of revelation and of the teaching of the hierarchical magisterium in the light of the signs of the times." The

293

function of the theologian, in his view, involves a combination of subordination to the authority of the magisterium with independent interpretation of the received teaching in a developing human and social reality.

In his suit against Catholic University Curran was determined to test how far the new canonical regulations governing ecclesiastical faculties could accomodate the realities of academic freedom in an American university as he understood them. If taken literally, he was convinced, the apostolic constitution was in clear and direct conflict with the new view of Catholic higher education which had emerged in the decade of the 1960's. He had earlier declared,

> If the apostolic constitution is literally applied, it
> will mean that such canonically erected Catholic
> institutions cannot be true universities in the accepted
> meaning of the term in the United States. Likewise,
> the theology done in such universities will not have the
> necessary academic freedom to perform its function
> properly, and the good of the whole Church will
> suffer.[29]

Curran's suit against Catholic University was for breach of contract. He sought "specific performance" of his contractual right to teach in the Department of Theology even without a canonical mission, or failing that, his contractual right to teach Catholic theology in some other department of the University. He alleged that the University's action in withdrawing his canonical mission and barring him from teaching theology in the University violated his contractual rights to academic freedom. He did not contest the finding of the Vatican concerning his unsuitability to teach theology with a ecclesiastical commission.

In seeking the support of American law in his search for vindication of academic freedom, Curran found that he had only a narrow ground of action. (It may be that he never expected to win his suit.) No constitutional principle

294

of academic freedom could be invoked. The court's decision turned entirely on the issues whether Curran's contract with the University required him to have a canonical mission; whether without the canonical mission the University could allow Curran to teach within the theology department, as long as he taught subjects where there was no conflict between himself and the church or as long as he did not teach students seeking "ecclesiastical" degrees; and whether the university owed Curran an appointment under which he would be allowed to teach Catholic theology in some other department of the University.

The University defended on a number of levels. The University denied that either Prof. Curran's contract rights or his academic freedom had been violated. It contended that, while academic freedom is an important value at Catholic University, it is limited both by the discipline of Catholic theology and by the nature of the institution in which the discipline is practiced. It argued that for the court to require the University to ignore these limits would violate the University's Free Exercise rights under the First Amendment. And it argued that because of its papal charter and its ecclesiastical faculties, the University is governed not only by civil law but also by canon law; and that, to the extent that its actions respecting Prof. Curran's appointment at the University were dictated by a definitive interpretation of canon law by church authorities, they were beyond the jurisdiction and review of civil courts.

The Superior Court saw the issue in this case as "part of a larger struggle that has been raging within Catholic higher education for many years." It viewed this struggle as a symptom of the tension between two allegiances in an American Catholic university, the allegiance to "the goal of robust academic inquiry in an environment free of external control or influence," and "a common bond of faith and a mission to preserve and protect the Church's doctrine." Nowhere, said the court, is this tension more acute than in a case involving the teaching of theology at a Catholic university, and especially at The Catholic University of America.

The Curran case, however, is a contract law case, not a First Amendment case. The basis of the court's decision was entirely an analysis of what was stated or implied in the terms of Curran's faculty contract and tenure award at Catholic University. The meaning of academic freedom, in so far as the court could address that question at all, was entirely a matter of the contractual terms established between Curran and his university.

Curran contended that the terms of his contract at Catholic University gave him the right to academic freedom as a teacher of theology. As a tenured professor he had the right to continuing appointment and was subject to dismissal only for cause. Both parties in this action agreed that Curran had not been dismissed for cause after peer review of his competence. The University consistently took the position that its actions respecting Prof. Curran's faculty appointment were not based on its own judgment of his competence as a professor, but only on the judgment of the Holy See that he is not eligible to exercise the function of a professor of Catholic theology, teaching in the name of the Church, and on the decision of the Board of Trustees that the papal judgment is binding on the University.

The court found the case unique and unprecedented. It was not governed by clear principles or rules of procedures on academic freedom and tenure as propounded in the University Faculty Handbook. Nor was there any custom or practice at the University or elsewhere that could be cited as a source of the contractual rights of the parties under these particular circumstances. "The fact is," said the court, "that it has never happened before, at this university or anywhere else."

The dispute centered on whether the faculty contract provides a specific guarantee of academic freedom and, if it does, whether there are limits to such academic freedom with respect to theology positions at Catholic University and what those limits are. The dispute also concerned the question of the extent to which the University's customs and practices with respect to academic freedom constitute part of the contractual relationship between the University and its faculty.

The specific terms of the faculty contract are, of course, the point of departure for determining the contractual rights and obligations of the respective parties. The Superior Court took the view, however, that, under District of Columbia law, the employee handbook was also part of the contract, and that "in a university setting, the employment contract can also include the customs and practices of the university."[30] If the contract is imprecise or ambiguous, said the court, it would then have to determine "what a reasonable person in the position of the parties would have thought the contract meant."

Applying these tests the court found that the University had not breached its contract with Prof. Curran when it withdrew his canonical mission to teach Catholic theology. No established university procedures or policies of the University had been violated. The question, said the court, "comes down to what the contract says and what the parties to it intended." The court thought that certain things were "unmistakably known" to the respective parties: 1) that the University served under a pontifical charter; 2) that the Archbishop of Washington is the chancellor of the University and serves under the bylaws as the liaison between the University and the Holy See; and 3) that all the University's self-descriptions, in the Faculty Handbook and elsewhere, emphasize its unique relationship to the Holy See and its concomitant responsibility to the Roman Catholic Church. Accordingly, said the court, there can be no doubt that Prof. Curran's contract with the University was subject to the right and duty of the University to act upon definitive judgments of the Holy See.

As the court saw it, Curran's suit amounted to the requirement that the University's guarantee of academic freedom to a professor of theology should be understood to mean the following:

297

(1) The university will take no adverse action against the professor based on the moral and religious content of his speech, writing, or teaching;

(2) If it is determined that the professor requires a cacnonical mission to teach in the Department of Theology, and if the Holy See attempts to withdraw, or directs the chancellor to withdraw, the professor's canonical mission based on the moral or religious content of the professor's speech, writing, or teaching, the university will defend the professor's right to hold the canonical mission;

(3) If, notwithstanding the foregoing, the professor's canonical mission is withdrawn, the university will guarantee the professor the right to teach Catholic theology in an appropriate department or faculty in which a canonical mission is not required, subject to all the rights and privileges customarily associated with the concept of academic freedom in an American university.

It goes without saying, said the court, that the University would never have written such a contract. Nor had the plaintiff adduced any evidence to establish that such were the terms of the contract he actually had with the University. Instead, said the court, the plaintiff had sought support for his interpretation of the contract in certain historical trends in Catholic higher education and at Catholic University in the late 1960's, which had in his view "transformed the university into a place where academic freedom reigned supreme, to the exclusion of all else, including the obligations imposed on the university by virtue of its pontifical charter and its relationship with the Holy See." What the plaintiff's evidence described, said the court, was, perhaps, "the university he wanted to work for, maybe even the one he thought he was working for, but not the one with which he had contracted."

The court saw the case as involving a "conflict between the University's commitment to academic freedom and its unwavering fealty to the Holy See." The court held that the University had the right to determine how it would resolve such a conflict and held that "nothing in its contract with Prof. Curran or any other faculty member promises that it will always come down on the side of academic freedom." Prof. Curran contended that academic freedom was good not only for himself as a scholar, but also for Catholic University and the Roman Catholic Church. He may be right, said the court, but a civil court is not the place to decide that issue. The question for the court was whether the terms of Curran's faculty contract gave him "the right to teach Catholic theology at CUA in the face of the definitive judgment by the Holy See that he is ineligible to do so." The court held that he had no such contractual right.

The case has attracted national attention in circles of higher education and is viewed in some quarters as raising serious questions concerning the state of academic freedom in Roman Catholic colleges and universities. Father William J. Byron, President of the University, sought throughout the controversy to advance a different interpretation, however. In an article published in America during the early days of the Curran controversy, Byron contended that academic freedom is strong at Catholic University, even though it is limited by the University's relationship to the Church. Indeed, all freedom is limited, he argued, and the only question is whether or not the limitations placed on it are proper.[31]

Byron, whose sympathies and commitments lie, as we have seen, with the Land O' Lakes concept of a Catholic university, emphasized that once an individual is appointed to the faculty of a Catholic university, whether in theology or in some other discipline, the university owes him a guarantee of freedom of inquiry - - full academic freedom. "Disciplined theological investigation and instruction (i.e. research and teaching conducted within the generally accepted norms of the particular academic discipline) must be protected," says Byron. "Both inquiry and communication of discovery should have no limits except the limits of prudence and of truth itself."

Thus far Byron is in agreement with the concept of academic freedom espoused by Prof. Curran in the Lovejoy/MacIver tradition. In the instance of a Catholic university, however, the question arises of the propriety of an externally imposed limit to freedom of inquiry, derived from an understanding of Church doctrine. Is there an appropriate limiting role for the Church in restricting the framework within which theological inquiry and instruction may be carried on <u>in the name of the Church</u>? Byron unhesitatingly answers that there is a proper role for the Church in this respect. But, he contends, "The limits the church might choose to set on theological research or teaching can be imposed without violence to academic freedom <u>only if the limits are themselves expressions of prudence and truth</u>." (Our emphasis)

The theory of freedom here is critical to the concept of a religiously affiliated institution of higher education, whatever its ecclesiastical tradition. Theological limits properly applied to inquiry and teaching within any academic discipline, says Byron, stem either from the force of prudence or from the "truths which faith knows with certainty." Where certainty is not yet found, theological investigation must continue to probe; and even where certainty has been achieved by the church, theology must continue to inquire in order to reach deeper understandings and new applications.

In the case of the Catholic Church, Byron observes, the Church on occasion defines "its points of certainty" through its formal teaching authority, the magisterium. This it does authoritatively, although rarely. The problem for the Roman Catholic theologian then becomes that of discerning how best to serve the interests of truth in those marginal areas where the Church has declared itself authoritatively, but not with complete certainty, clarity, and finality. "The theologian must decide how best to proceed in examining those questions on which the church does not hesitate to speak, but concerning which the truth is not yet completely and compellingly clear."

ACADEMIC FREEDOM

Father Curran's dissent from Church teaching is in the area of authoritative, but not infallible church pronouncements. Most of the Catholic Church's teaching in matters of morality fall within this range of official teaching, which has not been identified as complete, clear, and final, although it often carries the weight of traditions of long standing. Curran's disagreement with the Church in these matters in no way jeopardizes his personal standing in the Church. Indeed, there is always the possibility that the views he advances might some day become official Church doctrine. His problem, however, is that his disagreement has led the Church, through its own duly established procedures, to withdraw his commission to teach theology in its name.

The church, the university, and the theologian take somewhat different views of the freedom to inquire. The theologian is free to pursue truth wherever it leads. The church is free to decide who may or may not teach in its name. The university must respect the freedom of both, while maintaining its own integrity and autonomy. As Byron puts it,

> It cannot . . . be said as easily in the case of theology, as it might be said with reference to other academic disciplines, that there should be no limits on teaching and research except the limits of prudence and truth. But with due allowance for the fact that Catholic theology searches for understanding in the light of the Catholic faith and thus in an ecclesial context, that is exactly what must be said if officially commissioned theologians are to serve the church effectively and if theology is to be respected as a discipline in a university setting. . . It is precisely there, in the guarantee of responsible freedom to the theologians on its faculty, that the church-related university, as university, makes its proper contribution to theological progress.

We share Byron's view that the Curran case raises no serious questions concerning the status of academic freedom

301

in Catholic or other religiously affiliated higher education. There are no indications of an emerging hierarchical initiative to impose new external constraints on Catholic colleges and universities generally. Confirmation of the right of the Vatican to exert certain kinds of control over Catholic University in the Curran case is not likely to have far-reaching effects on the relationship between the Church and the American system of Catholic higher education generally. On the contrary, there is every indication that the recent trend toward enlargement of the tradition of academic freedom in religiously affiliated higher education will continue indefinitely.

Following the decision delivered by the Superior Court, Father Curran announced that he would not appeal, saying, "Now that the university has publicly said that it does not have academic freedom, and the judge agrees that it does not, the principle of my case has been taken care of." He disagreed that the implications of the decision were limited to the unusual organizational circumstances of Catholic University. Curran warned, "In principle, what happened to me can happen elsewhere, because other institutions can declare an identity with the Vatican or the Vatican can impose its will on an institution."[32]

NOTES TO CHAPTER EIGHT

1. Robert M. MacIver, Academic Freedom in Our Time, New York, Columbia University Press, 1955, p. 14.

2. John Cogley, "The Future of an Illusion," Commonweal, June 2, 1967.

3. Harvey Cox, The Secular City; Secularization and Urbanization in Theological Perspective, New York, Macmillan, 1966 (Revised Edition),   p. 194.

4. Report of the Harvard Committee, General Education in a Free Society, Harvard University Press, 1945, p. 39.

5. Manning M. Pattillo, Jr. and Donald M. MacKenzie, Church-sponsored Higher Education in the United States, Washington, D.C. American Council on Education, 1966, p. 100.

6. Theodore M. Hesburgh, The Hesburgh Papers: Higher Values in Higher Education, Kansas City, Andrews and McNeel, Inc., 1979, pp. 64,65.

7. Ibid., p. 41.

8. Ibid., p.58.

9. William J. Byron, S.J., Quadrangle Considerations, Chicago, Loyola University Press, 1989, pp. 20,25.

10. Nels F.S. Ferre, The Finality of Faith, New York, Harper, 1963, p.61.

11. Arnold O. Lovejoy, "Academic Freedom," Encyclopedia of the Social Sciences, Vol. 1, p. 384 (1930).

12. William Van Alstyne, The Specific Theory of Academic Freedom and the General Issue of Civil Liberty, originally published in The Annals of the American Academy of Political and Social Science, Vol. 404, 1972; reprinted in Edmund L. Pincoffs, The Concept of Academic Freedom, Austin TX, University of Texas Press, 1975, p. 60.

13. "Academic Freedom and the Law," 46 Yale Law Journal 670 (1937). Reprinted in Walter P. Metzger, The Constitutional Status of Academic Freedom, New York, Arno Press, 1977.

14. David Fellman, "Academic Freedom in American Law," 61 Wisconsin Law Review 3, 17 (1961). By this time the term "academic freedom" was at least recognized as a legal term in Words and Phrases, which carried the following definition: "'Academic freedom' is the freedom to do good and not to teach evil." This remarkable definition was taken from Kay v. Board of Higher Education of the City of New York (1940), which upheld the termination of Bertrand

Russell's appointment at the City College of New York.

15.   William P. Murphy, "Academic Freedom - - An Emerging Constitutional Right," in <u>Law and Contemporary Problems</u>, Vol.28, No.3, Summer, 1963, published by Duke University School of Law, Durham NC.

16.   Thomas I. Emerson, <u>The System of Freedom of Expression</u>, 1970, p. 616. Emerson, a Yale professor, served as counsel to Paul Sweezy in the celebrated case of <u>Sweezy v. New Hanpshire</u>, 354 U.S. 234 (1957).

17.   Carr, "Academic Freedom, The American Association of University Professors, and the United States Supreme Court," in 45 <u>AAUP Bulletin</u> 5,6,20 (1959).

18.   Thomas I. Emerson, <u>The System of Free Expression</u>, 1970, p. 614.

19.   Robert M. O'Neil, "Academic Freedom and the Constitution," <u>Journal of College and University Law</u>, Vol. 11, No. 3, 1984, pp. 275-292.

20.   Mark G. Yudof, "Three Faces of Academic Freedom," <u>Loyola Law Review</u>, Vol.32, No.4, Winter, 1987, pp. 831-858.

21.   Edmund L. Pincoffs, ed., <u>The Concept of Academic Freedom</u>, Austin TX, University of Texas Press, 1975, p. viii.

22.   Cf. <u>Gerende v. Board of Supervisors</u>, 341 U.S. 56 (1951); <u>Garner v. Board of Public Works</u>, 341 U.S. 716 (1951);   <u>Adler v. Board of Education</u>, 342 U.S. 485 (1952); <u>Wieman v. Uppdegraff</u>, 344 U.S. 183 (1952).

23.   Robert MacIver, <u>Academic Freedom in Our Time</u>, p. 138.

24.   Ibid., p. 288.

25.   Perry A. Zirkel, "Commentary: Academic Freedom of Individual Faculty Members," <u>West's Education Law Digest</u>, Vol. 47, 1988, p. 812.

26. Charles E. Curran, "Academic Freedom: The Catholic University and Catholic Theology," The Furrow, 1980, p. 740. Also published in Academe, Vol. 23, 1980, p. 126.

27. Reported in Edward Manier and John W. Houck, Academic Freedom and the Catholic University, 1966.

28. See above, pp. 261,262.

29. Curran, "Academic Freedom: The Catholic University and Catholic Theology," in The Furrow, 1980, p. 754.

30. The opinion cited such earlier decisions as McConnell v. Howard University, 260 U.S.App.D.C. 192, 196-97, 818 F.2d 58, 62-63 (1987); Greene v. Howard University, 134 U.S.App.D.C. 81, 88, 818 F.2d 1128, 1135 (1969); Bason v. American University, 414 A.2d 522, 525 (D.C. 1980); Pride v. Howard University, 384 A.2d 31, 35 (D.C. 1978); and Howard University v. Best (Best I), 484 A.2d 958, 967 (D.C. 1984) and (Best II), 547 A.2d 144, 151 (D.C. 1988).

31. William J. Byron, "Credentialed, Commissioned and Free," America, August 23, 1986, p. 69.

32. Charles E. Curran, quoted in a news article in The Chronicle of Higher Education, March 8, 1989, pp. 13,17.

CHAPTER NINE

SUMMARY AND RECOMMENDATIONS

The generalization which comes most readily to mind as we look back over the foregoing survey is that the law affecting the exercise of religious preference in employment decisions at religiously affiliated institutions of higher education falls short of a coherent theory. It is, perhaps, inevitable that the law should be somewhat less systematic than legal scholars and commentators would wish. Indeed, one would expect a certain incompleteness in legal analysis and judicial determination in the law of higher education, where there is much less activity than in some other areas of law. Furthermore, as William Kaplin observes, the development of the law of higher education continues to be affected by the traditional separation between academia and law and by the tendency of legislatures and courts to defer to the autonomy of academic institutions.[1]

This is by no means to say, however, that the law affecting preferential hiring is unpredictable or subjective. Our survey has indicated a number of lines along which this law has been developing in recent years, and we have identified a number of issues which have been clarified or resolved. Yet the result remains unsatisfactory in some respects, and there are steps which need to be taken in the near term to confirm or extend the principles propounded to date.

We contend that the exercise of religious preference in employment is indispensable to maintenance of the distinctive purposes of religiously affiliated higher education. These purposes have, in our judgment, a significant social utility as an element in the preservation and adaptive development of the values underlying the common life. We contend that the rights associated with the pursuit of religious purposes in the higher learning emerge not from the American tradition of toleration of sects (even the most extreme), but from the social importance of religiously affiliated higher education.

306

SUMMARY AND RECOMMENDATIONS

Religiously affiliated higher education has no interest in being viewed as a sect. What it needs is recognition of the social and educational appropriateness of its religiosity as an important resource in the American culture. The rights of religiously affiliated institutions of higher education emerge from recognition of the contributions which religious understandings can make to civilization and from the compatibility of religiously oriented programs of higher education with the traditional ideals of civil rights and academic freedom.

Our survey has shown that the right to exercise religious preference in employment decisions in religiously affiliated higher education is recognized in American law, although the precise dimensions of such recognition remain somewhat indeterminate. We have observed, too, that the larger academic community itself recognizes this right, albeit with considerable misunderstanding of its nature. We wish now to summarize the findings of our survey and to present a series of recommendations for future development.

1. Institutional Integrity

The first line of defense of the right of preferential hiring is non-legal. It involves identification and adaptive development of the ideals by which a religiously affiliated institution of higher education lives. The autonomy of independent and religiously affiliated higher education lies in its own hands. If it is unclear about its own selfhood and integrity, its role in society and in the larger system of education will be vague and its relationships with government will be correspondingly uncertain.

Recommendation 1

Religiously affiliated institutions should review their educational programs and reassess their employment policies and procedures, with a view to clarifying the basis on which they may exercise religious preference in employment decisions.

SUMMARY AND RECOMMENDATIONS

Religiously affiliated institutions of higher education are assured the right to exercise broad control over their employment policies and practices, subject to certain limitations of law. The law often defers to the autonomy of institutions of higher education, both public and private. In certain respects the law is even more deferential to the autonomy of religiously affiliated institutions. The exercise of such autonomy is the best means of assuring its continuance.

We believe that there are steps which need to be taken, both by institutions and by educational associations and consortia, to clarify and reaffirm the implications of religious affiliation and orientation in undergraduate learning and employment policy. Such clarification should not be expected to follow a monolithic model, of course. Each institution or group of institutions will find its own way. But a new national effort in restating the aims and needs of religiously affiliated higher education is urgently needed if its role in American education and society is to remain dynamic and vital.

The first step is a comprehensive evaluation of present employment policies and practices at the institutional level. The urgency of this step will vary from institution to institution, of course. But every institution needs a periodic review of its policies and documentation and a reassessment of existing mechanisms for implementation and enforcement, so as to keep abreast of institutional and environmental change and to evaluate performance. We believe that a new examination of the practice of religiously preferential hiring would be timely for most religiously affiliated institutions.

The reassessment must begin with identification of the central institutional values which define the framework for employment decisions. Special attention should be paid to the basic concept of nondiscrimination in employment, and to the promulgation of criteria for the exercise of religious preference within the context of renunciation of forms of discrimination (particularly discrimination on the basis of race or sex) which are inconsistent with religious ideals.

SUMMARY AND RECOMMENDATIONS

There should then be a position-by-position review of the applicability of religious qualifications for appointment or promotion. Particular attention needs to be paid, obviously, to the ways in which religious preference is to be exercised in faculty employment. Finally, there should be a review of all policies and procedures related to appointment, discipline, promotion, or termination and of the documentation of those procedures to assure that due process (however it is defined by the institution) is clearly understood and followed.

Part of this reassessment will involve comparison of institutional policies and procedures with the requirements of law. For this purpose legal counsel is required, of course. The assessment should focus on preventive legal planning to avoid problems and conflicts before they arise. But in addition, programs of staff development on the legal basis of the exercise of religious preference in employment are very much needed at most institutions. There should be broad discussion of current legal issues related to the exercise of religious preference in employment at the institution, so as to strengthen the consensus regarding policies and procedures and to enhance faculty and staff understanding of underlying legal and administrative principles.

Some of the national higher education organizations or associations might be prepared to take a fresh initiative in seeking to strengthen the autonomy and viability of religiously affiliated higher education, with particular reference to the exercise of religious preference in employment decisions. Consideration might be given to offering programs and services to assist member institutions to deal more effectively with the legal issues affecting employment policies and practices in this area. Denominational agencies and consortia for interinstitutional cooperation are another means for further study and joint action.

SUMMARY AND RECOMMENDATIONS

2. Pervasively Religious Institutions

Pervasively religious institutions of higher education have a number of distinctive needs and concerns with respect to the exercise of religious preference in employment. Such institutions, both individually and in association, need to take a number of steps to defend their distinctive programs and roles.

Virtually all seminaries, schools of divinity, rabbinical schools, and Bible schools and colleges fall within this category of institutions, but we suggest that a significant number of colleges and universities are of this type as well. Among the baccalaureate institutions there are also a number of strongly religious (although not pervasively religious) institutions which exercise religious preference in employment decisions quite non-selectively over the entire range of academic and staff positions.

Such institutions are concerned to be protected in their right to a broad exemption from the Title VII proscription against religious discrimination in employment. Their need is not met by the BFOQ exemption, which involves the potential of case-by-case judicial determination as to whether or not religion is a bona fide occupational qualification for specific positions. The question is whether federal and state statutes, administrative regulations, and judicial decisions provide the broader exemptions which such institutions require.

Recommendation 2

Pervasively religious institutions of higher education should anticipate that their right to a broad exercise of religious discrimination in employment will be vindicated by the courts, but they should be prepared to depend more heavily than they might like on the bona fide occupational qualification exemption. They should be prepared to endure expensive and time consuming litigation from time to time in defending their right to

**a broad exemption from the general proscription of
religious discrimination in employment.**

The U.S. Supreme Court decision in Amos has confirmed
the constitutionality of the broad exemption provided to
churches and religious organizations under Section 702 of
the Civil Rights Act. The law is clear as to the exemption
for religious organizations as a class. The question is how
the Amos precedent applies to pervasively religious
institutions of higher education. A number of these
institutions have been quick to embrace the Amos decision
as providing assurance of their eligibility for a
comprehensive exemption from the general proscription
under Title VII against religious descrimination in
employment. We suggest, however, that the Amos precedent
has only limited application in religiously affiliated higher
education.

The key factor affecting the eligibility of institutions of
higher education to exercise religious preference in
employment non-selectively, across all or virtually all
positions, is how the courts will construe their religious
purposes and organizational relationships. The Amos
decision is unambiguous in declaring that the courts will not
attempt to determine, in the case of churches and religious
organizations, what particular positions or types of positions
are governed by the exemptions of Title VII. But there are
judicial precedents which leave no assurance that a
religiously affiliated or religiously oriented school will be
treated by the courts as a church or religious organization.

If an institution has a close organizational relationship
to a church or religious organization ("is, in whole or
substantial part, owned, supported, controlled, or managed
by a particular religious corporation, association, or
society") or if it "is directed toward the propagation of a
particular religion," it is eligible for the broad exemption of
Section 702(e)(2). But there are indications in lower court
proceedings that religiously affiliated colleges and
universities cannot be sure how these descriptors will be
judicially applied in individual cases. Furthermore, there is

the complicating factor that if an institution is found eligible for the broad exemption, through being classified as analogous to or organizationally part of a church or religious organization, its eligibility for public funds may be brought into question, since such funding is conditioned on the separability of religious and secular functions in educational programs.

We find that seminaries, schools of divinity, rabbinical schools, and Bible schools and colleges may rely on the broad exemption with respect to their minister-like positions, specifically with respect to all faculty and senior administrative appointments. However, the judicial precedents do not assure such institutions that they may rely on the broad exemption with respect to junior administrative and non-academic staff positions. Nevertheless, we believe that, with respect to junior administrative and non-academic staff positions, such institutions should have little difficulty establishing the applicability of the BFOQ exemption, on the ground that all positions in the institution affect the integrity of the religious functioning of the institution. To express our conclusion in other words, the courts cannot be expected to treat institutions of theological education as the equivalent of a church or religious organization (and thus as governed by the Amos precedent), but rather as analogous in certain respects to a church (and thus as governed by the Southwestern Seminary precedent).

The situation is a bit more uncertain with respect to pervasively religious or strongly religious colleges and universities. Again, such institutions should have no difficulty vindicating their claims to the exercise of religious preference in all positions on the basis of the BFOQ exemption. The problem is that their practice may be subject to a challenge which would require a judicial determination of the bona fide character of the religious qualification in positions which might be alleged to be separable from the religious purposes of the enterprise. We see no assurance thata religiously pervasive college or university will be viewed by the courts as governed by the

SUMMARY AND RECOMMENDATIONS

<u>Amos</u> precedent and as eligible for a broad exemption <u>as an institution</u>.

The bottom line is that pervasively religious institutions should have no difficulty maintaining their right to exercise religious discrimination in all their employment decisions, but the legal basis on which they may successfully do so may be more narrow than they would like it to be. From the perspective of constitutional law, we find no basis for predicting that such institutions will succeed in claiming a constitutional right to a broad exemption from religious discrimination based on the Free Exercise Clause. For one thing, it is generally difficult to obtain a vindication of an institutional right of Free Exercise. (Even the <u>Amos</u> case was decided on Establishment Clause grounds.) And the recent tendency of the courts to identify compelling state interests which justify a burden on free exercise further erodes the Free Exercise base. But such limitations aside, the problem concerns the way in which courts are likely to identify a Free Exercise right of religiously affiliated institutions of higher education. It seems likely that the court will continue to employ general descriptors of colleges and universities which remove them a step or two from the actual practice of religion (as members of a different class of institutions, say, from parochial elementary and secondary institutions) and thus to reduce the availability of a Free Exercise defense.

As for the broad statutory exemptions of Title VII, it is hard to predict what the courts will say. It seems likely that they will prefer to employ the BFOQ exemption if constitutional questions can be thereby avoided. That procedure, of course, may involve a case-by-case determination of whether or not a religious test is a bona fide occupational qualification in the instant position.

The potential for litigation exists, therefore. But institutions may find it preferable to endure the risk of litigation in exchange for retaining their present classification as institutions eligible for public funds, as long

313

as those funds can be restricted to nonreligious or secular programs.

We urge pervasively religious institutions to exercise a strong initiative in serving the national concern to prevent employment discrimination on the basis of race and sex. A few of these institutions have strongly and sincerely held convictions about the religious basis for defining social and familial roles of the sexes and for maintaining separation of the races. We happen to believe that such convictions are often based on a misunderstanding of the religious traditions on which it is claimed that they rest. And we believe that educational institutions bear a special social responsibility and accountability to exercise leadership in the national effort to eradicate all forms of discrimination unrelated to individual merit. If some religiously affiliated institutions, however, find it necessary, on grounds of conscience, to exercise employment discrimination on the basis of race or sex, they must be prepared for the eventuality that they may lose their tax-exempt status or their eligibility for public funding, should their policies and practices be subjected to legal challenge.

3. Statutory Revision

We have found a number of respects in which federal and state statutes provide an inadequate basis for legal determination of the rights of religiously affiliated institutions of higher education with respect to the exercise of religious preference in employment decisions. The law is vague at points and is not entirely consistent, with the result that judicial determinations are less predictable than would be desired. Furthermore, the language of the law tends to misunderstand or misrepresent the nature of religiously affiliated higher education and to use pejorative terminology in describing their educational purposes and instructional methods.

SUMMARY AND RECOMMENDATIONS

Recommendation 3

A series of higher education amendments to federal law should be enacted to clarify the rights of religiously affiliated institutions of higher education in employment decisions, and to confirm the intentions of Congress relative to such rights and the eligibility of religiously affiliated institutions of higher education for particular forms of federal aid.

We believe that an act to reform the federal statutes affecting religiously affiliated institutions of higher education is needed to clarify and/or confirm the status of religiously affiliated institutions of higher education with respect to the jurisdiction of the law of nondiscrimination in employment and the eligibility of such institutions for particular forms of federal aid. A bill for action by the Congress might be prepared following the format of the Civil Rights Restoration Act and providing clarifying amendments to the Civil Rights Act (especially Title VII), the Higher Education Act (especially Titles VII and IX), and other federal statutes which contain language applying to religious discrimination in employment in religiously affiliated higher education. The bill might be called the Religiously Affiliated Higher Education Act.

The purpose of such legislation should not be to substantively reform the current scope and structure of federal programs in higher education, but only to clarify the intention of Congress with respect to the applicability of specific provisions of the law of higher education to religiously affiliated institutions. For example, we would hope that consideration of such a series of amendments would not require the Congress to return to the protracted controversies which disturbed the debate on the Civil Rights Restoration Act. Hopefully, however, fresh consideration might be given to several questions concerning the application of that Act and others to religiously affiliated institutions, which the polarizations and time pressures of the previous debate prevented the Congress from addressing on the merits.

315

SUMMARY AND RECOMMENDATIONS

The language of the law in characterizing religiously oriented institutions of higher education is often offensive to responsible educators who serve in such institutions. The law assumes that institutions which are eligible for a broad exemption from federal regulation as religiously oriented or religiously affiliated will be engaged in "indoctrinating" methods of teaching, in "inculcating" certain religious "tenets," or in "propagating" a particular religion. Such characterizations of the educational process fail to recognize the freedom of teaching/learning at pervasively religious institutions and the inclusivist and non-sectarian approach to the study of religion which is generally found in such institutions. It would be highly desirable if less pejorative language could be found to specify the identifying characteristics of those religiously affiliated institutions which the law wishes to recognize for special treatment.

We suggest that the purposes of such legislation might be understood in such terms as the following:

1. To clarify the scope of the intended coverage of the law of nondiscrimination in employment in religiously affiliated institutions of higher education, and to confirm the basis on which such institutions might be judged eligible for exemptions from the general requirement of nondiscrimination on the basis of religion.

2. To clarify the distinction between religious and secular programs in religiously affiliated institutions of higher education and to clarify the method by which federal support for and regulation of the secular programs of such institutions might be effectively and constitutionally implemented.

3. To revise statutory language to more accurately reflect the actual situation of religiously affiliated higher education with respect to educational missions and instructional methods, and to eliminate, to the extent possible, pejorative language which might unnecessarily and offensively attribute indoctrinative and sectarian purposes to those

institutions which the law views as eligible for exemptions from a general proscription against religious discrimination in employment.

4. To confirm the intention of Congress with respect to the requirement that religiously affiliated institutions colleges and universities (not including institutions engaged in the professional education of clergy and religious) may exercise nondiscrimination in employment on the basis of race or sex, irrespective of possibly conflicting religious convictions or tenets.

Two types of provisions would be needed in such amendments: revisions to definitions and revisions to exemptions.

Definitions

We do not favor introduction of a prescriptive definition or criterion of religion in such legislation. We believe that the controversy associated with any such attempt would be protracted and counterproductive, and its use is likely to involve serious constitutional challenges. We recommend a loosely analogical approach in the legal definition of religion and believe that any attempt to provide a substantive definition of religion in either statutory or judicial determinations would result in serious constitutional conflicts.

Nevertheless, we see the need for clarification of an operational criterion for certain terms which are employed in the statutory language defining the intended coverage of the law of nondiscrimination for religiously affiliated higher education. We suggest a series of definitions like the following:

Religiously Affiliated Institution of Higher Education

Our study has re-emphasized earlier findings of research conducted by the Center for Constitutional Studies, indicating that there is a wide variety of organizational relationships between institutions of higher education and the churches or traditions with which they are affiliated. We believe that the current law is inadequate in its recognition of this variety.

The Center for Constitutional Studies has long advocated a more inclusive term than "church-related institution of higher education," in order to recognize the rights of institutions which, though definitely oriented towards a religious tradition and purpose, are independently incorporated and have no formal relationship to a church, religious organization, or association of churches. An earlier recommendation of the Center called for revision of the exemption from nondiscrimination on the basis of sex under Title IX of the Higher Education Act by deleting the term "controlled by" and substituting language employed by the Internal Revenue Service in its commentary on a regulation governing the filing of financial information by a church viz.: "The term 'affiliated' means either controlled by or associated with a church or with a convention or association of churches."[2] Such a revision would provide a more inclusive exemption as follows: "This section shall not apply to an educational institution either controlled by or associated with a church, religious organization, convention or association of churches, or religious tradition if the application of this subsection would not be consistent with the religious tenets of such church, religious organization, association of churches, or religious tradition."

Similar language was recommended by the National Association of Independent Colleges and Universities at the time of the Civil Rights Restoration Act of 1987, in the context of Section 908 of that Act, which specifies the "programs" covered by its provisions. The NAICU recommendation, which was not endorsed by the Congress, would have provided an exemption as follows: "except that such term ['program'] does not include any operation of an entity which is controlled by or which is closely identified with the tenets of a religious organization if the application of Section 901 [of the Higher Education Act, Title IX] would not be consistent with the religious tenets of such

318

organization." NAICU argued that the Congress had already created a precedent for use of such broadened language in the Higher Education Amendments of 1986, where it had added an identical "religious tenet" provisionn under the College Construction Loan Insurance Association Program.[3]

We propose a similar statutory revision here, but with a broader application to the full range of federal regulatory programs affecting religiously affiliated higher education. We suggest the approach of introducing a clarifying definition of the term "religiously affiliated institution of higher education," so that the term may be employed in the substantive provisions of law to carry out the intentions of Congress with respect to coverage of such institutions. The definition we recommend is as follows:

> A religiously affiliated institution of higher education is an institution of higher education which is, in whole or substantial part, owned, supported, controlled, or managed by a particular church, association of churches, religious corporation, religious society, or other corporation organized for religious purposes, or which is closely identified with a particular religious tradition, or whose curriculum is directed or oriented towards the nurture of religious faith.

Institution of Professional Theological Preparation

The law also needs to have a device for providing for special treatment of seminaries, schools of divinity, rabbinical schools, seminary colleges, and Bible colleges and institutes as a sub-class of religiously affiliated institutions of higher education. We suggest that the important feature which needs to be recognized in such institutions is their involvement in the terminal or professional preparation of clergy and religious, since, as we have seen, the law treats the employment of such personnel by churches and religious organizations in a unique way. For example, the law might be drafted so as to accord to such institutions the same general employment rights accorded under the Amos decision to churches; or it might, alternatively, be drafted so as to limit the scope of a nondiscrimination exemption to the range of exempt positions identified in Southwestern Seminary decision. Accordingly, we propose the following definition for such a class of institutions:

> An institution of professional theological preparation is a recognized institution of higher education which is involved, in whole or in part, in the terminal or professional preparation of persons to enter upon, or be ordained into, clergy, priestly, religious, or ministerial professions within a church, religious organization, or religious tradition. Such institutions include theological seminaries, schools of divinity, rabbinical schools, Bible colleges and Bible institutes, and other institutions organized for the training of religious.

Religious Educational Programs

As we have observed, Establishment Clause jurisprudence affecting higher education depends on the distinction between religious and secular programs. The law must have a method for assuring that public funds which are received by a religiously affiliated institution are restricted to secular programs intended to be covered and do not flow to religious programs which it would be impermissible to support with public funds. The same distinction is critical to the theory of governmental regulation of the employment policies and procedures of religious and religiously affiliated organizations. The regulation of religious employment would, presumably, involve an infringement of First Amendment rights, while the protection of discrimination in areas of secular employment would, presumably, be inconsistent with national policy and, possibly also, with constitutional principles.

The distinction is central to such Supreme Court decisions as Tilton, Hunt, and Roemer, and to the entire theory underlying the tendency of the law to treat religiously affiliated institutions of higher education differently from parochial or religiously affiliated elementary and secondary schools. It is a long established legal precedent that the distinction is a viable one at the higher education level. For our purpose we do not need to resolve the question whether or not the distinction is also viable at the elementary and secondary levels.

The problem in this area is that of drawing the distinction between religious and secular programs of higher education institutions without creating an unconstitutional governmental entanglement in religion. We have seen that the Supreme Court has had only the narrowest majority in deciding the circumstances in which such a distinction is feasible. We anticipate that the divisions within the judiciary will continue indefinitely. We see the need, however, for a clarification of Congressional intent with respect to this distinction. We suggest that the statutory language related to this distinction should be narrowly discriminating, so as to reduce the risk of extensive factual explorations in the courts concerning what programs are religious and what programs are secular. We suggest the following definition:

> A religious educational program is a curricular or academic program or institutionally organized extra-curricular program of an institution of higher education whose primary purpose is the nurture of religious faith or the encouragement of worship or religious practice. The term does not apply to programs of theological, religious, or philosophical education conducted by application of a critical scholarly method.

Exemptions

With the aid of such definitions it becomes possible to clarify the language of a number of sections of the law where exemptions are provided for the exercise of religious discrimination in employment decisions. For example, we suggest a revision of the Section 703(e)(2) exemption under Title VII of the Civil Rights Act which provides an exemption for religiously affiliated institutions of higher education as follows:

321

SUMMARY AND RECOMMENDATIONS

> It shall not be an unlawful employment practice for a religiously affiliated institution of higher education or institution of professional theological education to hire and employ persons of a particular religion or religious persuasion in carrying out its educational mission or conducting its activities.

With respect to employment discrimination on the basis of race or sex, we think some further clarifications are required. We suggest statutory language which explicitly prohibits religiously affiliated institutions of higher education (but not institutions of professional theological education) from exercising discrimination on the basis of race, color, or national origin, irrespective of religious scruples or tenets which might be advanced as the basis for such discrimination. We suggest that the broad exemption provided under Section 702 of Title VII should be revised to clarify this prohibition:

> This title shall not apply to a religious corporation, association or society with respect to the employment of individuals of a particular religion to perform work connected with the carrying on by such corporation, association, or society of its activities, or to . . . a religiously affiliated institution of higher education with respect to its employment of individuals to perform work connected with the educational activities of such institution; except that this subsection may not be interpreted to authorize a religiously affiliated institution of higher education (other than an institution of professional theological education) to discriminate in employment on the basis of race, color, or national origin.

With respect to the exercise of employment on the basis of sex, sexual behavior, or sexual orientation we find matters a bit more complicated and controversial than in the case of employment discrimination on the basis of race. For there are widely accepted religious reasons for treating certain kinds of sexual activity as immoral and as thus

322

possibly raising serious questions about the moral suitability of persons for serving as faculty or employees in religiously affiliated institutions of higher education. However, we believe that most provisions of labor law affecting employment and salary determination without regard to sex apply fully to religiously affiliated instituions of higher education. We see no religious grounds for a sexually discriminatory employment or salary policy, except possibly in the area of sexual behavior which is viewed as morally significant.

Some indeterminacy in the law affecting discrimination on the basis of extra-marital pregnancy, abortion, and sexual orientation is probably politically unavoidable, at least for the time being.[4] We suggest, however, that it would be desirable for the inconclusiveness of federal law in this area to be more explicitly acknowledged in a statutory provision such as the following:

> Nothing in this Title shall be construed to prohibit a religiously affiliated institution of higher education from establishing policies, procedures, or practices in the employment of personnel on the basis of sexual behavior, extra-marital pregnancy, abortion practice, or sexual orientation if such behavior, condition, practice, or orientation is inconsistent with the beliefs, tenets, moral standards, or values of the religious organization or tradition with which the institution is affiliated.

We suggest that such statutory language as the foregoing should be recommended to state legislatures as well as to the United States Congress. The Uniform Law Commissioners' Model Anti-Discrimination Act, approved in 1966, is closely modelled on federal enactments. Section 308 of the Model Act uses the exact language of Section 702 of the federal Civil Rights Act in providing a broad exemption for religious organizations. Section 309(2) provides a significant variant of the Title VII Section 703(e)(2) exemption by omitting any reference to the curriculum of the institution as a criterion of eligibility. The present exemption for religiously affiliated educational institutions in the Model Act reads as follows:

> It is not a discriminatory practice for a religious educational institution or an educational organization operated, supervised, or controlled by a religious institution or organization to limit employment or give preference to members of the same religion.

We find this language much preferable to that of the present federal statutes. We suggest, however, that it would be even clearer if it were recast in the terminology proposed above:

> It is not a discriminatory practice for a religiously affiliated institution of higher education to limit employment or give preference to members or adherents of the church, religious organization, religion or religious tradition with which the institution is affiliated.

4. Contract Theory and the Right to Educate

In this study we have raised the question, what is the basis of the private right to educate as our legal system accords it to individuals, to corporations, and to churches. And we have asked, What limitations are placed on that right by the social interest in education and by the accountability of educational institutions to the social, political, and legal system?

Many people would seek an answer to these questions in some kind of First Amendment analysis. That is, they would seek the basis of the right to educate in its being a special instance of the more general right to freedom of expression or the free exercise of religion. Certainly, there is an important aspect of the right to educate which is properly analyzed as a special case of First Amendment rights, and the Center for Constitutional Studies has in the past made its own contributions to such an analysis. But as our study has shown, First Amendment doctrine, especially its Free

SUMMARY AND RECOMMENDATIONS

Exercise aspect, is actually of limited application in the theory of independent, and especially religiously affiliated higher education. That assessment is supported by both educational and legal considerations.

In the American tradition, freedom of belief and expression has meant the right to <u>believe</u> just about anything whatever, the right to <u>advocate</u> most things, even highly unpopular points of view, and the right to <u>act</u> on the basis of such belief subject only to the broadest constraints of the national interest or security. Under the First Amendment our system of justice protects all kinds of subjectivity and extremism in matters of belief and expression. The courts have refused to restrict the right to freedom of expression, belief, or association by reference to some a priori concept of orthodoxy or social acceptance.

Education, however, is inherently understood as a responsible social function, and the educational community is guided by the canons of scholarship and of logical coherence in its search for understanding. The right to educate must therefore be balanced by recognition of the social and intellectual accountability of the educational function.

It goes without saying that in every educational system a dialectical exchange of differing understandings is of the essence. And academic freedom requires that every scholar be protected from the arbitrary imposition of limits on his freedom to inquire. Yet education is more than a forensic sharing of freely expressed opinions. It is the search for coherence in belief, and it accepts the discipline of the rule of truth. Furthermore, no society can abandon its collective interest in the quality of education. Anyone who undertakes the profoundly social function of a teacher must be prepared to accept a social evaluation of his work. The right to educate, in other words, is not just the right to sound off. It is the right to contribute to the social good through the pursuit of truth. Society's interest in education places certain limits on the rights of schools and defines their accountability.

SUMMARY AND RECOMMENDATIONS

Moving to the legal side, it is instructive to observe that the American courts have been reluctant to define the right to educate simply in terms of the right to freedom of expression or of the right to the free exercise of religion. We believe, indeed, that the more comprehensive and theoretically adequate foundation of the right to educate is to be found not in the First Amendment, but in the law of contracts. It is, in fact, on such a basis that the most celebrated case in the establishment of the private right to educate was decided in this country.

The Dartmouth College decision, which was handed down by the Marshall Court in 1819 during what some scholars have called the most momentous six weeks in American judicial history, was an important phase in the confirmation of the constitutional basis of government and of law for which the Marshall Court is universally honored. Yet the perspective in which the case was decided emerged only after many years of political and intellectual struggle.

The rhetoric of our national celebrations has sometimes conveyed the impression that the American Constitution and its institutional expression sprang full-grown from the creative genius of the founders. When we go back to the history of this extraordinary period of the Marshall Court, however, we are sometimes puzzled to discover that there was a time when many of the fundamental assumptions of our national life were deeply debated.

At the time of the Dartmouth College case Chief Justice John Marshall had emerged from his conflicts with the Jeffersonians over the authority of the Court. It was a bitter battle. In those early days of the Republic there were many who shared Jefferson's deeply held belief that a strong federalism, such as Marshall represented, was a profound threat to the American democracy. Marshall's leadership, however, confirmed three principles of the emerging constitutional system:

1. The Constitution is law and as such is enforceable in the courts.

2.   The Constitution is "the supreme law of the land" with which all legislation, both federal and state, must be consistent.
3.   While the function of making the law belongs to the legislative branch of government, that of expounding and interpreting the law in the light of the meaning of the Constitution rests with the judiciary.

After nearly two hundred years such propositions sound platitudinous. Yet the emergence of these propositions in the formative years of the republic was a development no less revolutionary than the original break with Britain. These were convictions not contemplated in the Articles of Confederation, the weakness of which it was the primary purpose of the Great Constitutional Convention to correct.

The Dartmouth College decision centered not on the idea of freedom of speech or the free exercise of religion, but on the law of contract and the authority of the federal Constitution over the states. Dartmouth had been founded out of the pre-revolutionary zeal of the Reverend Eleazer Wheelock of Connecticut, who, following his Yale studies and the clarification of his religious vocation through his encounter with Jonathan Edwards and the Great Awakening, had decided that he would establish (at his own expense) a school for instructing Indians in the Christian faith. Wheelock solicited contributions from sources in England and obtained a charter from King George III, which authorized the formation of a self-perpetuating Board of Trustees of twelve persons, with power to govern the institution, to appoint its officers, and to fill all vacancies. The Board had no organic relation to any particular church, although its orientation was clearly Christian and Congregational. The royal charter created an independent corporation. It is a classic case of an individual (and later a corporation) obtaining a legal right to educate.

At Hanover, on the edge of the wilderness, Wheelock discovered that the Indians were less receptive to the Christian gospel than he had supposed that they would be. The college began to develop on the then-current model of the liberal arts and served much the same kind of clientele as did the other colonial colleges, though its resources were somewhat restricted. At Wheelock's death the presidency of the institution passed, under a provision of the original charter, to his son John, who became involved after a number of years in an ecclesiastical controversy which created a rift between himself and the Board of Trustees. The controversy led to his being ousted by the Trustees in 1815.

In the midst of this controversy the Governor of the State of New Hampshire intervened by proposing to the Legislature an action designed to protect the public's interest in the continuing development of this institution of higher learning. He wrote to the Legislature proposing an act to assume public control of the college so as to protect it from decay.

The original charter of the college, the Governor told the Legislature, emanated from royalty and was based, accordingly, on principles which were not congenial to a democracy. The concept of a Board of Trustees which perpetuates itself is, he contended, "hostile to the spirit and genius of free government." He proposed that the Trustees should be elected in future by the state legislature, in order to assure the college's continuing public accountability, and he asked for legislation to accomplish that purpose. "The college was formed for the public good," the Governor argued, "not for the benefit and emolument of its Trustees; and the right to amend and improve acts of incorporation of this nature has been exercised by all governments, both monarchical and republican." The Legislature promptly obliged by passing an act which made the college Dartmouth University, governed by a Board of twenty-one trustees, to be appointed by the Governor.

The Governor, who had originally been a Federalist but had since 1812 been a leader of the Jeffersonian party in the state, sent a copy of his legislative message to Jefferson, who replied that he found the proposal "replete with sound principles." Jefferson, who at that time was

328

directing his own efforts to establishing the University of Virginia, observed, "The idea that institutions established for the free use of the nation cannot be touched nor modified, even to make them answer their end . . . is most absurd." Jefferson's principles would allow for the public interest in the operation of a private institution of learning to override the rights of private control if the social effectiveness and utility of the institution were at stake.

The Superior Court of Appeals took essentially the same view as Jefferson in deciding against the college and in favor of the state. "A corporation all of whose franchises are for public purposes is a public corporation," the Court declared - - hence a gift to such a corporation is actually a gift to the public. Funds solicited and received by Dartmouth College from private sources for the purpose of education are public, not private funds. Accordingly, said the Court, the office of Trustee of Dartmouth College is, in fact, a public trust, as much as is the office of Governor of the State of New Hampshire or of a judge of this Court. No provision of either the national or state constitutions, said the Court of Appeals, prevents the Legislature from exercising control over the college, since the constitutional provisions are intended to protect private interests only. The Legislature is entirely within its authority in exercising control over an organization which serves the public interest. Furthermore, declared the Court, even if the royal charter is viewed as a contract, there is nothing to prevent the Legislature from modifying the terms of the contract for the general good as conditions and times change.

The Dartmouth case was argued on appeal to the U.S. Supreme Court on March 10, 1818. The College was represented by a group of attorneys led by Daniel Webster, himself a Dartmouth graduate. Dartmouth College, argued Webster, is an eleemosynary corporation and should be treated by the law as a private charity. The founder and the donors, said Webster, acted on the belief that the rights held under the charter of the corporation would be inviolate.

SUMMARY AND RECOMMENDATIONS

Little did the founder suppose that the legislature would ever take his property and privileges away and give them to others. Little did he suppose that this charter secured to him and his successors no legal rights. Little did the donors think so. If they had, the college would have been what the university is now, a thing upon paper, existing only in name.

The plaintiffs contended, said Webster, that the action of the State Legislature in taking control of the college in the name of the public interest was unconstitutional under Article One, Section 10: "No state shall . . . pass any bill of attainder, ex post facto law, or law impairing the obligation of contracts." The granting of a charter to Dartmouth College was a contract just as surely as if it were a contract between consenting individuals. Furthermore, Webster pointed out, the courts recognize that a grant by a State before the Revolution is as much to be protected as a grant made since the Revolution. The case before the Court is therefore simply one concerning the inviolability of contracts.

Individuals have the right to use their own property for purposes of benevolence, either towards the public, or towards other individuals. They have a right to exercise this benevolence in such lawful manner as they may choose; and when the government has induced and excited it, by contracting to give perpetuity to the stipulated manner of exercising it, it is not law, but violence, to rescind this contract, and seize on the property. Whether the State will grant these franchises, and under what conditions it will grant them, it decides for itself. But when once granted, the constitution holds them sacred, till forfeited for just cause.

The case, said Webster, concerns not only "this little institution" but every college in the country. They are all based on the same principle, viz. the inviolability of contracts. It would be a most dangerous experiment, Webster warned, to render these institutions subject to the

330

rise and fall of popular parties and to the vagaries of political opinion. If the charter may be taken away at any time by action of the legislature, the higher learning will become "a theatre for the contentions of politics. Party and faction will be cherished in the places consecrated to piety and learning."

The Court's opinion was not delivered by Chief Justice John Marshall until almost a year later, on February 1, 1819. The opinion was a model of the analytical precision and constitutional exposition for which Marshall is famous. He agreed essentially with Webster, although Webster himself had not been confident of winning the case merely on the basis of the contract clause. Yet the law of contract was precisely the foundation of Marshall's judgment:

> The American people have said, in the Constitution of the United States, that 'no state shall pass any bill of attainder, ex post facto law, or law impairing the obligation of contracts.' . . . On the judges of this Court, then is imposed the high and solemn duty of protecting, even from legislative violation, those contracts which the constitution of our country has placed beyond legislative control; and however irksome the task may be, this is a duty from which we dare not shrink.

The college's charter, said the Court, is a contract. And on the basis of the provisions of the charter and of the modifications of its provisions reached by mutual consent, large contributions were made to the college as a religious and literary institution. In these transactions, said Marshall, "every ingredient of a complete and legitimate contract is to be found." The crux of the legal decision, as he saw it, concerned the construction to be placed on the college's charter as a contract.

If that instrument grants to the institution "political power" and creates a "civil institution" as an instrument of government, then the Legislature may do with it as it wills.

SUMMARY AND RECOMMENDATIONS

If, on the other hand, Dartmouth College be an eleemosynary institution, empowered to receive contributions unconnected with government, the matter is entirely different. Dartmouth, the Court found, is not an instrument of government and its actions are not (as we would say nowadays) state actions; it is a private corporation and is no more subject to the control of government, despite its social purpose, than is any other private corporation or individual. A private charity incorporated for purposes of education is not excluded from the rule of law as applied to other corporations.

The contract clause of the U.S. Constitution is part of this nation's fundamental law, said Marshall. That clause, in its "plain import," comprehends Dartmouth's charter. No individual or group would ever found a college if he could not be assured that the contractual basis of his action would continue unimpaired. Hence, Marshall concluded, it is the judgment of this Court that "this is a contract, the obligation of which cannot be impaired without violating the Constitution of the United States." The right of the Dartmouth trustees to carry on an educational service is based on the college's charter, which is to be viewed as an inviolate contract.

The right to educate is thus vindicated in this landmark case not by reference to the Bill of Rights, but by reference to key provisions of the unamended Constitution - - viz. the authority of the Constitution over the actions of the states and the sanctity of contracts. Marshall, like most of the Federalists, tended to view the Bill of Rights as superfluous. Of course, Marshall did not have our modern precedents on freedom of speech and of expression to which he might turn as the basis for establishing the right to educate. But it should be remembered that this was a precedent-setting time. Marshall might have focused on First Amendment rights in this momentous decision affecting the legal standing of private institutions of education and learning. It is significant that he chose, instead, to apply the law of contracts. In deciding for Dartmouth he argued from the inviolability of contracts. If a state can take over the governance of a college through its own action whenever it judges that the public interest requires it to do so, then the will of the state is effectively substituted for the will of the donors and the original charter (contract) no longer exists.

The Dartmouth decision was at first given little notice outside New Hampshire. But it was not long before the importance of the decision began to dawn on the American public. Of course, it had implications far beyond the realm of higher education. But our interest at the moment concerns what the decision suggests concerning the foundation and source of the right to educate.

We suggest that it is edifying for independent, and especially religiously affiliated colleges and universities to consider the right to educate as derived from a contract, indeed, from a series of contracts, between an educational institution and agencies of government representing the public interest, and that clarity concerning the nature of that right and the conditions under which it may be exercised arises from understanding of the provisions of these contractual agreements. It seems to us that at this moment in American society there is an increasing risk that the autonomy and quality of American education, as well as the coherence of American culture, will be adversely affected by inattention to the mutual obligations arising from the contractual foundations of the act of education.

Recommendation 4

Each religiously affiliated institution of higher education should review the rights and obligations which have been established, by charter and other documents, in agreements it has reached with the government, with the religious organization with which it is affiliated, and with individuals whom it has contracted or employed for services, and should develop strategies for confirming and protecting its institutional autonomy-rights within the context of its social accountability as an educational institution.

SUMMARY AND RECOMMENDATIONS

The creation of an independent college or university is based on a contractual agreement between an individual, corporation, or group, on the one hand, and the government, representing society, on the other, for the performance of a specified educational service. The educational entity is created by the contract, which commits the government to continuing and indefinite guarantees of the autonomy of the entity thus created.

Educational institutions enter into all kinds of contractual agreements in carrying out their functions. There are charters, articles of incorporation, and licenses which are the basis of the standing of such institutions before the law. There are contracts and agreements between and among institutions for the sharing of resources and for strengthening educational service through interinstitutional cooperation. There are contracts between the institution and the faculty, and there are at least quasi-contractual agreements between the institution and students. And there are forms of understanding between the institution and non-academic employees which essentially function as enforceable contracts.

The terms of such contractual understandings define certain rights and obligations of individuals functioning within the institutional system. They also define certain legal rights and duties of the college or university as a corporate person, and they identify appropriate forms of the regulation of education through both public and voluntary agencies functioning in the public interest. Uncertainty or confusion about these contractual understandings has at times invited chaos in the educational system and has caused legal and administrative conflicts which have been neither beneficial nor necessary.

As our study has emphasized, judicial decisions affecting conflicts over the exercise of religious preference in employment decisions in religiously affiliated institutions of higher education are not likely to be reached directly on constitutional grounds. Courts will avoid constitutional construction if another basis of decision can be found. Furthermore, there are few constitutional precedents for the special circumstances of higher education law. We believe that it is more realistic for religiously affiliated institutions of higher education to depend on the law of contracts as the primary basis for determination of individual and institutional rights and obligations in employment matters. And we emphasize our Recommendation 1 above, which urges institutions to exercise their own autonomy in applying sound educational and administrative principles in their own employment practices and procedures within the context of existing contractual understandings.

The protection of the autonomy-rights both of institutions and of faculty and employees depends, in our view, primarily on the law of contracts. The terms of faculty contracts normally define the rights and responsibilities of the faculty and of the institution, usually with specific reference to the system of institutional policies, regulations, and procedures by which both parties agree to be bound. It is these terms and procedures, rather than some First Amendment abstraction or some vague tradition of academic freedom, which define the principles which govern faculty personnel administration.

If contract terms are clearly drawn and if the system of policies and procedures is coherent and complete, there will be a firm basis for resolving questions affecting the exercise of religious preference in employment decisions, either within institutional due process or, if need be, through the courts. Contractual and quasi-contractual understandings with administrative and non-academic employees may be developed along similar lines to those which have been widely followed in faculty appointments. Careful attention to the nature of these contractual and quasi-contractual agreements is, in our judgment, the primary line of defense of the right of religiously affiliated institutions of higher education to exercise religious preference in employment decisions.

335

SUMMARY AND RECOMMENDATIONS

The right to educate, we submit, is not just the right to speak. It is a right to carry on a socially significant function on the basis of contractual agreements freely entered upon by individuals and by governments. It is both a tactical and a moral error for an institution to seek to preserve its autonomy and viability by doctrinaire legal defenses, rather than by responsible performance of purposive educational service on the basis of clearly stated contractual understandings. A return to Dartmouth would, we believe, be edifying as independent colleges and universities seek to achieve greater clarity and consistency in their understanding of the implications of the right to educate.

Governmental interest in higher education has always included concern for the strength of independent and religiously affiliated institutions as important to the national welfare. A college or university which meets a recognized social need and makes an important contribution to the general welfare has a basis for establishing a contractual understanding with the state for carrying out the function of education. It is this social usefulness of education which is the foundation of the right to educate, whether that right is held by a public educational institution or by an independent or religiously affiliated institution. Public service can be combined with institutional autonomy in a charter expressing shared purposes and values. Such an understanding provides the basis of collaboration between church and state, or between government and private corporations, for the pursuit of the general welfare, while assuring the protection of the right to educate under the concept of the sanctity of contracts.

We must ultimately ground the right of religiously preferential hiring in independent and religiously affiliated higher education in values which the college or university shares with the society which has chartered it. It is these shared values and contractual understandings which establish the common ground on which school and society may function cooperatively to achieve those educational benefits

336

which are distinctive for the independent and religiously affiliated sector.

We live in times of momentous decision for independent, and especially religiously affiliated higher education. We are convinced that there is a system of shared values which can unite private and governmental agencies in the joint consecration of talent and of resources for the common good. And we believe that there is much at stake, especially in the independent and religiously affiliated institutions, in our becoming clear about what those values are and how they might confirm the contractual understandings which define the right to educate. Clarity about the nature and basis of the educational function is the foundation of the new commitments which are required by cooperative activity in these unprecedented times.

NOTES TO CHAPTER NINE

1. Cf. William A. Kaplin, <u>The Law of Higher Education</u>, San Francisco, Jossey-Bass Publishers, Inc., 1985, pp. 3-10.

2. Rev. Reg. 1.6033-2(g)(5).

3. See Section 752(e)(2) of the Higher Education Amendments Act of 1986.

4. The Civil Rights Restoration Act left the abortion issue unresolved, refraining from requiring institutional policy on abortion to conform to any legal or ethical norm.

INDEX OF CASES

GENERAL INDEX

342